Law and Economics of Public Procurement Reforms

Appropriate laws and regulations are essential tools to direct the action of procurers toward the public good and avoid corruption and misallocation of resources. Common laws and regulations across regions, nations and continents potentially allow for the further opening of markets and ventures to newcomers and new ideas to satisfy public demand.

Law and Economics of Public Procurement Reforms collects the original contributions related to the new European Union Directives approved in 2014 by the EU Parliament. They are of both economists and lawyers, and have been presented in a manner that allows for exchanges of views and "real-time" interaction. This book features, for each section, an introductory exchange between two experts of different disciplines, made up of a series of sequential interactions between an economist and a lawyer, which enriches the liveliness of the debate and improves the mutual understanding between the two professions. Four sections characterize this book: supporting social considerations via public procurement; green public procurement; innovation through innovative partnerships; and lots – the economic and legal challenges of centralized procurement. These themes have current relevance of the new European Public Procurement Directives.

Written by an impressive array of experts in their respected fields, this volume is of great importance to practitioners who work in the field of EU public procurement in the Member States of the EU, as well as academics and students who study public finance, public policy and regulation.

Gustavo Piga is Professor of Economics at the University of Rome Tor Vergata, Italy.

Tünde Tátrai is Associate Professor at the Corvinus University of Budapest, Hungary.

The Economics of Legal Relationships

Sponsored by Michigan State University College of Law

Series Editors:

Nicholas Mercuro, Michigan State University College of Law

Michael D. Kaplowitz, Michigan State University

For a full list of titles in this series please visit www.routledge.com/The-Economics-of-Legal-Relationships/book-series/ELR

15 Patent Policy
Effects in a National and International Framework
Pia Weiss

16 The Applied Law and Economics of Public Procurement
Edited by Gustavo Piga and Steen Treumer

17 Economics and Regulation in China
Edited by Michael Faure and Guangdong Xu

18 Law, Bubbles and Financial Regulation
Erik F. Gerding

19 Empirical Legal Analysis
Assessing the Performance of Legal Institutions
Edited by Yun-chien Chang

20 Predatory Pricing in Antitrust Law and Economics
Nicola Giocoli

21 The Role of Law in Sustaining Financial Markets
Edited by Niels Philipsen and Guangdong Xu

22 Law and Economics
Philosophical Issues and Fundamental Questions
Edited by Aristides N. Hatzis and Nicholas Mercuro

23 Public Procurement Policy
Edited by Gustavo Piga and Tünde Tatrai

24 Legal Origins and the Efficiency Dilemma
Nuno Garoupa, Carlos Gómez Ligüerre and Lela Mélon

25 Law and Economics of Public Procurement Reforms
Edited by Gustavo Piga and Tünde Tátrai

*The first three volumes listed above are published by and available from Elsevier

Law and Economics of Public Procurement Reforms

Edited by Gustavo Piga and Tünde Tátrai

Routledge
Taylor & Francis Group
LONDON AND NEW YORK

First published 2018
by Routledge
2 Park Square, Milton Park, Abingdon, Oxon, OX14 4RN

and by Routledge
711 Third Avenue, New York, NY 10017

Routledge is an imprint of the Taylor & Francis Group, an informa business

British Library Cataloguing-in-Publication Data
A catalogue record for this book is available from the British Library

Library of Congress Cataloging-in-Publication Data
Names: Piga, Gustavo, 1964– editor. | Tátrai, Tünde, editor.
Title: Law and economics of public procurement reforms / edited by Gustavo Piga and Tünde Tátrai.
Description: Abingdon, Oxon ; New York, NY : Routledge, 2018. | Includes bibliographical references and index.
Identifiers: LCCN 2017027245 | ISBN 9781138296480 (hardback) | ISBN 9781315100005 (ebook)
Subjects: LCSH: Government purchasing—European Union countries. | Government purchasing—Law and legislation—European Union countries.
Classification: LCC JN30 .L3836 2018 | DDC 352.5/3094—dc23
LC record available at https://lccn.loc.gov/2017027245

ISBN: 978-1-138-29648-0 (hbk)
ISBN: 978-1-315-10000-5 (ebk)

Typeset in Times New Roman
by Apex CoVantage, LLC

Contents

Figures

Tables

Contributors

Antoinette Calleja is Director, International Affairs and Policy Development at Ministry for Health, Malta

Bernardo Nicoletti is Lecturer at the Master in Procurement Management at University of Rome Tor Vergata, Italy

Biancamaria Raganelli is Associate Professor of Administrative Law and Law and Economics and PhD Fellow of Economics Law and Institutions at University of Rome Tor Vergata, Italy

Boštjan Ferk is Founder at Institute for Public-Private Partnership, Slovenia

Francesco Decarolis is Associate Professor at Boston University, USA

Francesco Saverio Mennini is Professor of Economics and Health Economics at University of Rome Tor Vergata, Italy

Francois Lichere is Professor of Law at Aix Marseille University, France

Giancarlo Spagnolo is Professor of Economics at SITE-Stockholm School of Economics, EIEF, Sweden and Rome Tor Vergata, Italy

Gustavo Piga is Professor of Economics, Department of Economics and Finance at University of Rome Tor Vergata, Italy

Ilenia Mauro has a PhD in Economics Law and Institutions at University of Rome Tor Vergata, Italy

Josè Luis Guasch is Professor Emeritus of Economics at University of California, San Diego, USA

Lara Gitto is Health Economist, researcher EEHTA, at Faculty of Economics, University of Rome Tor Vergata, Italy

Lorenzo Castellani is Research Fellow EIEF at Einaudi Institute for Economics and Finance, Italy

Martin Trybus is Professor of European Law and Policy and Director, Institute of European Law at Birmingham Law School, University of Birmingham, UK

Mihály Fazekas is Research Associate at Cambridge University, UK

Nicola Dimitri is Professor of Economics at University of Siena, Italy

Nikola Komšić is Expert Associate for Public Private Partnership for Chamber of Commerce and Industry of Serbia

Pedro Telles is Senior Lecturer in Law at Swansea University, Wales, UK and Adjunct Law Futures Centre Griffith University, Australia

Petra Ferk is Founder at Institute for Public-Private Partnership, Slovenia

Sharlene Jo-Ann Shillingford McKlmon is Procurement Specialist Inter-American Development Bank, USA

Shirley Gayle Sinclair is Procurement Specialist for Inter-American Development Bank, USATis

Stéphane Saussier is Professor of Economics at Sorbonne Business School, Paris, France

Tünde Tátrai is Associate Professor at Corvinus University of Budapest, Hungary

Zornitsa Kutlinia-Dimitrova is Senior Economist for European Commission, Brussels, Belgium

Editor's introduction

After the 2013 "The Applied Law and Economics of Public Procurement" (edited by Gustavo Piga and Steen Treumer) that published the debates and papers of the First Interdisciplinary Public Procurement Symposium held in Rome and the 2015 "Public Procurement Policy" (edited by Gustavo Piga and Tunde Tatrai) that published the debates and papers of the Second Symposium held in Budapest, we are delighted to see in print our third book arising from the Third Symposium, held in Belgrade, on Routledge's "Economics of Legal Relationships" series.

As customary for this series, this book combines juridical and technical expertise so as to find a common terrain and language to debate the specific issues that a public administration in need of advancing and modernizing in its purchasing operations has to face. The format of the book features, for each section, an introductory exchange between two reputed scholars of different disciplines, made of a series of sequential interactions between an economist and a lawyer who write and follow up on one another. Our aim, which we hope we have achieved, is to enrich the liveliness of the debate and improve the mutual understanding between the two disciplines. Two more papers, possibly from experts from different disciplines again, conclude each section.

There are four sections in this book: local preferences in public procurement; joint public procurement; Big Data in public procurement; and finally renegotiation in public procurement.

We do hope that this book, as in the past, will attract the interest of policymakers, practitioners working in the field of public procurement as well as academics. As scientists, public procurement remains our passion and we continue to believe that investing in skills and professionalism in this delicate field of action of the public administration is the critical reform capable of positively impacting on the productivity of firms and on the social outcomes for citizens across the world.

Gustavo Piga is Professor of Economics at the University of Rome Tor Vergata, Italy.

Tünde Tátrai is Associate Professor at the Corvinus University of Budapest, Hungary.

The Academic partners of the Third Interdisciplinary Public Procurement Symposium were the Faculty of Law of the University of Belgrade and the Faculty of

Economics of the University of Rome Tor Vergata. The institutional partners of this edition of the Symposium, which we wish to thank for their support, are the Chamber of Commerce and Industry of Serbia and the European Bank for Reconstruction and Development. We gratefully acknowledge support from KPMG Serbia and Construccions Rubau.

Abbreviations

CARICOM	Caribbean Community
COTED	Council for Trade and Economic Development
CPARS	Country Procurement Assessment Reports
CSME	CARICOM Single Market and Economy
EAs	Executing Agencies
EC	European Commission
EPA	Economic Partnership Agreement
FRIP	Framework Regional Integration Policy on Public Procurement
FOC	Full and Open Competition
FTAA	Free Trade Area of the Americas
ICB	International Competitive Bidding
IDB	Inter-American Development Bank
IDPs	International Development Partners
IFIs	International Financial Institutions
IMF	International Monetary Fund
MAPS	Methodology for Assessing Procurement Systems
MFN	Most Favored Nation Treatment
NCC	National Contracts Commission
OECD	Organization for Economic Cooperation and Development
OECS	Organization of Eastern Caribbean States
PEFA	Public Expenditure and Financial Accountability
PIUs	Project Implementation Units
PPS	Pharmaceutical Procurement Service
RFQ	Request for Quotation
RFP	Request for Proposal
RFT	Request for Tender
SBD	Standard Bidding Documents
SOE	State Owned Enterprises
UWI	University of the West Indies
WB	World Bank

Introduction – Vendor rating, performance and entry in public procurement

Giancarlo Spagnolo and Lorenzo Castellani

1 Introduction

In the last two decades measuring and improving performance of public sector organizations has become an increasingly important and debated issue (Heinrich, 2002). Managerial techniques developed in the private sector for performance measurement and improvement have been imported and adapted for public sector organizations in practices and theories (Pollitt and Bouckaert, 2011).

One of the policy area in which this process is occurring is public procurement. Furthermore, public procurement is becoming increasingly configured as an interdisciplinary field of studies in which issues as local preferences, joint procurement, Big Data, renegotiation and reputational mechanism design for suppliers are becoming increasingly more relevant and debated by academics and policy-makers, as the exciting program of 3rd Symposium on Public Procurement, whose papers are found in this book, demonstrated.

In this note we examine which effects the introduction of a reputational mechanism linking future contract awards to suppliers' track record produces on suppliers' performance in public procurement by summarizing and discussing the findings from a firm experiment by Decarolis, Pacini and Spagnolo (2016). In the final part of the work we focus on the problem of market entry for suppliers when a reputational mechanism is introduced in awarding procedure, confronting the results of Decarolis, Pacini and Spagnolo (2016) with the ones in an experimental study of this issue by Butler et al. (2013).

In this context, public procurement policy is generally recognized as being characterized by an unstable tension between the public expectations of transparency and accountability, and of efficiency and effectiveness pursued by public management. Despite this tension, one of the practices that government can emulate from the private sector to improve performance in the public procurement process is the buyers' reliance upon preferred suppliers with the best past performance as a way to reduce procurement risk.

Because of competition requirements, regulations, socioeconomic programs and other concerns, government is often unable to follow the private sector's lead with respect to preferred suppliers (Kelman, 1990; Bovaird, 2006). In this context, the aim of this chapter is to give some policy suggestions on reputational mechanism and public procurement based on the evidences provided by the mentioned studies.

2 Literature

Studies on the private sector have investigated reputational mechanism effects. For example, research on the Indian software industry by Banerjee and Duflo (2000) develops a model of reputation formation as a signaling game in which each party can propose a type of contract and there is systemic overrun due to the complexity of the goods/services supplied. It finds that firms with a better reputation are more likely to be involved in time-and-material contracts and, in most cases, pay for a smaller share of cost overrun. It also shows less firm-generated overrun and less total overrun in contracts involving more reputable firms. Dellarocas, Dini and Spagnolo (2006) discuss some important dimensions in which Internet-based reputation mechanisms differ from traditional word-of-mouth networks and survey the most important issues related to their design, evaluation, and use in the context of public procurement.

The available evidence on the design and effects of reputational mechanisms in electronic platforms has been recently surveyed in Tadelis (2016). A frequent finding in this literature is that reputation regards the probability of selling, but the effect on price is typically small. A recent study on the private sector shows how certification and reputation can affect entry decision and increase the quality of entrants (Hui et al., 2017). The results of this study indicate that the availability and precision of past performance information are important not only for the rate of entry in a market, but also for the quality of who is actually entering, hence for how markets evolve in the long run. These findings have direct implications for the design of reputation and certification mechanisms in markets plagued by information asymmetries, as public procurement markets are. However, empirical evidence on reputation mechanisms in public procurement markets is still absent, although the theoretical debate on the issue has been rather lively (see e.g. Kim, 1998; Doni, 2006; Calzolari and Spagnolo, 2009; Albano, Cesi and Iozzi, 2011; Spagnolo, 2012).

3 Past performance in public procurement: public policy frameworks in the US and the EU

One method that public procurement officials can use to reduce procurement risk is to request information regarding a supplier's past performance and to use this information in source selection, as it is standard in private procurement. By now this method is largely applied in the US federal procurement system. With the Federal Acquisitions Streamlining Act of 1994 and the Federal Acquisition Reform Act of 1995, the US undertook a major policy change that saw the use of contractors' past performance as the pillar of a new approach to procurement aimed at reducing the rigidity of the procedures built in the Federal Acquisition Regulations and enabled public buyers to use more flexible purchasing methods similar to private sector management practices (Kelman, 1990; Osborne and Gaebler, 1992). During the policy implementation process some obstacles occurred in collecting and sharing past performance information, but recent legislation has reinvigorated the role of reputational systems for federal procurement. In the last years comments and policy initiatives on past performance have been numerous. In 2009 GAO recommended a transition to a single set of evaluation factors for use in contractor performance evaluations.[1] In the 2011 Office of Federal Procurement Policy's memorandum the Administrator confirmed the requirement of using the Contractor Performance Reporting System (CPARS) and also offered additional steps and strategies for improving the collection and reporting of quality past performance information into CPARS.[2] In 2013 the Obama Administration updated the FAR to standardize the factors used in evaluating contractors' performance,[3] and to require that all past performance information be entered into the Contractor Performance Assessment Reporting System.[4]

Past performance differs from experience, in that experience reflects whether contractors have performed similar work before, while past performance reflects how well contractors have done the work. It also differs from the idea of contractor responsibility, which relates to the capability to perform work. When lowest price is not the driving factor in procurement, officials are allowed to make best value determinations, such as trade-offs between cost or price, technical merit and past performance to ensure the best value to the government. However, the benefits of past performance mechanism in procurement are still today discussed by public policy-makers. There is a lack of consensus among them on the improvements that well-designed and well-managed past performance-based vendor rating systems can produce in public procurement.

This lack of consensus becomes readily apparent when comparing procurement policy in the US to procurement policy in the EU. As mentioned above, in the US the Federal Acquisition Regulation (FAR) requires that government agencies consider past performance when awarding contracts.

The EU, until the 2014 EU Procurement Directives, explicitly prohibited taking past performance into account when comparing bids among potential suppliers. The use of past performance was completely excluded. European regulation considered that the use of reputational indicators would have hindered entry of foreign suppliers in national procurement markets by, for example, allowing manipulations in favor of local incumbents or introducing undue subjectivity into the procurement process, which does not accord well with the EU's primary objective of common market integration (Gordon and Racca, 2014). However, many public procurers continued to request permission to take suppliers' past performance into account – requests EU regulators continued to deny until the last directive on public procurement.

With the Directive 2014/24 on Public Procurement the EU regulators opened to the use of suppliers' track record. They created yet another ground for exclusion based on poor past performance by the economic operator. Under this new ground, contracting authorities can exclude economic operators who have

> shown significant or persistent deficiencies in the performance of a substantive requirement under a prior public contract, a prior contract with a contracting entity or a prior concession contract which led to early termination of that prior contract, damages or other comparable sanctions.[5]

The introduction of past performance as an exclusion ground responds to the requests made for a long time by practitioners and brings the EU system closer to that of the US. Remarkably, this provision may overturn the practice and case law that prevented contracting authorities to take past performance into consideration. Even if good past performance should not be taken into consideration either for selection or award purposes, the EU regulator introduces its use for 'negative' purposes in order to allow contracting authorities to protect their interests by not engaging contractors prone not to deliver as expected.

Member States are implementing the EU Directive 2014/24 in different ways. For example, in the UK the legislature has undertaken a flexible implementation giving the largest discretion to civil servants in monitoring past performance under the EU regulation. With the Procurement Policy Note 04/15 the government has implemented the EU Directive 2014/24 designing a system to report and classify the last three years past performance and managing a database for public officials involved in public procurement process. In this case, the opportunity offered by EU regulation in the use of past performance is maximized by national legislation. Other countries such as Spain, France, Germany and the Netherlands have transposed article 57(4)(g) of the EU Directive in their national legislation without implementing a past performance reporting and classification system. In this legal framework, discretion for civil servants is reduced and strictly bounded to EU regulation. In this case policy implementation is weak and it satisfies only the minimum requirements imposed by the EU Directive. In other countries, such as Italy, discretion for public procurement officials is further reduced by a very detailed national legislation in the use of past performance. In this case, the implementation of European legislation is stronger but flexibility in the use of past performance by contract authorities is weakened by a too-rigid national legislation on the reputational mechanism. Indeed, the Italian policy-maker has issued a detailed legislation on what has to be monitored to gather past performance information and it has established a high rigidity on how information should be used.

To conclude on this point, whether there is a trade-off between reputation and entry and, if so, whether there are ways to improve reputation's effect on entry, are questions every procurement manager, in the private and public sector, should know how to answer. At the same time, policy-makers should understand if the use of past performance in public procurement process is a valuable policy to improve suppliers' performance or not and how the reputational mechanism should be designed to achieve optimal results. Unfortunately, the leading management, operations research and even public procurement textbooks offer little guidance. However some recent academic works, mentioned above, investigate benefits of past performance in public procurement and show how an effective reputational mechanism can be designed.

4 Past performance and procurement outcomes

Quantifying the costs and benefits of running a reputational mechanism in public procurement is essential, especially given the sheer economic size of this market, but little reliable evidence is available at present. The aim of the study by Decarolis, Pacini and Spagnolo (2016) is to analyze and quantify the costs and benefits of using an appropriately designed reputational/vendor rating system as a supplier selection tool in public procurement.

This study tries to overcome this problem by exploiting a rich set of data related to the experimental introduction of a past performance monitoring system in the procurement practices of a large Italian multi-utility company subject to public procurement law. This company provides water and power to a vast area in central Italy and is close to some of the main US operators in terms of several observables such as the number of employees, the customer base, the power grid size, the total turnover and the expenditures for maintaining and upgrading the power grid. For these firms, the quality and safety standards followed in the execution of the construction works performed to maintain and update the power grid are essential not only for an elective functioning of the grid, but also to limit both the number and the severity of the workplace accidents which characterize this industry.

The study observes the experimental introduction of a reputational mechanism in procurement made by this company in 2007 with the technical support of two of the authors. To build the reputational mechanism the company, the authors created a list of 136 observable parameters measuring both quality and safety features of the job executed. Three months after the new audits had begun, the company communicated through a public statement the introduction in the new audit system of a numerical "reputation index" and that, after a few more months of data collection, this index would be used to award new contracts. The aim of the company was to set out an experiment introducing a new audit system only for a subset of contracts, all of those involving public illumination and electrical-substation works, and its stated goal was to learn whether the new audit system could be beneficial for its overall procurement. The study investigates the evolution of both price and performance around the time when the new audit system was publicly announced, but before the scoring auctions incorporating reputation were first used. The audit system changed in late 2007, while the awarding system changed in mid 2010. For two and half years after the new audits were introduced, the company continued awarding contracts through lowest price auctions. During this period, the company recorded the performance of its contractors. The company established that the new audits would be used in the future to switch from price-only to price-and-rating auctions, with a linear scoring rule auction assigning 75 percent of the weight to the price offered and 25 percent to the reputation index. In the following four meetings, it informed contractors on the forthcoming award rule change and it disclosed how compliance with the 136 parameters was evolving across all the contractors audited. Furthermore, the company planned that the reputation index (RI) would apply exclusively to those bidders audited at least seven times in the relevant time window. Otherwise, a bidder would be assigned a RI equal to the *average* RI of the bidders in the auction. The same averaging rule was going to be used for new entrants in order to not compromise the entry of new bidders (i.e. firms never audited).

The study analyzes how compliance with the parameters monitored evolved in response to the announcements of the introduction of a past performance mechanism. The research shows that essentially all awarded suppliers improved their compliance in similar ways and they did it following the same strategy, with compliance increasing relatively more for those parameters with higher weights in the computation of the reputation index. Moreover, cost and time overruns – two proxies that are generally used for performance measurement, but that the Italian company decided not to include in the index – did not worsen.

The second part of the research investigates whether and to what extent the improvement in performance caused a change in procurement costs. This is key to evaluate the desirability of the policy change and is made feasible by the nearly ideal timing of the experiment. While the continued use of price-only auctions for more than two years after the announced switch to scoring auctions was due to legal constraints, this feature is what allows the authors to study the price effects linked to performance without confounding effects driven by changes in the market structure. Specifically, for the price-only auctions, all suppliers are treated symmetrically regardless of their rating and this reduces the chances that estimated price effects are driven by the barriers to entry that an immediate switch to price-and-rating auctions would have set up.

The empirical strategy used in this part of the analysis exploits a second dataset containing information on all the contracts awarded not only by the company, but also by all other Italian public contracting authorities (CAs) during the period 2005–2010. It used the variation across procurers and over time to develop a difference-in-differences estimation strategy.

The first set of findings shows that suppliers' quality and work safety increased from the date of the first announcement of the policy change. Compliance with the parameters monitored evolved in response to the timing of the five public announcements. Using audit data for the years 2007–2009, the authors show the clear evidence of a substantial change in contractors' behavior: compliance in the 136 parameters increased from 25 percent before the first announcement (t1) to more than 80 percent after the fifth announcement (t5). Authors find that essentially all active suppliers improved their compliance in similar ways and they did so strategically, with compliance increasing relatively more for those parameters with higher weights in the computation of the reputation index. While this is compatible with a strategic allocation of effort, multi-tasking likely occurred mostly within the set of parameters scored and did not cause a reduction in the effort on unmonitored tasks. According to the company's engineers the broad set of parameters chosen was exhaustive in terms of determining safety and quality for the chosen contract types. Indeed, the company's own evaluation of the policy change also found the increase in performance to be fully satisfactory.

Furthermore, considering the date of the first announcement to be the one characterizing the occurrence of the policy change, then there is no significant effect on the price paid by the company. More specifically, by looking at any symmetric window of time around the first announcement, prices remain stable on average. However, when the empirical model is extended to account for the evolution of compliance, the price response appears more nuanced.

Using the results from the first part of the analysis, the period analyzed by the study can be divided in two parts: a first phase, after the announcement of performance recording, in which suppliers' compliance grows, and a second phase when it consolidates at high levels. When the baseline difference-in-differences model is extended to account for these two phases, the result is that the original finding of no effect results from the combined effects of prices declining when compliance improves, but increasing after compliance stabilizes.

This evidence is interpreted by authors considering that winning a contract has the additional benefit of improving the chances of winning future contracts. After all contractors have earned a high reputation index, however, this benefit is compensated by the increased cost of high compliance, and auction prices become symmetrically higher. The estimates indicate that the overall cost increase of higher quality, after the phase of competition for reputation, ranges between 0 and 9 percent of the contract reserve price.

The study enforced these positive outcomes that came from the introduction of the reputational mechanism through a back-of-the-envelope cost-benefit calculation. Under the worst case estimate of the price increase observed in the final part of the sample, the increase in procurement cost amounts to 2.4 million per year. By using the OECD figures for the value of a statistical life together with the same statistical model employed by the company's engineers to map the relationship between changes in parameter compliance and the occurrence of fatal accidents, the authors estimate that the benefit from increased compliance on the safety parameters ranges between €3.5 and €5.3 million per year. This is a lower bound for the benefits that does not account for both quality improvements and safety improvements associated with non-fatal injuries. Hence, the fact that it exceeds the upper bound of the cost leads the study to conclude that the policy change was beneficial.

5 Entry and reputational mechanism

The final part of the paper by Decarolis, Pacini and Spagnolo (2016) studies whether the observed effects are the result of changes in the selection of contractors bidding or in their behavior. The evidence revealed by this study is compatible with the presence of moral hazard: authors find that suppliers who are observed bidding both before and after the new rating system is announced stop offering suspiciously low prices. These are precisely the anomalous, too-low bids often associated with poor contractual performance. On the other hand, the study finds only limited effects of selection and entry based on three features in the data. First, while several suppliers leave the market, the timing of their exit is not associated with the announcements. Second, both the firms that leave the market and those that remain have similar bidding patterns. Third, considering many observable characteristics, the firms leaving the company's auctions are no different from the suppliers who leave the auctions of another large multi-utility company that did not participate in the experiment and that are used as a benchmark.

Another recent study by Butler et al. (2013) tries to fill a part of the knowledge gap on the effects of past performance-based selection on entry in procurement markets, and it offers clear evidence-based results for future policy. Butler et al. (2013) build a simple model of repeated procurement with limited application and potential entry and implementing it in the laboratory. The authors consider reputation as an incentive system to limit moral hazard in the quality dimension as well as on the effect of reputation on selection through entry. The study assumes that some important costly to produce quality dimensions of supply, although observable for the parties, are too expensive to verify for a court to be governed through an explicit contracting and are therefore left to reputational governance. An additional assumption is made, considering that there is a potential entrant that is more efficient than all incumbents. In this context, the study investigates how quality, price, entry and welfare change when an ordinary and transparent reputational mechanism is introduced that rewards an incumbent firm that provides costly high quality with a bid subsidy in the subsequent procurement auction, but that may also award a bid subsidy, of varying size, to an entrant with no record of production, as often done for example in private construction procurement where all qualified supplier start with the same amount of "points", useful for selection, and then they can lose points by providing poor performance and regain them by improving it, but up to the maximum initial number.

The first set of results of the study by Butler et al. (2013) demonstrate that concerns about reputation-based selection hindering entry are indeed justified: naively introducing a "standard" reputational mechanism in which only good past performance is awarded with a bid subsidy in the following procurement auction enhances quality provision, but it also significantly decreases entry. However, in contrast to this first result and the convictions of policy makers, the study shows that *properly designed* reputational mechanisms in which new entrants, with no history of track record, are entitled to an averaged or high reputation score – as in the case of the company studied by Decarolis, Pacini and Spagnolo (2016) and as is often done in the private sector, or with point systems in driving licenses – actually *promote rather than hinder entry* while, at the same time, delivering a substantial increase in high quality provision. The third important result of this study is that, consistently with the findings in Decarolis, Pacini and Spagnolo (2016), the total cost to buyers does not increase significantly when a reputational mechanism is established, even though costly quality provision grows. The introduction of bid subsidies for good past performance seems to benefit the buyer/tax payer by expanding competition for incumbency, reducing winning bids sufficiently to compensate the potential increase in procurement costs produced by bid subsidies.

6 Conclusions

The interaction between the shape of explicit procurement contracts and the design and functioning reputational mechanisms remains an important topic for future research.

In the study made by Decarolis, Pacini and Spagnolo (2016) the merits of using past performance are to stimulate greater efforts from contractors when executing public works. The evaluation of the evidence from an experiment undertaken by an Italian large multi-utility company subject to public procurement regulation has highlighted strong improvements in performance – quality and safety at work – after the firm announced its intention to use past performance scores to award future contracts.

Once the merits of this kind of reputation mechanism in improving contractor performance are demonstrated, many aspects remain open and give room for future research. In their work, these authors suggest focusing on how to optimize the parameters' weight, how to select the rating for new entrants, how to structure the weights in the awarding criteria, and how to choose the optimal "length" of the indicator and how heavily older information should be discounted. Even the optimal timeline at which the switch to a reputation system should occur seems an interesting problem to assess in the future.

As far as concerned the issue of entry the market when a reputational mechanism is adopted by buyers, Butler et al. (2013) demonstrate that a trade-off is not necessary between an appropriately designed reputational mechanisms and entry by new firms into a procurement market, as a well-calibrated reputational mechanism may increase entry and quality provision simultaneously, without increasing the cost for the buyer.

If confirmed in further studies, these findings suggest that the Federal Acquisition Regulation in the US, which established past performance as a criteria for selecting bids, has introduced room for an effective policy that – if appropriately designed and implemented – creates incentives to improve quality and efficiency in public procurement without undermining entry of new or foreign firms, or even facilitating it – a policy that EU regulators have been forbidding for a long time.[6]

The results in Butler et al. (2013) and in Decarolis, Pacini and Spagnolo (2016) show however that a past performance-based vendor rating policy, which aims to improve suppliers' quality and to not undermine of facilitate market entry, can obtain a positive outcome only when the reputational mechanism is appropriately designed. European policy makers should therefore not debate about whether a generic past performance mechanism should be introduced in public procurement process, and focus instead on how such a mechanism should be designed.

Notes

1 GAO-09-374, *Federal Contractors: Better Performance Information Needed to Support Agency Contract Award Decisions*, April 23, 2009.

2 Office of Federal Procurement Policy (OFPP), *Improving Contractor Past Performance Assessments: Summary of the Office of Federal Procurement Policy's Review*, and Strategies for Improvement, 21 January 2011.

3 Office of Management and Budget (OMB) released the memorandum, *Improving the Collection and Use of Information about Contractor Performance and Integrity*, dated 6 March 2013. The purpose of this memorandum was to establish a baseline for reporting compliance, set aggressive performance targets that can be used to monitor and measure reporting compliance, and ensure the workforce is trained to properly report and use this information. This memorandum establishes a 100% Annual Reporting Performance Target for Fiscal Year (FY) 2015 for past performance, reporting compliance on contracts over the Simplified Acquisition Threshold (SAT). OFPP's strategy to improve past performance information and respond to section 853 of the NDAA for Fiscal Year 2013 is to increase oversight of contractor performance evaluations, develop government-wide

past performance guidance and revise the FAR. OFPP worked with the FAR Council to revise the FAR to implement provisions of the NDAAs for Fiscal Years 2012 and 2013 related to assigning responsibility and accountability, implementing standards for complete evaluations and ensuring submissions are consistent with award fee evaluations. Revisions by OFPP and the FAR Council to the timing of the contractor comment process in accordance with the acts became effective in July 2014.

4 A new version of CPARS was released in July 2014, which merged three separate modules (ACASS, CCASS, CPARS) into one module to standardize the past performance evaluation process.

5 EU Directive 2014/24, art 57(4)(g)

6 Also thanks to these studies, with 2014/24 EU Directives on procurement, European public procurement policy has shifted towards a framework that has opened to the use of past performance, even if only as an exclusion criterion.

References

Albano, G. L., Cesi, B., and Iozzi, A. (2011). *'Relational' procurement contracts: A simple model of reputation mechanism.* CEIS Tor Vergata Research Paper Series, 9(10), No. 209.

Banerjee, A. V., and Duflo, E. (2000). Reputation effects and the limits of contracting: A study of the Indian software industry. *The Quarterly Journal of Economics*, 115(3), 989–1017.

Bovaird, T. (2006). Developing new forms of partnership with the 'market' in the procurement of public services. *Public Administration*, 84(1), 81–102.

Butler, J. V., Carbone, E., Conzo, P., and Spagnolo, G. (2013). *Reputation and entry in procurement.* Discussion Paper Nr 9651, Center for Economic Policy Research, London.

Calzolari, G., and Spagnolo, G. (2009). *Relational contracts and competitive screening.* Discussion Paper Nr 7434, Center for Economic Policy Research, London.

Decarolis, F., Pacini, R., and Spagnolo, G. (2016). *Past performance and procurement outcomes.* Working Paper Nr 22814, National Bureau of Economic Research, Cambridge, MA.

Dellarocas, C., Dini, F., and Spagnolo, G. (2006). Designing reputation mechanisms. In N. Dimitri, G. Piga, and G. Spagnolo (eds.), *Handbook of Procurement* (pp. 446–482). Cambridge: Cambridge University Press.

Doni, N. (2006). The importance of reputation in awarding public contracts. *Annals of Public and Cooperative Economics*, 77(4), 401–429.

Gordon, D. I., and Racca, G. M. (2014). Integrity challenges in the EU and US procurement systems. In G. M. Racca and C. R. Yukins (eds.), *Integrity and Efficiency in Sustainable Public Contracts: Corruption, Conflicts of Interests, Favoritism and Inclusion of Non-Economic Criteria in Public Contracts* (pp. 115–143). Bruxelles: Bruylant.

Heinrich, C. J. (2002). Outcomes – based performance management in the public sector: Implications for government accountability and effectiveness. *Public Administration Review*, 62(6), 712–725.

Hui, X., Saedi, M., Spagnolo, G., and Tadelis, S. (2017). *Certification, reputation and entry: An empirical analysis.* Unpublished Manuscript.

Kelman, S. (1990). *Procurement and Public Management: The Fear of Discretion and the Quality of Public Management.* Washington, DC: American Enterprise Institute.

Kim, I. G. (1998). A model of selective tendering: Does bidding competition deter opportunism by contractors? *The Quarterly Review of Economics and Finance*, 38(4), 907–925.

Osborne, D., and Gaebler, T. (1992). *Reinventing Government: How the Entrepreneurial Spirit Is Transforming Government.* New York: Perseus Books.

Pollitt, C., and Bouckaert, G. (2011). *Public Management Reform: A Comparative Analysis-New Public Management, Governance, and the Neo-Weberian State*. Oxford: Oxford University Press.

Spagnolo, G. (2012). Reputation, competition, and entry in procurement. *International Journal of Industrial Organization*, 30(3), 291–296.

Tadelis, S. (2016). Reputation and feedback systems in online platform markets. *Annual Review of Economics*, 8, September, 321–340.

Part I

Local preferences in public procurement

1 Colloquium

Zornitsa Kutlina-Dimitrova and Pedro Telles

1 Zornitsa Kutlina-Dimitrova – local preferences: avenues for increasing efficiency in international procurement markets

Public procurement is gaining importance on the trade negotiation agenda, both under the aegis of the WTO and at bilateral level in various preferential trade agreements. These trends reflect the economic importance of public procurement markets in terms of GDP and trade flows, as well as the fact that to date a relatively small part of these markets has been committed internationally, both at the bilateral and multilateral levels. In terms of economic importance worldwide, the size of government procurement spending as measured in the most recent GTAP database 9 amounts to 6–32 percent of GDP. In the EU alone, in 2011, public procurement expenditures including state-owned utility providers stood at €2.4 trillion, corresponding to almost 19 percent of EU GDP in that year (Cernat and Kutlina-Dimitrova, 2015).

Looking at the impetus from trade policy measures, the potential of committing public procurement markets is deemed increasingly important in an environment in which import duties are globally at a low level and efforts linked to regulatory cooperation has been largely unsuccessful.[1] In this context, in April 2014, additional liberalization rounds at the multilateral level led to the signature of the revised Government Procurement Agreement (GPA). Similarly, at bilateral level, an analysis of all regional trade agreements (RTAs) announced at the WTO shows that before the year 2000 only 17 RTAs featured a separate public procurement provision whereas, after the year 2000, the number of bilateral trade agreements with a stand-alone procurement chapter or article increased to 88. A similar analysis of all bilateral trade agreements notified by the EU to the WTO confirms this trend (Cernat and Kutlina-Dimitrova, 2015).

Coinciding in time, but particularly during and after the global financial crises, several governments opted to support domestic demand by introducing stimulus packages in order to sustain and boost domestic production. Several of these funding programs were subject to buy-local conditions.[2] Moreover, domestic preferences are not a phenomenon specific to crisis times; in fact many of these buy-local policies existed in a number of countries before the financial crises. Having this in mind, it is necessary to examine the presence of prevalent local preferences, or the so-called home bias, and to analyze why governments decide to buy goods and services from local versus foreign suppliers and the determinants of international government procurement.

In fact, a recent analysis by Cernat and Kutlina-Dimitrova (2016) of the Global Trade Alert (GTA) database makes clear that the number of newly introduced discriminatory measures in international public procurement markets has augmented markedly from two in 2012 to 66 in 2014. The analysis also shows that some governments have put more frequently discriminatory measures in place than others and that some states have been more often affected by discriminatory measures.

This rise in protectionist measures is worrying as we know from economic theory that domestic preferences in procurement markets can have non-trivial impact on production and welfare. 'Home-biased' procurement can distort international specialization and significantly impact on international trade flows especially in sectors where government spending is substantial compared to total spending and in sectors characterized by monopolistic competition (see Trionfetti, 2000).

Moreover, increasing the efficiency of public procurement markets is particularly important in times marked by fiscal consolidation pressure, as reducing (unproductive) expenditures is often considered the right way to stimulate cost-efficient general government expenditures and procurement of good and services in particular. Given the size of government procurement expenditure of 19 percent of GDP in the EU, for example, a cut in public procurement spending of 5 percent would imply a substantial cost reduction of almost 1 percent of EU GDP.

In spite of the size and importance of international public procurement markets there is currently a lack of economic analysis of the presence of 'home bias' in international public procurement and even more so on the determinants of a cross-border procurement award. In terms of the former, the literature by Trionfetti (2000), Brülhart and Trionfetti (2001), Shingal (2015) and more recently Rickard and Kono (2014) seem to provide empirical/data-driven evidence for the presence of 'home bias' in government procurement markets. Most of these papers look at the import penetration of governments compared to the one of the private sector. If a persistent difference between these two shares is identified, it is assumed that there is a 'home-bias' presence. Following somewhat different methodological approach, the econometric analysis by Rickard and Kono (2014) assesses the presence of 'home bias' in a gravity model of trade. The authors find that the coefficient of government procurement spending is significantly and negatively linked to bilateral imports. This result is similar to the one found in Crozet and Trionfetti (2002), where government public has a negative impact on trade flows in EU Member States.

This type of literature however does not analyze the determinants of cross-border procurement; that is, what is shaping governments' decision-making process on procuring from abroad versus domestically. This gap is filled by a recent paper of Kutlina-Dimitrova and Lakatos (2016) on the determinants of cross-border award. The authors explore all public procurement awards in EU Member States in the period 2008–2012 and assess econometrically the factors determining the probability of a cross-border award. The most important drivers from a policy perspective, all of them statistically significant, are presented in the following:

- Product market regulation indicators: The analysis shows that product market regulation indicators such as: (i) scope of public enterprises; (ii) regulatory protection of incumbents; and (iii) barriers to foreign direct investment (FDI) have a negative impact on the propensity of governments to source goods and services from abroad. This finding strongly supports the theoretical prediction by Evenett and Hoekman (2005) on the importance of competition restraining practices for procurement markets.
- Macroeconomic factors: Trade openness and per capita GDP also influence the probability of a cross-border win. These results are not surprising as public bodies of countries with more liberal trade regimes are expected to procure relatively more foreign goods and services. In the same vein, government authorities of wealthier countries should be inclined to source more foreign goods and services after controlling for openness.
- Government procurement level: There is a strong negative relationship between the public procurement purchases at the local level versus the central/federal level and the probability of a cross-border win. This finding is supported by the fact that, internationally, there are almost no commitments of government entities at the local level in bilateral and the plurilateral GPA agreement(s).[3] International procurement commitments are usually made at central/federal level as opposed to sub-central/local level.
- Contract value: The analysis shows that there is a stable positive relationship between the contract value and the propensity of a foreign firm winning a contract. This finding is intuitive as foreign companies are expected to face higher costs related to monitoring the foreign market and also compliance costs linked to the tender specifications, such as the need to translate the tender documents and comply with specific requirements.

The abovementioned results have important trade policy implications. Particularly, the fact that all three product market regulation indicators impact highly significantly, strongly and negatively on the probability of a cross-border bid shows that 'behind-the-border' measures such as barrier to FDI, entry-impeding legal provisions and the scope of public enterprises are affecting indirectly but strongly the distribution of foreign versus domestic contract awards. This result, coupled with the empirical literature that finds inconclusive evidence of the impact of the GPA on procurement flows, suggests that there are additional benefits to be reaped from extending the scope and the coverage of the GPA agreement. Moreover, other policy strategies such as the general trade openness in respect to FDI and non-tariff measures and competition fostering legislation may be at least as equally important.

The fact that it is at least likely to award a contract at the local level means that greater liberalization efforts at the sub-central level are required if one wants to achieve a substantial increase in international public procurement flows. This applies at the bilateral and multilateral level likewise. The recently negotiated free trade agreement between the EU and Canada sets a precedent in this respect: it is the first time a country has bilaterally committed to substantially open its public procurement market at the provincial and local level. Moreover, Canada has also granted market access to European companies to the so-called Crown corporations at provincial level, which were also not committed in the GPA.

The abovementioned findings also make clear that the probability of a cross-border award increases with the contract value. This also reflects the fact that the higher the contract value, the more likely it is that a foreign company submits a bid, as these companies are facing higher foreign market penetration cost. This has important implications for the likelihood of a SME participating in and consequently winning international public procurement tenders.

Another important aspect to be borne in mind when talking about local preferences is the fact that the empirical findings presented above cover direct cross-border procurement only. This international procurement vehicle is called modality 1 procurement (Cernat and Kutlina-Dimitrova, 2015). However, there are other government procurement modalities such as modality 2 (procurement through foreign subsidiaries) and modality 3 (value-added procurement through sub-contractors) that are more important for the way public authorities procure goods and services from abroad. Due to lack of data, however, we don't know which are the factors determining international public procurement through modalities 2 and 3.

Moreover, there was no economic assessment at the macro-level of the impact stemming from elimination of local preferences, which is indispensable in order to evaluate the cost of 'home-biased' procurement for the economy. This is largely due to the fact that until recently there was no input-output database and model accounting for the specificities of government procurement markets. In a first attempt Kutlina-Dimitrova (2017) provides an assessment of a cut in domestic preferences in GPA countries and hereby an indication of the likely impact of extending the scope of the GPA and the cost of price preference policies.

Another area of great importance for assessing local preferences is the identification and assessment of public procurement barriers. So far there is a collection of public procurement barriers in the framework of the GTA report. This database, however, although a very encouraging first attempt, is not complete. Even more importantly there is no taxonomy of public procurement barriers which would ensure a structured, coherent and harmonized approach from an economic and legal point of view. This work is crucial, as to be able to assess the impact of explicit (de-jure) barriers on international procurement flows there is a need for a sound methodological approach (taxonomy of procurement barriers) and an empiric estimation of the corresponding trade cost these barriers are causing for businesses.

The same applies to transparency provisions, which in theory should improve the visibility and accessibility of procurement opportunities for companies bidding for a tender from abroad and hence lead to more foreign awards. However, there is no in-depth assessment of transparency provisions so far.

To sum up, the above-presented findings and stylized facts suggest that in order to increase the international participation in public procurement markets several factors play a role. First, trade policy efforts should aim at ensuring commitments at the state/provincial and local level of procurement. The general more strategic focus on trade and FDI openness as well as on pro-competitive provisions and measures seems to be an important factor fostering international procurement. In terms of the increased protectionist trend observed in past years, abolishing local preferences as buy-local provisions would foster competition and stronger international participation in public procurement markets.

Furthermore efforts targeted at increasing transparency and ensuring certainty and predictability of the business environment for international companies through eProcurement, for example, are expected to be another adequate instrument for boosting international procurement.

Finally, public procurement in general and international procurement in particular are areas characterized by severe lack of data on both: the flows side – i.e. data is available (if at all) only for direct cross-border procurement (modality 1) – and on the barriers side – i.e. so far there is no taxonomy of procurement barriers and collection of explicit and implicit barriers. As a consequence, international efforts for data collection and analysis should be strongly encouraged.

2 Pedro Telles – localism: legal view

2.1 Introduction

The reason why we have a EU-wide regulation of public procurement is to open up the public sector markets to economic operators based in other Member States. The idea is that the only way to implement and conclude the single market is by ensuring that cross-border competition for public contracts can flourish. Success measured in cross-border procurement, however, proved elusive over the last 50 years.

Current direct cross-border procurement figures are abysmal. After 50 years of regulation and successive rounds of Directives, only 3.6 percent of procurement spend is won by economic operators based in other Member States (Ramboll, 2011). We do not know though what is the participation rate of foreign economic operators in contracts tendered by contracting authorities in the EU. Are they simply not turning up, thus explaining why the success rate is low? Or if they do turn up are they simply not competitive enough? Knowing this piece of information is crucial to really assess the reasons behind those cross-border procurement figures.

In absence of such data point, one must try to look at the numbers in context. If we use Member States' trade openness as a proxy for the ability of economic operators to sell cross-border, we find that the single market is working well overall (Fazekas and Skuhrovec, 2016). What can explain the poor showing in procurement then? In a word, localism.

I am using "localism" as an umbrella term for a number of different activities which amount to trade barriers or an unspoken preference for local economic operators. In this chapter I will be focusing my analysis on what may be four localism strategies that amount to trade barriers and what could be done to reduce their impact in direct cross-border procurement. These strategies are legal, and either exist for clear protectionist objectives or their protectionist nature is at least tolerated within the legal framework.

2.2 Social considerations

The first modern manifestation of localism worth referring to is the introduction of social considerations in public procurement. Their original premise seems reasonable though: who can really object to procurement pursuing social objectives which are within the role of the State anyway? The problem with (some) social considerations is their progressive detachment from the contract object nexus. In traditional procurement, any award criteria and technical specification need to be connected with the contract object. The logic behind this approach is also quite simple – allowing for any requirement to be set as a contract award criterion would simply leave too much discretion in the hands of the contracting authority, thus making it easier for rules to be bent in favour of specific economic operators. Furthermore, as it will be seen below the real objective of these clauses in practice is not to improve social conditions in general but to obtain local concessions. They amount to local social considerations and protectionism comes right in tow as a consequence.

Scotland (Scottish Government, 2008) and Wales (Welsh Government, 2014) are two good examples of social considerations being used to obtain local benefits and not a generic improvement to the public good. This can be seen even by looking at the name under which they are called by the respective regional governments: community benefits. In addition, they are presented as examples of good practice to avoid the "Scottish pound" and "Welsh pound" leaking to other economies (i.e. England).

It is now accepted within the EU legal framework that social considerations which are not connected with the contract object may be set as performance clauses. This approach raises a number of different problems. First, if any scope is left to the contractor to decide how the clause will be performed by allowing relevant information to be included in the tender, then the award decision may be influenced by a non-disclosed award criterion, making it challengeable. In this scenario the decision would be based on an illegal award criterion. Second, it forces economic operators to develop additional competencies in what will probably not be their core business. This may have an impact on SMEs which are by definition less able to accommodate requirements outside their core business. For the purposes of this chapter, local social considerations are also a problem for foreign economic operators, constituting an additional barrier to their participation in public procurement. As to comply with the local social consideration set as a performance clause, the foreign economic operator may have to price in a cost it is not used to price for social clauses which may be alien to their knowledge. In other words, economic operators need to become proficient in their core business and a potential minefield of different "social consideration" practices. In consequence, a local/national economic operator will be exposed to a more limited range of social considerations, giving it an advantage in comparison with a foreign one. This advantage is compounded if the social considerations at hand include the need to perform locally the services associated with them, which in my opinion is what contracting authorities would be looking for. For example, setting up an apprenticeship scheme has the same public good value irrespective of where it is done, but no contracting authority would accept a scheme set in a different country as counting towards its "social considerations".

There is another argument against social considerations as a performance clause disconnected from the contract's object: they are nothing else other than offsets with a new name. Offsets have a long and polarising history in defence procurement (Transparency International, 2010), where acquirers of defence material usually insist on unrelated "benefits" to the local/national economy to be provided by the contractor as a means to offset their cost. There is ample evidence they do not work in general and that they foster corruption, probably because breaking the nexus between the contract and unrelated services open the door for corruption to occur on those side deals.

2.3 Financial thresholds

Financial thresholds are the second current manifestation of localism as a trade barrier (Telles, 2013, 2016). They effectively guarantee that each contract valued above the set limits will be subject to the full EU rules, namely the Treaty principles and relevant Directives. Below said thresholds, however, contracting authorities are mostly subject to national rules and have to comply only with Treaty principles if any given contract is certain to generate cross-border interest. Recent(ish) data indicates that over 80 percent of procurement spend in the EU is actually spent below thresholds and not above.

It is difficult to define certain cross-border interest in advance, as the reality is that contracting authorities do not have the incentive to investigate possible cross-border interest and will defer to national rules when those exist or their own objectives. Therefore, there is limited chance that contracts designed to be won by local economic operators will actually be found out in breach of EU law.

Although there is no consistent data collected in most Member States, logic would imply that the reality for cross-border procurement is even worse below thresholds and certainly the case in Portugal (IMPIC, 2016) and Spain (Commission Staff, 2017). Although there is evidence that foreign economic operators tend to be more successful in larger contracts, the fact that we have had thresholds in place for almost 50 years certainly deters SMEs from ever wanting to do business directly with a contracting authority in another Member State for contracts with a value below thresholds.

There are talks – and certainly an ambition – of reforming threshold levels in the next few years as per Article 92 of the Directive 2014/24/EU, probably with the objective of raising them. If that indeed happens, the only logic behind such a move would be a protectionist one. Having said that, recent changes in some legal regimes below thresholds such as mandatory electronic procurement or the obligation to advertise most contracts may open the market in unanticipated ways, particularly in sectors with low opportunity and transaction costs.

2.4 Language

When it comes down to localism as a trade barrier, the issue of language is not usually taken into account. Language has been flagged already as the "elephant in the room" (Sanchez-Graells, 2012) and mentioned by economic operators as one of the elements leading to not bid for contracts based in other Member States. This can be observed in data for contracts tendered by Maltese and Irish contracting authorities which are done in English and in which UK economic operators have a success rate above the average (Ramboll, 2011).

Currently, Member States are free to determine what languages contracting authorities may adopt in their tendering procedures. It is no surprise that these tend to be limited to the official language(s) of the state in question. Using the national language for the tendering (and contract) puts foreign economic operators at a disadvantage in the tender, thus leading to the conclusion that only really motivated economic operators will make the go/no-go decision of tendering for a contract in another Member State. Economic operators which opted to establish a presence via a subsidiary in another Member State are not affected by language issues, but then they are not taken into account on the direct cross-border statistics.

While some Member States do offer some flexibility to contracting authorities in terms of choice of language, there is no evidence that contracting authorities actually take advantage of said options. Such approach by contracting authorities can easily be understood from an incentive perspective. Whereas private economic operators have a direct incentive in finding the best price for whatever they are buying – be it national or otherwise – contracting authorities answer to additional objectives, as can be seen above with the reference to social considerations.

2.5 Applicable contract law (and jurisdiction)

The final current example of localism acting as a trade barrier is the contract law applicable to the contract. Whereas in the private sector parties are (mostly) free to pact what law will be applicable to the contract, when it comes down to public contracts tendered within the EU, by definition the applicable law is going to be that of the host state. For a national economic operator or a foreign owned subsidiary this poses no problem, but for foreign ones this is yet another example of a barrier which puts them at a disadvantage as by definition they will not know all the intricacies of said law. This means an increase in perceived risk (even if it is not real) and as it is assessed before making the go/no-go decision it would also imply an immediate transaction cost of hiring local lawyers to provide assistance. This also can also explain why foreign economic operators appear more successful in larger contracts, as the added risk and transaction costs are defrayed over a bigger sum.

The differences between applicable contract law should not be minimized, from civil law systems where good faith is a fundamental principle and *culpa in contrahendo* a cornerstone of the system to common law ones where "buyer beware" principle applies instead. In addition, legal systems have evolved differently over the years also in the body of law applicable to public contract performance: in some, it is a branch of public law, in others, private law.

To really level the playing field between national and foreign economic operators, regulatory change should focus as much in the harmonisation of the law applicable to the contract's performance as we have applied to the procurement stage.

3 Zornitsa Kutlina-Dimitrova – response to paper 2

The author of the note 'Localism: legal view', Pedro Telles, makes the point that there are "behind-the-border" barriers in public procurement which are acting as trade barriers, hence deterring the access of foreign suppliers to international procurement markets. In general this is described as one of the reasons why foreign participation in procurement markets is limited and direct cross-border procurement in the EU stands at 3.6 percent. The author then presents four approaches in public procurement which presumably act as trade barriers and points to their detrimental impact on cross-border procurement.

These four approaches concern:

- Social considerations;
- Financial thresholds;
- Use of languages;
- Applicable contract law (and jurisdiction).

In respect to social considerations in public procurement, Pedro Telles argues that taking such consideration into account is not wrong per se but that problems arise when the pursuit of those is detached from the contract object nexus. In simple words, allowing for any additional requirements to be set as contract award criteria leaves much of a free space for the contracting authority to possibly favor specific (local) economic operators. Moreover, it may be particularly difficult for SMEs, for example, to comply with requirements which are outside the scope of their core business.

The author also makes a case for lowering the financial threshold above which EU rules should be applied as below threshold procurement is generally subject to national rules and thus relevant EU Directives do not apply to this type of procurement. Moreover, Pedro Telles argues that the import penetration of below threshold procurement is lower than the one of above threshold procurement for the same reasons.

The use of different languages by contracting authorities is also according to the author an important trade barrier, as many economic operators have pointed to the use of different languages as one of the main reasons for not bidding for a cross-border contract. Finally, the fact that in public contracts the law applicable to the contract is set to be the law of the jurisdiction where the contracting authority is located is potentially another factor putting foreign suppliers at a disadvantage.

The fact that the import penetration of direct cross-border public procurement is lower than that of private economic operators is not surprising at least for two reasons. First, the direct cross-border procurement is only one vehicle for international public procurement. As introduced by Cernat and Kutlina-Dimitrova (2015), the concept of modalities of international public procurement shows that in addition to modality 1 (direct-cross border procurement), there are two other vehicles through which foreign suppliers bid for public procurement contracts. The most important one is modality 2 (commercial presence procurement) where a domestic subsidiary of a foreign company bids "locally" for a public procurement contract. Modality 3 (value-added indirect international procurement) describes a situation where foreign companies participate in a tender indirectly along the value-chain as sub-contractors or in lots. Moreover, a study by Ramboll (2011) shows that in fact the most important modality for international procurement in terms of the total value awarded is modality 2, followed by modality 3, while modality 1 is a distant third in terms of economic relevance.

This is also implicitly reflected in the note by Pedro Telles which draws attention to the fact that language barriers and the problems arising from the applicable contract law do not affect (or affect to a lesser extent) foreign subsidiaries. This may also mean that foreign subsidiaries are aware of the barriers mentioned by the author and have managed to avoid them by being locally present in the foreign market.

Second, the spending patterns of contracting authorities are different from the ones of the private sector. Government bodies are more heavily orientated towards purchasing services and works (construction) which naturally are less tradable than goods. This explains partly why the import penetration of governments is lower than the one of the private sector. Having said that, it is beyond doubt that behind-the-border barriers or de-jure discriminatory provisions prevent foreign suppliers from bidding and winning public contracts.

In respect to considering social objectives in public procurement, there is certainly a need for a thorough discussion and cost-benefit analysis of their potentially discriminatory impact on cross-border procurement and the degree with which they succeed to achieve the socially desired objectives.

In respect to lowering the threshold for public contracts under which EU law would apply, the argument presented by Pedro Telles is meaningful. I also think that the cross-border share of below threshold procurement is likely to be significantly lower than the one of above threshold procurement. However, a discussion on the compliance burden of procuring entities with the EU Directives would be appreciated, as it will be a comment upon the trade-off between loss of flexibility of public authorities to choose the preferred procedure to procure low-value contracts and an increase in the probability of awarding a procurement contract to a foreign company.

4 Pedro Telles – response to paper 1

Kutlina-Dimitrova presents in her paper a number of interesting ideas behind the low cross-border direct procurement which I alluded to in my first paper and how the so-called 'home bias' could explain said figure. Kutlina-Dimitrova cites Cernat and Kutlina-Dimitrova (2016) and earlier research from economics to show that protectionist measures have been on the rise when one compares the delta between import penetration by the private sector and that of the public sector. She then proceeds to provide some more specific clues about the determinants behind the numbers such as product market regulation indicators, macro-economic factors, government procurement level and contract value. Looking at these in some more detail appears to be a good starting point for this commentary.

After four or five decades of regulation one would expect that at least the first factor (product market regulation indicators) would have subsided by now. The same can be said for macro-economic factors and contract value. After all, if it is possible and cost effective for a citizen to buy low-value goods cross-border, why would it not be as such for the public sector? Therefore, it is possible to conclude that the problem is not with the goods or services themselves or free movement in general but with conditions which are specific to public procurement, be it incentives/objectives followed by contracting authorities or how the buying is carried out. It is interesting to note that those determinants reside outside the public procurement procedures and that at most these are simply instrumental to achieve other goals and objectives.

In face of the findings presented by Kutlina-Dimitrova and Lakatos (2016), one has to wonder if the policy-making emphasis of regulating procurement processes to the detriment of associated areas of intervention by public bodies may explain said conclusions. It may well be that we are achieving "diminishing returns" at each passing generation of regulation of public procurement procedures. Just by looking at the increase on the total number of procedures with similar objectives in the current Directive 2014/24/EU that we are now "splitting hairs" to find the differences between them (Telles and Butler, 2014). If improving the procedures is no longer the low-hanging fruit of changes in procurement regulation that could yield significant improvements for the single market – in the sense that it is more accessible by economic operators based in other Member States – the work by Cernat and Dimitrova highlights what areas EU regulation should focus on in the near future.

From an economics perspective it would be interesting to probe those various factors in more detail as more procurement data become available for empirical research. It would be especially interesting to see if contract value holds up as a predictor of success by foreign economic operators in all markets/sectors or if other factors play a causal part as well such as competition levels or regulatory regimes.

As for a potential taxonomy of current procurement barriers, in addition to the potential determinants put forward by Kutlina-Dimitrova and Lakatos (2016) as well as those I suggested in my first submission (social considerations, financial thresholds, language and applicable law/jurisdiction), perhaps there is still work to be done at the procedural level to improve the attractiveness of supplying goods and services cross-border. While it is true that the move to electronic procurement, full deployment of the European Single Procurement Document and getting rid of burdensome pre-qualification questionnaires will lower the transaction cost for participants, there is still scope for procedural improvements. Good examples of this spirit are the work being done by the Government Digital Service (https://gds.blog.gov.uk/about/) in the UK and 18F (https://18f.gsa.gov) in the US. While the work carried out is not directly meant to increase cross-border procurement or to specifically attract bidders based in other Member States, lowering the transaction costs (especially for digital services or "goods") may actually provide a boon for foreign economic operators. At this time, all of the above are simply conjectures and a few ideas worth exploring with further research, preferably in quasi-natural experiments (Angrist and Pischke, 2010) which could help define what works or not.

It is, however, important not to forget that Kutlina-Dimitrova's dataset covered only contracts above the EU thresholds and that over 80 percent of public procurement spend in the EU still occurs below thresholds (Eurostat, gov_oth_procur descriptor – discontinued in 2010). This spend is subject mostly to national rules, making it prime candidate for localism or local preferences. Under the current legal regime, as long as the contracts do not have a certain cross-border interest (Treumer, 2012; Telles, 2013; Bogdanowicz, 2015) then Member States are free to award them as they see fit, and localism or local preferences is perfectly legal. The problem with the leeway given to Member States below thresholds is that the slope from legal localism to illegal localism by gaming the system as to avoid external competition for national incumbents is quite short. There is now a growing body of empirical evidence (Palguta et al., 2015; Fazekas and Skuhrovec, 2016; Bobilev et al., 2015) that Member States are engaging in the strategic definition of contract values right below thresholds as to avoid them being subject to further competition and naturally the bulk of EU regulation. It seems there is a clustering of contracts right beneath thresholds which would otherwise be subject to more transparency and competition. While it may be too early to conclude that corruption is a leading cause behind this strategic behaviour it is certainly implied by that research (Palguta et al., 2015) and questions should be asked about this practice.

It appears that if we are to effectively achieve a single market which covers public procurement, the way forward may well be to create a taxonomy of the reasons and practices which lead to legal and illegal localism, so that further empirical research and policy priorities can be devised. It may well be the most promising area will be found outside public procurement procedures and related practice.

5 Zornitsa Kutlina-Dimitrova – conclusions

The current economic research on international public procurement including my own analyses briefly reviewed in the above note 'Local preferences: avenues for increasing efficiency in international procurement markets' shows that the factors determining the probability of a foreign public procurement award are multidimensional and complex. Surely local preferences (de facto and de jure) among others play an essential role in shaping the decision of government authorities to purchase domestically versus from abroad. The trend observed in several countries during the economic crisis to implement explicit buy-local preferences as a mean of boosting domestic production and favoring local firms has been reinforced in past years.

In that respect, as mentioned in the note, clear evidence of the impediments to international government procurement in numerous countries can be derived from the GTA database, which tracks newly introduced discriminatory measures around the world, including in the field of public procurement. As shown in a recent analysis by Cernat and Kutlina-Dimitrova (2016), the number of newly introduced almost certainly discriminatory measures has increased considerably between 2012 and 2014 from two to 66. The database also provides information on the country implementing the measures and it can be shown that some countries make use of explicit discriminatory measures in cross-border government procurement more frequently than others.

Having said that, it cannot be claimed that discriminatory buy-local policies are the only drivers of international public procurement flows. In fact, economic theory and empiric research as the ones presented above show that there are various determinants behind the decision of government authorities to purchase goods and services domestically versus from abroad. For example, and to respond to the question raised by Pedro Telles, the contract value holds as a predictor for direct cross-border public procurement award across sectors, as we included sectoral fixed effects in our econometric analysis (see Kutlina-Dimitrova and Lakatos, 2016).

Moreover, additional factors, which have not been yet analyzed econometrically due to lack of data or for methodological reasons, may play a role in cross-border public procurement purchases. In that respect, procedural improvements such as a reduction of the administrative burden faced by companies have the potential to affect positively the probability of a cross-border award. This of course can only happen if foreign companies were facing higher share of the burden before the procedural improvements were put into place.

To conclude on the empirical research, much more analysis and essentially better data is needed in order to be able to adequately assess the various determinants of cross-border government procurement and their interplay. This research should focus not only on direct cross-border awards (modality 1) but also on government procurement through foreign affiliates and subsidiaries (modality 2) and indirect value-chain procurement through subcontractors (modality 3).

Finally, in respect to the remark on the taxonomy of public procurement barriers, this taxonomy should cover both implicit and explicit public procurement barriers, as not only de jure discriminatory provisions prevent governments from buying foreign goods and services, but also various other implicit barriers may impede companies from bidding abroad.

6 Pedro Telles – conclusions

It is interesting to note that across two very different disciplines such as law and economics there is some commonality in terms of concepts and issues arising from localism. There is not, however, a complete super imposition in findings and that is to be celebrated as an example of cross-pollination between our disciplines. This final submission will touch a couple of points raised by Kutlina-Dimitrova in her reply to my original paper. First, I will consider the comments about the different cross-border procurement modalities and second the potential implications of lowering financial thresholds as a measure to reduce localism.

As for the three different cross-border procurement modalities (direct, commercial presence procurement and value-added indirect international procurement) introduced by Cernat and Kutlina-Dimitrova (2015) and Ramboll (2011), it is important to distinguish between which modalities are a product of specific public procurement regulation and those arising from general internal market principles such as freedom of establishment or movement of goods. Looking at those three modalities, only direct cross-border procurement can be attributed to public procurement.

The others are not controlled/decided by the contracting authority and are simply the consequence of general principles of EU law. Economic operators can establish and operate in other Member States because of freedom of establishment and not procurement rules. The same can be said about foreign value-added goods imported and integrated into a bid presented by a national economic operator. While these successes are to be celebrated they should not be taken into account when measuring the success or failure of EU procurement rules, as they simply add noise and not signal to the data.

Kutlina-Dimitrova raises a relevant point about the transaction costs implied by my suggestion of lowering the EU procurement financial thresholds. When putting forward and idea for legal reform it is important to consider the costs side by side with the benefits. As such, simply submitting contracts currently excluded to the EU principles with cross-border advertising would not entail significant transaction costs in comparison with simply national advertising. They would however be more demanding to run instead of negotiated procedures without prior call for competition, but at least in the UK there has been a movement to reduce the scope for this type of discretionary procedures (Cabinet Office, 2011), so the fairer comparison is between the improved practice now developing and the suggested EU-wide advertising alternative. It is entirely possible that improved contract visibility arising from national advertising practice by itself would raise the participation and success rate of economic operators based in other Member States, but such hypotheses can only be tested with appropriate tender data.

The other option would be to simply apply current EU public procurement rules (i.e. Directive 2014/24/EU) to all contracts irrespective of value. While the transaction costs would be higher than the alternative above it is important the comparison is a proverbial "apple to apples" one. It is one thing to discuss the 2004-era rules and another the 2014-era ones, yet to be fully implemented in most Member States. The newer set of rules does take steps to limit transaction costs by forcing the use of the European Procurement Single Document, reducing timescales and mandating electronic procurement from 2018 onwards. Only when that happens will we be able to truly measure the real transaction costs in EU-compliant public procurement today.

In conclusion, after almost 50 years of positive procurement obligations arising from EU Directives on procurement aiming to reduce discrimination against foreign economic operators it is clear there is still significant scope for regulatory improvements. However, reducing localism as to achieve the aim of an internal market will require fresh thinking and a focus on regulatory areas such as language, thresholds, applicable contract law and contracting authority incentives which have not been targeted so far.

Notes

1 An assessment of the successes and failures of regulatory cooperation efforts is provided in Hamilton and Pelkmans (2015).
2 See OECD (2015), Evenett (2009).
3 The negotiated free trade agreement between the EU and Canada is an exception, as Canada has committed its local level procurement in a bilateral free trade agreement for the first time. See European Commission (2013).

References

Angrist, J. D., and Pischke, J. S. (2010). The credibility revolution in empirical economics: How better research design, is taking the con out of econometrics. *Journal of Economic Perspectives*, 24(2), 3–30.

Bobilev, R., Guglielmo, A., Paltseva, R., and Spagnolo, G. (2015). *Public procurement thresholds and data in Sweden*. Uppdragsforskningrapport 2015, 3.

Bogdanowicz, P. (2015). *(Still) qualitative approach to a cross-border interest and application European Union Law to concessions?* Some Remarks on C-388/12 Comune di Ancona Judgment, 2015 24 PPLR p. NA22–27.

Brülhart, M., and Trionfetti, F. (2001). Industrial specialisation and public procurement: Theory and empirical evidence. *Journal of Economic Integration*, 16(1), 106–127.

Cabinet Office (2011). Procurement policy note – Guidance on implementing requirements for greater transparency in Central Government procurement and contracting – Information Note 02/11.

Cernat, L., and Kutlina-Dimitrova, Z. (2015). *International public procurement: From scant facts to hard data*. RSCAS Policy Papers PP 2015/07, Robert Schuman Centre for Advanced Studies, European University Institute, Florence.

Cernat, L., and Kutlina-Dimitrova, Z. (2016). *TTIP and public procurement: Going beyond the tip of the iceberg*. CEPS Policy Brief No. 339, March.

Commission Staff Working Paper (2017). Country report Spain 2017 including an in-depth review on the prevention and correction of macroeconomic imbalances COM (2017) 90 final.

Crozet, M., and Trionfetti, F. (2002). Effets-frontières entre les pays de l'Union européenne: le poids des politiques d'achats publics. *Economie International*, 1(89–90), 189–208.

European Commission (2013). *Facts and figures of the EU-Canada free trade deal*. memo. Available at http://europa.eu/rapid/press-release_MEMO-13-911_en.htm.

Evenett, S. J. (2009). The emerging contours of crisis-era protectionism. In S. Evenett (ed.), *Broken Promises: A G-20 Summit Report by Global Trade Alert* (pp. 15–24). London: Centre for Economic Policy Research.

Evenett, S. J., and Hoekman, B. (2005). Government procurement: Market access, transparency, and multilateral trade rules. *European Journal of Political Economy*, 21(1), 163–183.

Fazekas, M. I., and Skuhrovec, J. (2016). *Universalistic rules-particularlistic implementation: The EU's single market for government purchases*. 2016 OECD Integrity Forum.

Hamilton, D., and Pelkmans, J. (2015). *Rule-Makers or Rule-Takers? Exploring the Transatlantic Trade and Investment Partnership*. Rowman & Littlefield Int.

IMPIC (2016). *Contratacao Publica em Portugal – 2015.*

Kutlina-Dimitrova, Z. (2017). Can we put a price on extending the scope of the GPA? First quantitative assessment. DG TRADE Chief Economist notes 2017–1 Directorate General for Trade, European Commission.

Kutlina-Dimitrova, Z., and Lakatos, C. (2016). Determinants of direct cross-border public procurement in EU member states. *Review of World Economics*, 152(3), 501–527.

OECD (2015). Emerging policy issues: Localization barriers to trade. Trade and Agriculture Directorate, Working Party of the Trade Committee, TAD/TC/WP(2014)17/FINAL.

Palguta, Pertold, Asfhenfelter, Bauer, Dusek et al. (2015). *Corruption and Manipulation of Public Procurement: Evidence From the Introduction of Discretionary Thresholds*. Prague: CERGE-EI

Ramboll (2011). *Cross-border procurement above EU thresholds*. Final report for the European Commission, Copenhagen. [Online] Available at http://www.eipa.eu/files/topics/public_procurement/cross_border_procurement_en.pdf

Rickard, S., and Kono, D. (2014). Think globally, buy locally: International agreements and government procurement. *The Review of International Organizations*, 9(3), 333–352.

Sanchez-Graells, A. (2012). Are the procurement rules a barrier for cross-border trade within the European Market? In G. Olykke, C. Risvig, and C. Tvarno (eds.), *EU Procurement Directives – Modernization, Growth and Innovation* (pp. 107–133).

Scottish Government (2008). *Community Benefits in Public Procurement.*

Shingal, A. (2015). Econometric analyses of home bias in government procurement. *Review of International Economics*, 23(1), 188–219.

Telles, P. (2013). The good, the bad and the ugly: EU's internal market, public procurement thresholds and cross-border interest. *Public Contract Law Journal*, 43(1), 3–25.

Telles, P. (2016). Public procurement financial thresholds in the EU and their relationship with the GPA. *EPPPL, 11*.

Telles, P., and Butler, L. (2014). Award procedures in the Directive 2014/24/EU. In F. Lichere and M. Burgi (eds.), *Modernising Public Procurement: The New Directive* (pp. 131–184). European Law Series. Djof.

Transparency International (2010). *Defence offsets: Addressing the risks of corruption and raising transparency*.

Treumer, S. (2012). Cross-border interest and application of EU law principles in the public procurement context at national level. Dragos D., Caranta R. (eds.), *Outside the EU Procurement Directives – Inside the Treaty?, European Procurement Law Series vol. 4, DJØF Publishing, Denmark.* (pp. 335–358).

Trionfetti, F. (2000). Discriminatory public procurement and international trade. *The World Economy*, 23(1), 57–76.

Welsh Government (2014). *Delivering Maximum Value for the Welsh Pound.*

2 CARICOM

Small market – big money. Amalgamating the procurement market to transform small size into an economic advantage

Sharlene Jo-Ann Shillingford McKlmon and Shirley Gayle Sinclair

1 Introduction

1.1 Economic profile of the region

Trade is recognized as a catalyst for economic development. It follows therefore that public procurement, as a vehicle to facilitate trade, can be a major driver for national development. The small economies of the Caribbean Community (CARICOM) face several challenges in achieving economic integration and economic development. These include geographic location and spread, physical and population size, import dependency as well as dependency on tourism and few export markets, transportation (air and sea) and customs, among other issues. CARICOM is comprised of fifteen countries of the Caribbean, being mostly island states. The countries are far from homogenous and reflect many differences in population and physical size and levels of economic development. Table 2.1 shows the GDP, size and population of the Region.

GDP Per Capita varies greatly with the Bahamas, Trinidad, Tobago and Barbados at the top end and Belize, Guyana and Haiti at the bottom end. Geographically the region comprises small islands as well as large continental territories. Guyana, Suriname, Belize and Jamaica are the largest territories. Guyana at 214,000 sq. km is the largest. The combined size of the other 14 countries is 247,282 sq. km. Essentially almost every single CARICOM country can fit within Guyana. Haiti has the largest population of almost ten million while Montserrat has the smallest population of just over nine thousand, for a total regional population of 17.387 million.

Figure 2.1 depicts the market size in relation to population. Haiti clearly has the largest population. While it has a comparatively low GDP to the other countries, its public procurement would be very large owing both to the size of the population and to the development and structural needs.

With the transition from agro-economies, and the protection including special and differential treatment which characterized the non-reciprocal trade agreements of the past, services has emerged as the dominant sector across the region contributing the most to GDP. The recent recession in the US and Europe had

Table 2.1 Economic and geographic profile of CARICOM

Name of state	*GDP US$ billions*	*GDP per capita US$ thousands*	*Physical size (sq km)*	*Population*
Antigua/Barbuda (A&B)	1.287	14414.302	442	88,000
Bahamas (BAH)	8.705	23902.805	13,940	352,000
Barbados (BAR)	4.412	15773.555	431	278,000
Belize (BEL)	1.763	4,841.735	22,966	343,000
Dominica (DOM)	0.497	7,030.145	754	71,000
Grenada (GND)	0.954	8936.578	344	105,000
Guyana (GUY)	3.164	4125.021	214,970	775,000
Haiti (HA)	8.618	804.564	27,750	10,413,000
Jamaica (JA)	13.924	4948.018	10,991	2,752,000
Montserrat* (MON)	0.04378	8,500	102	5,189
St. Kitts & Nevis (SKN)	0.896	16109.707	261	57,000
St. Lucia (SLU)	1.416	8191.984	616	168,000
St. Vincent & Grenadines (SVG)	0.757	6,882.286	389	110,000
Suriname (SUR)	5.192	9,305.687	163,270	546,000
Trinidad & Tobago (TT)	27.268	18,085.759	5,128	1,329,000
TOTAL	**78.8967**			**17,387,000**

Source IMF WEO 2016

* Figures for Montserrat from CIA World Factbook – GDP figures are 2006

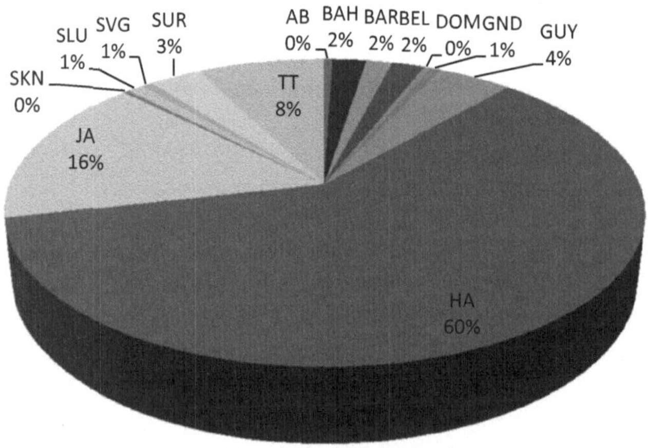

Figure 2.1 Market distribution based on population

severe repercussions in the region, further devastating economies that were in many cases already under stress. Several of the countries saw a decline in economic activity resulting from sharp decreases in tourism income and remittances, as well as escalation in the cost of food and other imports. Many of the countries are highly indebted, reflecting debt-to-GDP ratios in excess of 80 percent, with two, Jamaica and Grenada, in excess of 100 percent, thereby limiting governments' ability to fund much-needed public services. As a region, the Caribbean has had a negative annual balance of payments for the past 20 years.

1.2 The Caribbean community (CARICOM) single market and economy (CSME)

The CARICOM Single Market and Economy (CSME) was introduced in 2001 with the Revised Treaty of Chaguramas. It was intended to serve as a platform to better position the small vulnerable countries of the region to meet the challenges and better exploit the opportunities of the changing regional, hemispheric and global environment and to achieve the region's objectives. Some of its expected benefits are: accelerated, coordinated and sustained economic development and convergence; expansion of trade and economic relations with third states; and enhanced levels of international competitiveness. The single economic space is intended to bring with it optimal allocation and utilization of the region's resources; access for national producers to the entire CARICOM market in the first instance and then to market opportunities further afield and; and increased opportunities for CARICOM nationals for investment, production, provision of services and for employment in a new CARICOM environment. The CSME is to be governed by two key principles: non-discrimination on grounds of nationality only; and most favored nation (MFN) treatment, which prohibits treating a third country (or a third State) better than another CARICOM Member State.[1]

The integration process within CARICOM accelerated seven years ago when 12 of its 15 Member States declared themselves CSME compliant. Thus far, all of the Member States have taken legislative actions which are sufficient to establish and make the Single Market a functional entity. However, full implementation of the legal provisions is still outstanding. Today, the CSME remains mostly legally established but not fully operational. It should be recognized that the CARICOM Single Market was never intended to be implemented in a single undertaking. Article 239 of the Revised Treaty of Chaguramas addresses the Built-in Agenda, which includes contingent rights, government procurement, e-commerce, free zones and similar jurisdiction, and free circulation.

2 Pubic procurement within a single market and economy

2.1 Background: the regional regime for public procurement within CARICOM

The authority for developing a protocol on government procurement is Article 239 of the 2001 Revised Treaty of Chaguaramas establishing the Caribbean Community (CARICOM). Article 239 mandates that CARICOM Member States elaborate a regime for government procurement within the Single Market (CSME). This was to be achieved through the negotiation of obligations and rights to be contained within the Procurement Protocol, which is to be integrated into the Revised CARICOM Treaty.

The first stage for building a regime for public procurement consistent with the CSME began in 2001. With the support of Canada and the IDB, between 2001 and 2005, 15 Country Procurement Assessment Reports (CPARS) and 15 procurement statistical reports were produced. The reports found that procurement expenditure for central government was spread out among 500-plus central procuring entities with goods being the highest contributor to total government procurement. Based on data from the IMF World Economic Outlook, at 15 percent of the 2005 GDP, the region would have spent US$7.7 billion on public procurement.

At the end of the period of research and review, while acknowledging that some progress had been made in Jamaica to tackle procurement reform and while Guyana had introduced a dedicated procurement act, author Hagop Angaladian in his work "Public Procurement in the CARICOM – A Comparative Assessment 2005" concluded that "competitive public procurement in all remaining CARICOM States are obsolete and shallow . . . and the result is dysfunctional procurement regimes which translate into segregated pockets of procurement practices and not national systems". Very little has changed since 2005. Essentially, with the absence of dedicated legislation governing public procurement, and with the heavy reliance on outdated Financial Administration and Audit Acts, the provisions do not entail a strategic vision and fail the key tests of economy, efficiency, reliability, fairness, competitiveness, transparency and accountability.

The research that was conducted and the abovementioned reports that were produced between 2001 and 2005 contributed to the development of the first draft Framework Regional Integration Policy on Public Procurement (FRIP) in 2006. The policy went through six iterations before it was approved seven years later in May 2011 by the Council for Trade and Economic Development at its 32nd Meeting in Georgetown, Guyana. During those seven years between the first presentation of the policy and its approval, multiple simultaneous national reform initiatives began, all of which are ongoing and which will require imminent convergence if regional harmonization is to be strategically tackled, and successfully and effectively achieved.

2.2 Current state of public procurement

Over the past decade several of the countries with the support of international development partners such as the IDB, Canada, the World Bank and the EU have engaged in some aspect of modernization or reform of their procurement system. Much of this work has been focused on first generation reforms including developing new legislation to regulate procurement. Countries such as Jamaica and Guyana have undergone varying levels of reform, with Jamaica leading in the breadth and depth of the reform, including the establishment of a comprehensive institutional framework, but lacking in a primary procurement law. Guyana, in 2003, passed a Procurement Act; however, some of its key institutional bodies, including the Public Procurement Commission and the Bid Protest Committee are yet to be established. Both Trinidad and Barbados are at the early stages of reform, with both attempting to develop procurement acts. Haiti has had procurement legislation for several years; however, the IDB-financed operations are challenged by low institutional capacity, lack of trained personnel and disproportionate level of procurement activity due to the reconstruction following the earthquake of 2010. Within the Eastern Caribbean group (OECS) the support of the World Bank has led to several drafts of a harmonized public procurement model act for implementation in the six OECS territories. Only two countries, Antigua and Barbuda[2] in 2011 and Dominica[3] in 2013, had their Parliaments successfully approve dedicated public procurement legislation. In the case of Dominica, however, the Act is not yet in force.[4] Beyond the steps of legal reform, very little advancement has been made in transforming and modernizing public procurement. The current state reflects procurement systems that are outdated and structurally out of alignment with current demands, continuing to treat public procurement as an afterthought rather than a strategic function where planning is key. Public procurement management is weak and processes are inefficient and do not achieve value for money objectives. Human resource capacity is lacking due to a deficit in trained and competent professionals. Tables 2.2 and 2.3 provide a panoramic view of the systems in the Caribbean.

In short, procurement reform has been slow, sometimes incomplete, and in some countries not attempted. The countries face significant challenges due to the lack of (i) well-functioning administrative systems and processes; (ii) legislative and regulatory framework and guidelines; (iii) distinctive leadership at the national level with a strategic vision of public procurement and what it can achieve; and (iv) Project Implementation Units (PIUs) and Executing Agencies (EAs) that absorb the better public officers, who then rarely return to public service.

Strengthening initiatives have been proposed in the Strategic Plans which accompany the Methodology for Assessing Procurement Systems (MAPS), Public Expenditure and Financial Accountability (PEFA) and other public financial management diagnostics. However, implementation of the proposed interventions has been slow and in some cases not at all administered. The reasons for this vary and include the lack of political will for the changes, absence of funds, weak interest on the civil society side or a combination of all.

Consequently, we find that there are countries which have undergone comprehensive legislative reform and which, despite the new legal framework, have failed to deliver even moderate improvement of knowledge, capacity and quality in the procurement processes and procurement function, and have achieved little progress toward international standards. Conversely, there are countries which have not established dedicated procurement legislation but have worked on the development of administrative norms and the establishment of institutional bodies to support the procurement processes; however those institutions alone have failed to yield efficient, strategic, well-planned and effective cost-saving procurement. This is in large part due to the fact that the governments of the region have not committed to investing resources in procurement reform. The reform process has been largely donor driven and funded. This trend has been described by Andrews, Pritchett and Woolcock (2012) as "isomorphic mimicry" where there is a "tendency to introduce reforms that enhance an entity's external legitimacy and support, even when they do not demonstrably improve performance". The authors further note that an outcome of this is the formation of "capability traps: a dynamic in which governments constantly adopt reforms to ensure ongoing flows of external financing and legitimacy yet never actually improve". When donor prompting relents and funding dries up, reforms come to a virtual standstill.

In effect, as a region, the countries of the Caribbean have not been able to gain, much less maximize on the benefits of, planning, strategizing and organizing effective public spending. The state of the capability of Public Procurement Systems is very low and with severe deficiencies in the corresponding condition of human capital. Table 2.2 attempts to capture at a glance the state of procurement in each of the CARICOM countries. Essentially, the matrix shows the strength of some 20 indicators (also found in MAPS diagnostics) in each of the national systems. The scoring is based on a 0–5 measurement basis, the Shillingford-Gayle Scale (SGS), as follows:

0- It does not exist;
1- It exists in draft form; it is not yet implemented and/or it does not impact on the operations of the system;
2- It may exist but it is weak;
3- It exists. Its use is not mandatory hence occasional. It cannot always be found. It does not always work. It needs updating.
4- It exists; it is used. It functions though not exactly as it should. It needs strengthening to do a better job. It is on the right track.
5- It exists. It has the qualities of and functions according to good international practices.

In essence, ten countries rank in the range 0 to 1 indicating that for ten countries while there are some arrangements in place, they are rudimentary, do not constitute procurement "systems" and there is no positive impact on operations. Three countries are ranked in the 1 to 2 range, meaning that whatever "system" exists is weak and does not always work. One system, ranked at 4, is on the right track.

On examination of the average among the 15 countries, within the context of the four MAPS pillars, the "Legislative and Regulatory Framework" at a score of 1.8 is weak. The "Institutional Framework and Management Capacity" at a score of 0.6 does not exist or does not impact on operations. The "Procurement Operations and Market Practices" at a score of 2.1 is weak and "Integrity and Transparency" at a score of 1 does not exist or does not impact positively on operations within the system.

2.3 Size of the public procurement market

While the accepted estimate for public procurement in OECD countries is 15 percent of GDP, some developing countries cite up to 35 percent of GDP is spent in public procurement. In the Caribbean public procurement is likely between the 20 percent to 30 percent range. This is because the private sector is not very strong and so the government is the greatest economic driver. In addition there are annual spikes in public spending following the annual hurricane season. For the purpose of this chapter, 20 percent of GDP is used as the estimate of public procurement

Table 2.2 Caribbean public procurement matrix 1

Shillingford-Gayle scale: It does not exist. **0**; It exists in draft form; It is not yet implemented and/or it does not impact on the operations of the system. **1**; It may exist but it is weak. **2**; It exists. Its use is not mandatory hence occasional. It cannot always be found. It does not always work. It needs updating. **3**; It exists; It is used. It functions though not exactly as it should. It needs strengthening to do a better job. It is on the right track. **4**; It exists. It has the qualities of and functions according to good international practices.**5**

INDICATOR	*COUNTRY*														*Indicator Average*
	AB	*BAH*	*BAR*	*BEL*	*DOM*	*GND*	*GUY*	*HA*	*JA*[i]	*SKN*	*SLU*	*SVG*	*SUR*	*TT*	
Start of reform	2008	2011	2010	2011	2008	2008	2000	1999	1998	2008	2008	2008	2011	2012	
Legislative and regulatory framework	1	1	1	0	1	1	4	4	4	1	1	1	1	1	**1.8**
Complaints mechanism	0	0	2	0	0	0	0	2	4	0	0	0	0	0	**.6**
Standard bidding documents	0	0	0	0	0	0	4	3	5	0	0	0	1	0	**1**
Regulations and guidelines	0	0	0	0	0	0	5	5	5	0	0	0	1	1	**1**
User guide or manual	0	0	0	1	0	0	4	3	4	0	0	0	1	1	**1**
Institutional framework and management capacity	0	0	0	0	0	0	2	2	5	0	0	0	0	0	**.6**
Normative or regulatory body	0	0	0	0	0	0	1	3	4	0	0	0	1	1	**.7**
Central or accessible system providing procurement information	0	0	0	0	0	0	2	2	3	0	0	0	1	1	**.6**
Electronic information system	0	0	0	0	0	0	2	2	4	0	0	0	1	1	**.7**
Capacity -building program	0	0	0	0	0	0	0	0	4	0	0	0	1	1	**.4**
Procurement operations and market practices	2	2	2	2	2	2	2	2	4	2	2	2	2	2	**2.1**
Training of government and private sector	0	0	0	0	0	0	0	0	3	0	0	0	1	1	**.4**
Tools and technology	1	1	1	1	1	1	1	1	3	1	1	1	1	1	**1**
Records safekeeping	1	1	1	1	1	1	1	1	5	1	1	1	1	1	**1.3**
Integrity and transparency of the public procurement system	1	1	1	1	1	1	1	1	5	1	1	1	1	1	**1**
Audit and control systems	1	1	1	2	1	1	1	1	5	1	1	1	1	1	**1**
Appeals mechanisms	0	0	0	0	0	0	2	2	5	0	0	0	0	0	**.6**
Access to information	0	0	0	1	0	0	1	1	4	0	0	0	0	1	**.5**
Anti-corruption bodies	0	0	0	0	0	0	0	0	5	0	0	0	0	3	**.5**
Code of ethics	0	0	0	4	0	0	0	2	5	0	0	0	0	2	**1**
Public is engaged and interested in the integrity of the system	1	1	1	1	1	1	3	1	5	0	0	0	3	4	**1.5**
Country average	**0.5**	**0.4**	**0.4**	**0.7**	**0.4**	**0.4**	**1.7**	**1.8**	**4**	**0.3**	**0.3**	**0.3**	**0.9**	**1.1**	

[i] While the system in Jamaica is on average a 4 out of 5, meaning that it possesses most required systems, the public procurement system in general is not as efficient as it could be. This results from a combination of multiple weak points from procurement planning and budgeting, overlapping authority of relevant entities, numerous and slow layers of approval, and project and contract management issues.

Table 2.3 Caribbean public procurement matrix II

Indicator	*AB*	*BH*	*BA*	*BE*	*DM*	*GN*	*GY*	*HA*	*JA*	*SK*	*SL*	*SV*	*SU*	*TT*
Legislative and regulatory framework														
Complaints mechanism														
Standard bidding documents														
Regulations and guidelines														
User guide														
Regulatory body														
Central procurement system														
Electronic information system														
Capacity-building program														
Training														
Tools and technology														
Records and safekeeping														
Audit and control														
Appeals mechanism														
Access to information														
Anti-corruption bodies														
Code of ethics														
Civil society														

Table 2.4 Procurement as a percentage of 2015 GDP (US$ '000)

Country	*GDP*	*15%*	*20%*	*30%*
Antigua and Barbuda	1.287	0.19305	0.2574	0.3861
The Bahamas	8.705	1.30575	1.741	2.6115
Barbados	4.412	0.6618	0.8824	1.3236
Belize*	1.763	0.26445	0.3526	0.5289
Dominica	0.497	0.07455	0.0994	0.1491
Grenada	0.954	0.1431	0.1908	0.2862
Guyana	3.164	0.4746	0.6328	0.9492
Haiti	8.618	1.2927	1.7236	2.5854
Jamaica	13.924	2.0886	2.7848	4.1772
Montserrat	0.04378	0.006567	0.008756	0.013134
St. Kitts and Nevis	0.896	0.1344	0.1792	0.2688
St. Lucia	1.416	0.2124	0.2832	0.4248
St. Vincent and the Grenadines	0.757	0.11355	0.1514	0.2271
Suriname	5.192	0.7788	1.0384	1.5576
Trinidad and Tobago	27.268	4.0902	5.4536	8.1804
Total	**77.519**	**11.62785**	**15.5038**	**23.2557**

Source: International Monetary Fund, World Economic Outlook Database, October 2016

* Figures for Montserrat from CIA World Factbook – GDP figures are 2006.

** Dominica was hit by Tropical Storm Erika 27th August 2015. The entire annual GDP of the country was wiped out in one day. Government procurement has risen dramatically and is estimated to exceed 70 percent following this tropical disaster.

*** Belize was hit by Hurricane Earl August 2016. Preliminary estimates indicate damage in excess of US$115 million. Government procurement is expected to soar in the coming 24 months.

in the Caribbean. Table 2.4 below shows public procurement in the Caribbean at 15, 20 and 30 percent of GDP.

Calculated at 20 percent of GDP, the estimated annual public procurement spend in the Caribbean is US$15.5 billion. Because the economies are small and the government plays the leading role in stimulation of the economies, the national spending practices and the efficiency of the spending is of utmost importance. Governments procure a diverse range of goods and services to both enable direct delivery of public services and as inputs to other productive processes. In the Caribbean, the weight of the government as the chief spender is even stronger because of state ownership in various sectors such as telecommunications, health, utilities and hospitality/tourism. With relatively weak procurement systems in the Caribbean and with only donor funds going through rigorous procurement oversight and procedures, the amount of money at risk is about US$8–12 billion per annum.

Figure 2.2 below shows the distribution of the US$15 billion by country.

2.4 International development partners in the region

As mentioned earlier, several international development partners (IDPs) have given support to various related aspects of public financial management (PFM) reform over the past decade. Beyond the conduct of fiduciary diagnostics, the IDPs have not substantially coordinated their interventions in the Caribbean region and have been working largely in isolation. Figure 2.3 shows the various national and international players who have been working in the region. The effect of this failure to coordinate has resulted in multiple overlapping interventions as well as several isolated projects, some of which have failed to achieve the intended results. The interventions have further failed to leverage the benefits of

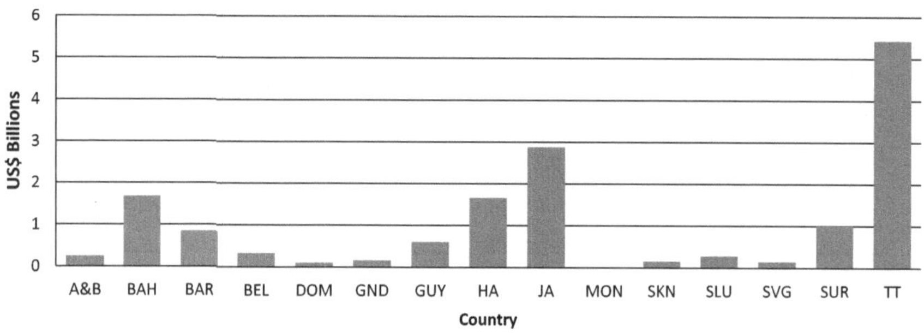

Figure 2.2 The distribution of the US$15 billion by country

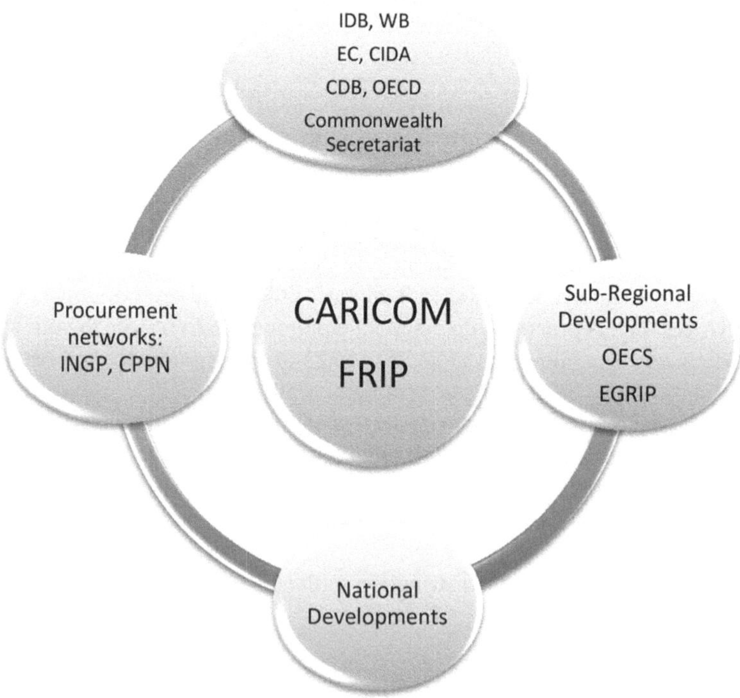

Figure 2.3 Players in the region

cross collaboration and economies of scale that would result from a more strategic and coordinated approach. Therefore, even the IDPs have failed to obtain optimal results from the use of their funds. Currently, the IDB and the World Bank provide funding through loans and technical cooperation grants and the EU has provided regional funding through the European Development Fund. The IDB is the major financier of development projects in the region.

3 Challenges

Public procurement within CARICOM is an unrecognized, under-valued, and unused potential driver for economic growth and development.

3.1 High debt

In general, the region currently faces significant economic challenges. Economic growth is low, foreign debt is high, with some countries facing serious balance of payments challenges. Managing public spending has become a delicate act involving significant cuts, juggling budget allocation. Those national challenges affect the national economies and, in a holistic manner, affect the entire region. Even the IDPs have been affected through the reduction in donor-financed operations and loans and the negative impact on project implementation. Reducing national debt to open up fiscal space and enable adequate provision of public goods and services is critical. Figure 2.4 below depicts the debt-to-GDP ratio across the region and compares 2013 and 2015 figures. Ten countries surpass 60 percent. Six surpass 80 percent and four 100 percent. It should also be noted that, for Haiti, the figures shown reflect the fact that part of its debt has been forgiven. Between 2013 and 2016 the debt-to-GDP ratio has increased in six of the countries featured.

3.2 Vulnerability to natural disaster and climate change

The Caribbean region is geographically located in a hurricane belt. In addition to the effects of climate change which are on the rise with an ever-growing impact on everyday island life, the Caribbean is annually hit by the passage of tropical storms and hurricanes that damage and destroy infrastructure, wipe out agricultural crops and often take the lives of many. The entire GDP of a country can be wiped out through the passage of one storm. In August 2015, Dominica was hit by Tropical Storm Erika. After 22 hours of rainfall, 50 people were dead or missing; there was major infrastructural damage. Ninety percent of roads and bridges were completely destroyed and many taken by the sea; an entire season of crops was lost. The preliminary estimated damage was US$300 million. Similarly, Belize was hit in August 2016. Preliminary estimates of damage are at US$115 million. The marked increase in public procurement after the passage of annual storm is a big reality for the Caribbean. Consequently, the absence of sound emergency procurement procedures and policies is very concerning.

While it is recognized that public procurement in the region faces a major challenge of limited financial resources, there are several other issues that stymie effective procurement.

3.3 The need to maximize benefits to the economy through improved procurement

Procurement expenditure within CARICOM is composed of activities funded by international donor agencies and those funded with internal resources, being either the national budget or the earnings of state-owned enterprises (SOE), which in some cases are self-financing and, in others, receive transfers from central government. In an environment of tightening fiscal constraints, the capacity of the governments of the region to finance the delivery of public goods and services such as health, education and infrastructure is becoming more limited. Funding from international lending agencies and donors therefore plays a major part in public procurement. As several CARICOM countries have risen to 'middle income' classification status based on GDP per capita, they have graduated from receiving grants from some donor agencies. This combined with their high debt burden, see Figure 2.4 above, which has served to limit their capacity to borrow from international lending agencies, has severely constrained resources available to procure goods and services to support social and economic development. The

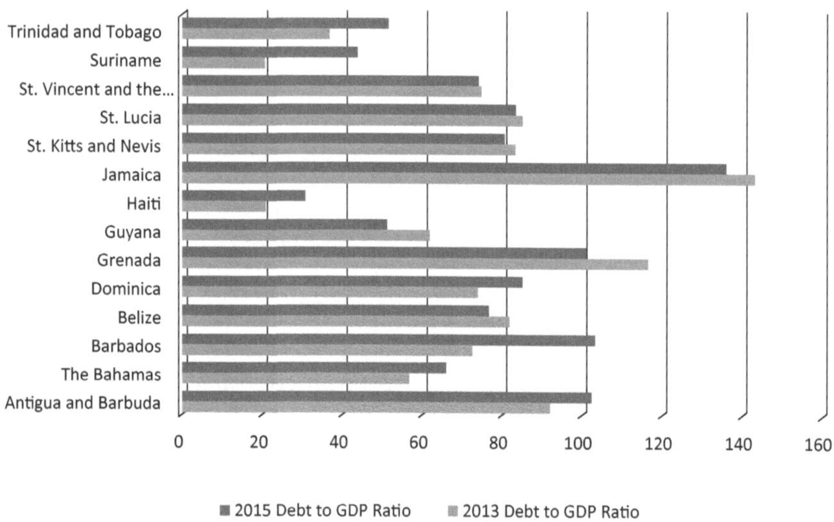

Figure 2.4 Compares 2013 and 2015 debt-to-GDP ratio

International Monetary Fund, World Economic Outlook Database, 2016. General Government Gross Debt as Percent of GDP[1]

[1]IMF WEO. General government gross debt consists of all liabilities that require payment or payments of interest and/or principal by the debtor to the creditor at a date or dates in the future. This includes debt liabilities in the form of SDRs, currency and deposits, debt securities, loans, insurance, pensions and standardized guarantee schemes, and other accounts payable.

need for public expenditure and, more specifically, procurement expenditure to be leaner, deliver better value and be managed by way of more efficient business processes is becoming more urgent, if not critical.

3.4 Underdeveloped country systems

Within CARICOM, while work is ongoing to develop systems in Jamaica and Barbados, there are no electronic systems in use. In Jamaica however, there is quarterly reporting on contracts awarded through the National Contracts Commission (NCC) portal, but very limited advertising. Jamaica is the only country where framework agreements are used, although it is limited. Very few use standard bidding documents beyond donor-funded international competitive bidding (ICB) and there are manuals in use in only two countries – Jamaica and Guyana. Practices continue to vary by procuring entity. In short, beyond the developments in Jamaica over the past 15 years, there are insufficient laws, policies, manuals and tools to consider the existence of true "national systems" elsewhere in CARICOM.

The countries of CARICOM, like many other countries, have been challenged with having to employ a different set of procurement policies for each IDP with which they work. This has frequently caused much confusion among the various policies to be implemented and a strain on human resources. In response to a cry from developing countries, through the Paris Declaration on Aid Effectiveness, donors agreed and have been working to harmonize policies. They have advanced fairly well with standard bidding documents (SBD), prohibited practices and some e-procurement. In addition, donors, recipient countries and international financial Institutions (IFIs) agreed to work together to improve and strengthen country systems for use in donor-funded operations. The use of national procurement systems would be validated for systems or portions of systems that display similarity to internationally accepted practices. After 15 years of reform, Jamaica is the only CARICOM country where a sub-system (price comparison) has been approved for use in operations funded by just one of the IDPs, the IDB.

3.5 Weak human resource capacity

With the increasing focus of IDPs on countries' procurement frameworks and capacity, there has been some effort in a few countries to train procurement staff and build the technical capacity to support procurement. However, there remains a long way to go to ensure that a professional cadre is developed in each country and across the region. Only one country, Jamaica, has a sustained and coordinated procurement training program, which is continuous and mandatory. In others, courses are delivered on an ad hoc basis and mostly by donors to their Project Implementation Units (PIU) staff teams. The human resource deficit presents a major obstacle to successful procurement planning and management and should not be underestimated. IDPs continue to express concern with the slow pace of execution of development projects around the region, as procurement is a key driver of project execution. The evidence has shown that project execution is suffering from the dearth of trained and competent procurement professionals. Executing Agencies face severe difficulty in filling procurement positions in PIUs. The deficit leads to many compromises with the result that positions are often filled with under-skilled persons who lack the knowledge-base and competencies to perform effectively and to use their discretion and professional judgement when needed.

3.6 Limited supplier base

The market for procurement in the Caribbean is further challenged by a limited supplier base at the national level. Small geographic size, few areas of comparative advantage, limited diversification, limited consumer base and purchasing power are all contributing factors. The small supplier base constrains procurement in many ways. First, the range of available goods and services is narrow. It limits competition and gives rise to monopolies and other forms of market dominance. Procuring entities feel compelled to contract the sole supplier of a particular good because it is the easiest and most natural thing to do. Suppliers are not pressed to distinguish by quality service, and in many cases do not treat their clients as valued business partners, failing to meet agreed contractual obligations. With little or no competition, pricing is distorted and goods and services cost more. These are some of the factors that often contribute to not obtaining best value for money.

3.7 Lack of procurement planning and specialized management of procurement processes

Procurement planning, a critical element of the procurement cycle, is lacking. Procurement is carried out in an ad hoc manner, creating urgencies that further reduce the scope for proper planning and encourage the practice of direct contracting. A review of the governing documentation for procurement across the countries will show that only a small minority show any recognition of procurement planning as a distinct activity in the process. Additionally, procurement processes have to interact with inefficient structures that act as stressors which cause undue delay. A recent IDB study (2013)[5] validated observations that systemic weaknesses in the public administration are a major contributor to slow procurement execution. Institutional structures that act as part of the mainstream process as well as those that are peripheral to it are inefficient and poorly organized to support the process. Ultimately, there is a lack of coordination and synergy among the various entities involved in the procurement process.

3.8 Inadequate use of modern procurement tools

Procurement in the region largely continues to take place without making use of more recent tools and techniques that would allow for transparency and optimal efficiency. As alluded to above in many of the smaller states, direct contracting is common as well as shopping based on familiarity with suppliers. This seems acceptable to practitioners given the small supplier base and the perceived reliability involved in procuring from a supplier who is known. The downside is that some suppliers are always assured of business while some are excluded. The use of more modern methods such as framework agreements and electronic tendering would increase transparency and efficiency, provide for more competition on more equitable terms and reduce the process costs.

3.9 Local preference and national policy space

The use of local preference is currently enshrined in one procurement act and only a few procurement policies in the Caribbean. It is in fact rarely used in the Caribbean. While this may be considered a lost opportunity it has been viewed by some as being in conflict with fundamental public procurement principles including full and open competition and impartiality. The Caribbean region has been deliberating for more than a decade on the use of regional thresholds to secure "national policy space", which is intended to secure for the region the same and implied benefits as with the use of the local preference margin. The region contemplated using a three-tier system of contract value thresholds to give market access preference at certain levels to national suppliers, then to regional and finally to international suppliers. Consideration of this harmonized three-tiered market access threshold was intended to improve the local economies by implementing key national policies and programmes, to foster the growth and development of selected sunrise industries such as information technology and e-commerce based services, etc.

The CARICOM Draft Regional Policy set out the following rules for application of the three-tier system:

1 CARICOM countries would continue the existing practice of allowing non-national bidders to participate;
2 Each Member State would freely select the procurement method which it considered to be efficient for any values below the agreed harmonized transparency threshold value;
3 Rules on transparency would be obligatory for any values above the threshold;
4 Each Member State may operate an offset mechanism that allows the procuring entity to apply a margin of preference at the point of selection of the qualified bidder. This would apply to extra regional suppliers only;
5 Full and open competition (FOC) procedures must be used for all values above the thresholds, such as Request for Proposal (RFP), Request for Tender (RFT), Request for Quotation (RFQ), etc.

To date the region has not concluded discussions on the harmonized contract value thresholds which would clearly differentiate access for the national suppliers as well as regional and international suppliers, and allow for the application of a margin of preference.

4 Opportunities

4.1 It's a much bigger market than assumed!

Small geographic size has often been postulated as a limitation for the countries of CARICOM. Indeed, size and the fact that most of them are islands bear connection to some of the challenges recognized in public procurement. Chief among these are limited human resources and market size. Small size means a smaller population, which in turn means a smaller manpower base. Without concerted and deliberate intervention, the professional demographics of the countries would present constraints for not only the procurement discipline but for many other areas of professional practice in both private and public management. Market size means a limited supplier base.

Small size, however, does not indicate small value. The countries of the region require similar goods and services as any of their larger counterparts in the rest of the developing world. The scale of certain physical services such as road construction will vary proportionately with size; however, it is arguable that the demand for intellectual services is similarly high. As previously shown, the CARICOM procurement market is estimated at US$15 billion. This is a substantial sum by any measure. This market represents numerous opportunities for business and professionals alike. The regional procurement market has been fertile ground for firms from across the world in all categories of procurement: works, goods and services. But, what opportunities does the market present for the region itself?

In a paper discussing the importance of size to economic growth in the Caribbean, IDB economist Ruprah (2013) compares economic growth in the Caribbean to that of other small economies with similar characteristics that could be described as causing a negative impact on economic growth and development. He addresses diseconomies of scale, high indivisible fixed costs and vulnerability. By way of the comparison with other small economies, he concludes that "size is not a binding constraint for economic growth" and that "countries can escape from size related disadvantages." He however points out that since achieving the high economic growth that followed the transition of its economic model from agriculture to services, the Caribbean region has not been able to overcome the challenges which feed the growth gap. Ruprah sums up that "policymakers and analysts should focus on the Caribbean's specific problems that could account for the growth gap; size cannot be the reason." To illustrate the discussion on size, the case of the Eastern Caribbean States (OECS) Pharmaceutical Procurement Service (PPS) is poignant.

Benefits of regional pooled procurement – the case of the OECS PPS

The Eastern Caribbean States (OECS) is a grouping of nine[6] *countries located in the Eastern Caribbean. With a combined population of 550,000, this small group has been able to turn around an alliance originally forged to address a significant market disadvantage into an "excellent cost-benefit model of economic and functional cooperation"*[7] *now hailed as an international best practice.*

With funding from USAID, the Pharmaceutical Procurement Service (PPS)[8] *was established in 1986 and became self-sufficient in 1989. Though annual cost savings are approximately 30 percent, the OECS PPS website reports that during the 2001/2002 tender cycle the 20 most popular drugs were purchased for 44 percent lower than the individual country prices.*

Factors of success in this model include the strong political will and financial backing of the governments, the formation of a public sector monopsony and the purchase of products exclusively through annual framework agreements. Purchasing of pharmaceuticals in the Eastern Caribbean has been transformed with a centralized restricted tendering process in which suppliers from a pool of 75 are pre-qualified to assess quality standards and technical competence.

In 2009 regional purchases peaked at US$21 million, with a portfolio of 700 products. Going forward, this sub-region of the Caribbean Community (CARICOM) has already moved toward pooled procurement of medical supplies, contraceptives and x-ray consumables.[9]

In the Eastern Caribbean PPS model we see the total package of an efficient and effective public procurement system. There have been clear and unquestionable economic benefits, with economies of scale being achieved and delivering an average annual savings of 30 percent. Under the PPS model there has been a move from the traditional purchase-and-store approach to pharmaceutical procurement, eliminating the risk and high cost associated with storage. Instead, the onus has been placed on suppliers to deliver according to the terms of the framework agreements and specific purchase orders. Apart from the savings on up-front purchase price, significant savings have been realized due to the reduction in storage. The other non-economic and cyclically enabling benefits include transparent and rational procurement (International Competitive Bidding – ICB), enhanced quality assurance; regional cooperation and integration; harmonized formulary manuals and standard treatment guidelines (STGs); and coordinated training and sharing of information.

The disadvantage of diseconomies of scale led the OECS group to pooled procurement. In this case, and based on what was being purchased, pooled procurement naturally led to the application of international good practices such as ICB. The resulting cost savings, transparency, improved planning, and enhanced service and product quality has transformed the initial disadvantage into an undisputable advantage bringing international recognition.

After 28 years of successful operation, the OECS PPS stands as a model of pooled procurement that should be emulated and replicated within the Caribbean and for goods beyond pharmaceutical and medical products. With a common examination curriculum, the opportunity exists for pooled procurement of other supplies including school books. Potential also exists in commodities, agricultural inputs and insurance, among other areas, the depth of which needs to be properly explored. The PPS has been showcased in Africa and other parts of the world as a best practice model. Does size matter? It does, but it is not a deterrent to growth. Speaking on competitiveness and innovation, IDB Principal Technical Leader, Competitiveness and Innovation Division, Juan Carlos Navarro, noted (in a presentation entitled "Competitiveness and innovation in the Caribbean", February 2014) that size may be seen as a weakness as the Caribbean is below its counterparts in innovation; however, size may not matter significantly anymore due to globalization. It is arguable, therefore, that the region stands to better face the opportunities and challenges of globalization as a united region.

4.2 Financial terms – when it all comes down to the money

As previously noted, at 20 percent of GDP, public procurement within CARICOM is US$15 billion annually. What does the US$15 billion compare to? It compares to the GDP of Senegal, Georgia, Mozambique and Papua New Guinea. It is 57 percent of the amount spent ($26 billion) by the World Bank in 168 countries in 2013[10] (Christopher Brown, Chief Procurement Officer, 19 February 2014 – Procurement Delivering Development Outcomes). It is larger than the value of projects approved by the IDB in 2012. The IDB 2012 annual report states that as the leading source of multilateral credit for the countries of Latin America and the Caribbean; it approved 169 projects totalling US$11.4 billion in 2012. The IDB has stationed a procurement specialist in each of its 26 borrowing member countries because US$11.4 billion is significant enough to care about how it is spent and also to provide assistance and support in the strengthening of country systems. How about US$15 billion within CARICOM?

A procurement spend of US$15 billion in CARICOM is exactly the same sum of money that the Corruption Eradication Commission in a 2011 study found to be at risk owing to "misuse due to corrupt and inept procurement practices" in Indonesia. The Millennium Challenge Corporation (MCC) of the US agreed on a $600 million compact with Indonesia. US$50 million of this amount is dedicated to the Procurement Modernization Project of Indonesia.[11] What, therefore, is the level of investment that the Caribbean would warrant and who is prepared to make this investment?

Under current market operations within CARICOM, that US$15 billion is imprisoned and along with it is the potential market access which would have allowed for growth of SMEs. Development of the CSME remains significantly constrained due to the continued segmentation of the regional market for goods, services and works. Figure 2.5 below shows the segmentation of the public procurement market.

It is possible that by applying internationally accepted best practices to public procurement, CARICOM members could save between 20 percent to 25 percent of the total procurement, which is equivalent to about US$3.75 billion annually. How could this US$3.75 billion impact on the five-year regional average negative balance of payments of US$1.5234 billion? In addition, implementing a program of strategic and pooled procurement the CARICOM region stands to save at least 30 percent on goods and services. The OECS PPS model is proof of this. What, therefore, could be the cause of the reluctance of Caribbean Community national governments to do what could likely lead to gains both to the governments and the citizens of the Caribbean Community? Table 2.5 below illustrates the panoramic economic profile of the region and demonstrates potential savings in public procurement, per country.

4.3 Operationalize the regional regime to overcome challenges

The CARICOM Framework Regional Integration Policy on Public Procurement (FRIP) was approved by the Counsel for Trade and Economic Development (COTED) on 20 May 2011. This is a significant development within the CSME.

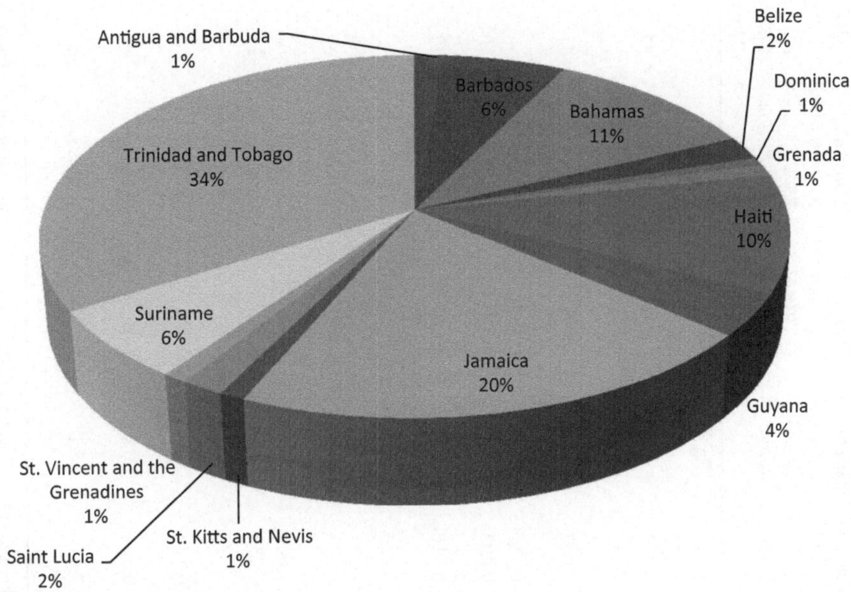

Figure 2.5 Showing segmented market

The CARICOM Regional Procurement Policy is intended to facilitate the establishment of an open and competitive regional government procurement market pursuant to Article 239 of the Revised Treaty of Chaguaramas. The policy was first developed in draft in 2006 and was reviewed of numerous occasions by various bodies of the Caribbean Community. With the policy approved, the region has commenced work on the legal protocol on public procurement which would amend the Treaty of Chaguramas and enable national implementation. Some of the critical next steps and binding commitments of the CARICOM public procurement regime include, inter alia:

1. Community Model Law
2. Capacity Building and Training
3. Electronic Procurement Regional Information System
4. Professionalization of Public Procurement Staff
5. Permanent Joint Council on Public Procurement
6. Joint Bidding Facility
7. Development of Standard Bidding Documents
8. Supplier Registry
9. Catalogue of Goods
10. Development of Infrastructure for Procurement Administration
11. Permanent Committee on Public Procurement
12. e-enabling Legislation

Table 2.5 Panoramic economic profile

Country	*Size Sq. KM*	*Population*	*GDP US$ Billions*	*GDP Per Capita*	*Dominant Economic Activity*	*Debt to GDP[i] Ratio 2015 US$ Billions*	*Balance of Payment[ii] US$ Billions*	*Strength of PP System on 0–5 Range*	*Public Procurement @20% of GDP US$ Billions*	*Potential Savings in PP 25% US$ Billions*	*2012–2013 Transparency International Corruption Perception Index*
A&B	442	88,000	1.22	13,428.64	Tourism/Services	102.085	–0.15	0.5	0.244	0.0588	–
BAH	13,940	352,000	4.262	22,832.91	Tourism/Services/Sugar	65.688	–1.135	0.4	0.852	0.2245	15
BAR	431	278,000	8.373	16,151.70	Tourism/Services	103.012	–0.255	0.4	1.674	0.4022	22
BEL	22,966	343,000	1.637	4,535.50	Agriculture/ Eco-Tourism	76.25	–0.04	0.7	0.327	0.0777	–
DOM	754	71,000	0.495	7,022.04	Agriculture/ Eco-Tourism	82.419	–0.067	0.4	0.099	0.0249	41
GND	344	105,000	0.811	7,496.46	Agriculture/Tourism	100.832	–0.181	0.4	0.162	0.0395	–
HA	27,750	10,413,000	8.287	758.849	Manufacturing/textiles/ small scale agriculture	30.435	–0.368	1.8	1.657	0.3951	165
GUY	214,970	775,000	3.02	3,596.43	Minerals/Agriculture Sugar/Seafood gold/ timber	50.854	–0.316	1.7	0.604	0.1394	133
JA	10,991	2,752,000	14.389	5,540.67		135.615	–1.817	4	2.877	0.76245	83
MON	102	5,189	0.0438	8,500	Agriculture/Rum/ Tourism Textiles	–		NA	0.009	0.002189	NA
SKN	261	57,000	0.767	12,803.52	Tourism/Services/Sugar	80.205	–0.099	0.3	0.153	0.0367	–
SLU	616	168,000	1.377	7,276.09	Tourism/Agriculture/ Small Scale Manufacturing	82.98	–0.234	0.3	0.275	0.061	22
SVG	389	110,000	0.742	6,489.25	Tourism/Services/ agriculture	73.588	–0.198	0.3	0.148	0.0356	36
SUR	163,270	546,000	5.009	8,685.81	Mining/alumina, gold, oil/timber	43.322	0.304	0.9	1.002	.2369	88
TT	5,128	1,329,000	27.13	19,018.21	Oil and Gas/Cement/ Manufacturing	51.061	3.07	1.1	5.426	1.26385	80

[i] IMF WEO. General government gross debt consists of all liabilities that require payment or payments of interest and/or principal by the debtor to the creditor at a date or dates in the future. This includes debt liabilities in the form of SDRs, currency and deposits, debt securities, loans, insurance, pensions and standardized guarantee schemes, and other accounts payable.

[ii] IMF WEO. General government gross debt consists of all liabilities that require payment or payments of interest and/or principal by the debtor to the creditor at a date or dates in the future. This includes debt liabilities in the form of SDRs, currency and deposits, debt securities, loans, insurance, pensions and standardized guarantee schemes, and other accounts payable.

Since 2006, when the first draft FRIP was prepared, nine CARICOM countries have commenced the process of modernizing national procurement systems with projects ranging from US$5 million loans to grants and technical cooperation of as little as US$30,000. Through these multiple simultaneous interventions, tax payer dollars are being spent to support multiple national initiatives that may be only partially implemented but which might affect implementation of the regional obligations if the systems are not compatible and/or interoperable.

The twelve pillars of the CARICOM procurement regime outlined above point to the foundation necessary for the transformation of public procurement in the region. Within these pillars lie the opportunities for efficient procurement development. A key example is the Electronic Procurement Regional Information System. This contemplates the establishment of a regional e-procurement platform that would enable, inter alia, the publicizing of procurement opportunities across the region, facilitating ease of access to this information. It would enable ease of tendering from any Member State and offer open and transparent administration of procurement processes. In short, a common electronic procurement system for the entire region. Because of the collective failure of the region, as a community, to advance on these elements, a few states have begun to pursue e-procurement development independently. If this continues, 15 states will singly go through the process of developing specifications and issuing calls for tenders to acquire e-procurement systems. The result will be a motley set of systems built on different platforms and sold by different providers at varying costs. With estimated average cost of approximately US$500,000 for an e-tendering system with limited functionality (excluding hardware), one thing is certain: the individual pursuit will cost each country far more than contributing to the purchase of a single system to serve the region.

Currently, there is a severe lack of systematic and reliable procurement statistics. There is no central repository for complete procurement statistics in any of the countries and procurement data is not being captured in a structured way. The application of electronic systems in the region will also support the collection of data and allow for the generation of statistics that are not only key to strategic procurement development but to economic planning in general. A related concern is the lack of a unified codification system for goods and services. A classification system will be necessary to underpin e-procurement; however, for the region to gain collectively from a coordinated approach to procurement development, a common procurement language must be spoken. In this regard, a unified codification system will be required across the region in order to ensure market synergy and importantly market access.

Capacity Building, Training and Professionalization are also key pillars. It has already been noted that there is a shortage of trained procurement personnel. It is noteworthy however, that the distribution of personnel is not even across the states. Some states have more resources than others. A real opportunity is presented to address the human resource deficit through the channels of the CSME. One of the primary tenets of the CSME is the free movement of labour (skilled persons). If the interventions for training and professional development could be coordinated region-wide so that a professional cadre is developed, implementation of free movement of persons would allow Member States to tap into the pool of personnel, regardless of the nationality.

The CSME, through the Joint Bidding Facility, offers the opportunity for business enterprises of all sizes and micro, small and medium enterprises (MSMEs) in particular to expand their expertise, resource base and market through joint ventures and other forms of collaborative tendering. Ultimately an expanded market base would allow these enterprises and their respective sectors to grow. The narrow supplier base of some states would be significantly expanded, thereby allowing for stronger competition and better prices. It becomes apparent how procurement could fuel economic growth and development in the region.

4.4 A regional regime as a platform for international trade negotiations

Public procurement is increasingly recognized for its important potential contribution to trade and, for more than a decade, it has featured prominently on the agenda of both multilateral and regional trade initiatives. When in early 2001 the regional effort to collect data and diagnose the strength of the public procurement systems in the Caribbean began, it was intended to develop the FRIP and be ready to face the EU in negotiation of the Economic Partnership Agreement (EPA), which was to be the successor to the Cotonou Convention wherein the trading relationship between Europe and the Caribbean had been defined for a decade following the end of the Lomé Conventions.[12]

Indeed, that regional policy in its goal to harmonize public procurement law and operations in the Caribbean was also intended to prepare the Caribbean for negotiation under the Free Trade Area of the Americas (FTAA) and for bilateral negotiations with Canada and the US. The region failed to develop a common approach on public procurement and therefore the opportunity to be truly prepared with endogenous policies for negotiations of the public procurement chapter of the EPA with the EU was missed. Nevertheless, at the end of 2007, CARIFORUM and the EC initialled the EPA, which came into effect in the Spring of 2008. Negotiations with Canada for an agreement to replace CARIBCAN[13] are ongoing, while negotiations of government procurement under the FTAA have stalled. Despite there being a precedent set in the provisions of the public procurement chapter of the EPA, CARICOM should continue its efforts to complete the regional regime for public procurement in order to engage other trade negotiations with a common approach on public procurement.

4.5 Enhancing the participation of small business

There is an argument put forward that the thresholds for market access and transparency in the region should be high in order to allow for national policy space to protect MSMEs, etc. With a very limited number of small business laws and policies in operation, and with the national market share not transparently nor evenly distributed, few small businesses are in reality protected. The firms participating are usually larger and in a better position to access what is required to participate and meet the criteria in a public tender process, including: access to credit, bank guarantees, years of business experience, reputation, business and supplier registration, and updated payment of taxes. This is where government policy would need to intervene to balance the scales in support of small business. The limited participation of the small business sector, which is regarded as a key engine of growth and employment, in the national market further compounds the problem of limited supplier base. It further perpetuates high and rising costs of goods and services to consumers. The ones left to carry the brunt of the financial cost of protectionism are the consumers.

If ultimately, already struggling consumers pay the high price of protection and small business being bound to their small share of already limited national markets do not realize their growth potential, who wins? What continues to hold the regional public procurement market hostage when, as it stands now, many businesses and consumers do not win?

4.6 Agree on thresholds and open the market!

Among the challenges facing the region is the lack of agreement on regional transparency threshold. Theoretically, within a single market such as the CSME, the threshold for both transparency and market access should be zero. Because the CSME is not fully implemented and consequently does not yet function as a single market, measures should be put in place to ensure that there is enough visibility of each national market at the regional level. As a matter of priority, transparency thresholds should be established to ensure that suppliers from across the region can access information about procurements and, by extension, the CSME public procurement market to bring to life some of the fundamental principles of the CARICOM FRIP including, inter alia, transparency, market access, competition, fairness, efficiency and value for money. With little to none of the governments advertising national opportunities electronically, competition and market access remains low and the price of goods and services high.

Given the thresholds agreed in the EPA with the EU, of Special Drawing Rights (SDRs) 150,000 for goods and services and 6.5 million for works, CARICOM needs to establish thresholds that promote rather than restrict competition and which are low enough to allow access but high enough to be consistent with internationally negotiated commitment. Thresholds of no greater than US$50,000 for goods and services and US$500,000 for works should be considered as transparency thresholds. This should in no way be a barrier to regional access to tenders not regionally advertised and which are below these thresholds.

5 Recommendations

5.1 Awakening civil society through transparency

The passage of Access-to-Information Legislation in some countries has served to increase civil society scrutiny of government actions. In Jamaica, for example, various individuals and groups including the media have used this avenue to request information on specific procurements, taking the matter further to force inquiry by regulatory bodies. Similar legislation is also present in Trinidad and Tobago. This kind of involvement and scrutiny by citizens is as important as regulatory oversight in maintaining accountability. Notwithstanding, as the biggest of all stakeholders, CARICOM's civil society is, for the most part, silent. Getting the populations engaged in demanding transparency and accountability regarding public spending is a key to taking the reform process to an entirely different level. Until citizens understand that national debt is a taxpayer burden passing from one generation to another and that every cent spent must be properly accounted for, public procurement will happen in a space that that is not subject to transparency, efficiency, fairness and accountability. Two key questions must be brought to the fore of a civil society conversation with governments: "Where is the money to come from"? and, "What was done with the money?"

With the goal of genuine implementation, it must be recognized that integration of the Caribbean Community is only partly a political process. To a greater extent, it is a people process. The body politick has been marginalized in the process largely due to the fact that binding Community obligations agreed through Ministerial Counsel meetings are not public and online. Civil society therefore relies on the press releases and communiques that do not give the complete picture of the Ministerial deliberations. It is therefore almost impossible for civil society to hold national leadership accountable to its Community obligations. The Community should work to ensure the bringing online of government throughout the region.

5.2 Supporting the creation of a regional regime

Notwithstanding the efforts to build the CSME and to harmonize public procurement systems, there has been an approach that seems to favour singular and national initiatives. Often Caribbean countries are treated as second tier because (a) the national markets are "small", (b) nationally public procurement is considered to be "small", (c) loans are small and (d) risks, while they are considered medium to high, the value on which there is risk, is considered to be "small". At US$15 billion, with a legally binding mandate for a harmonized regional public procurement system, the time has come to acknowledge the real value and potential impact of public procurement within CARICOM, not as national entities, but as a region. IDPs ought to consider investing in the region to support the development of both national and regional procurement systems that, despite concerns of small value, would serve to reduce the gaps with international practices. Operating on the premise that the portfolio and risk is small and not worthy of serious investment would serve only to widen the gap. The future of the Caribbean countries, like their past, is linked to their regional interrelationships, regional initiatives and regional identity in a manner which is very profound and symbiotic. The model of the OECS PPS, the most vulnerable group within CARICOM, has convincingly demonstrated the potential impact of regional economic initiatives earnestly and strategically implemented. As yet, no other solution has been proffered to the lingering ailments of the Caribbean either in fact or in theory that can rival the potential of an implemented CARICOM single market and economy and its institutions. A more coordinated and harmonized approach from the IDP community could bolster the ongoing efforts of the Community and give life to the sub-structures mandated in the CSME and the Framework Regional Integration Policy on Public Procurement (FRIP). Even as IDPs continue to work on national projects with the CARICOM members, the regional obligations and mandates to which these countries are legally bound should be at the fore of discussions, given due consideration and remain in full sight.

5.3 Be proactive – own the change

There are some critical aspects of the economy and of development that are outside the full realm of government control and over which government has little or no immediate influence, such as tourism and foreign direct investment. However, there are other aspects such as public spending where the political authority has immediate and full direction. It is in the latter that the opportunities lay to turn around the trajectory of public procurement in the CARICOM region. In an economic environment in which every dollar counts, there are US$15 billion reasons to take advantage of the opportunities that lay within an open regional public procurement market. And if there are any doubts about the impact of US$15 billion, there are 17 million human reasons that will weigh in when special concessions and aid for trade are exhausted and the reality of the economic situation sets in. The region should acknowledge and value public procurement as a potential driver for economic growth and bring a concerted regional political will and commitment to enable and develop the regional procurement regime.

When treated each as separate and distinct entities, the countries of CARICOM are more susceptible to the limitations of being small and vulnerable, with several characterized as economically sub-optimal. However, if the region were to implement the single market and economy as envisaged in the Revised CARICOM Treaty, its market size would expand; with the free movement of goods, services and skills, it could potentially balance human and natural resource needs as well as market needs and further possibly withstand if not repel constant external shocks. This position is supported by a belief that the tools and the resources needed by the region are already within the region, requiring only reallocation and realignment. There are countries with vast unutilized agricultural land and others with alkaline soil. There are some with great and some with little agricultural produce. There are some with high rates of unemployment and some territories where their nationals choose not to take up certain types of employment. Giving the CSME a chance could bring balance to these challenges.

With the small size of national markets, limited natural resources, high imports and low and narrow exports and domestic outputs, the countries of CARICOM are clearly small and vulnerable. However, despite half a century of using these characteristics to argue for special and differential treatment, without lasting success, the region has the opportunity to not be defined by these limitations but by its true potential that collectively can be harnessed from making strategic economic and procurement decisions. National governments of the Caribbean Community are one decision away from realizing their potential. Holding on to a model of protection is unrealistic and unnecessary.

Table 2.6 Problem-driven approach to procurement-related challenges facing the region

#	*Problem*	*Impact*	*Opportunity*	*Priority*	*Indicator*	*Authority and Influence*
1	Domestic market size	Diseconomies of scale; limited competition; high prices	Amalgamate the market	1	CSME operational; lower prices	Political directorate; private sector
2	Limited transparency obligations	Limited publicity and advertisement; limited market access; narrowly informed civil society	Establish regional transparency thresholds to facilitate opening of the now-segmented US$15 billion public procurement market; establish regional public procurement notice board	1	Thresholds established; regional public procurement notice board operational; national opportunities published on regional public procurement notice board	Political directorate
3	Lack of strategic procurement	Procurement is fragmented and has been subsumed under Finance and Administration or Audit Acts; policies developed to address finance and administration concerns; high costs of the majority of goods and services.	Reclassify procurement from an administrative function to a strategic function; consolidate and pool procurement of certain goods/services through a central, fully capacitated entity	1	Procurement repositioned as a strategic area of public financial management	Civil service; political directorate; private Sector
4	High cost of goods including pharmaceuticals and school text books	Shrinking budgets due to fiscal constraints; low-quality products provided to consumers; inadequate supply of goods	Pool procurement in pharmaceuticals and other feasible areas	1	Use of framework agreements	Civil service/political directorate
5	Low number of bidders	Unequal access; few contractors control the bulk of the market	Develop harmonized electronic procurement system; advertise all opportunities above US$50,000 regionally	1	e-tendering modalities in use; increase in number of bidders per call	Political directorate; private sector

6	Weak Human resources capacity	Inadequate supply of trained persons to manage procurement; frontline workers provide low-level service to private sector; inefficient spending	Professionalize public procurement; train personnel in public procurement, project and contract management, by sector; partner with a regional institution such as the UWI to develop a sustainable training program (diploma, certificate, degree) in public procurement; UWI to partner with national universities and colleges to provide diploma training	1	Structured and contextually relevant training/ certification program rolled out and maintained across the region	Civil service/political directorate
7	High cost of electronic systems	Multiple donor-funded national initiatives; failure to maximize scarce resources	Pool national and donor resources to develop regional or interoperable; harmonize national systems	1	Integrated e-procurement and financial management systems in place	Political directorate; IDP community; CARICOM Secretariat leadership
8	Small businesses participating minimally in procurement; no incentives for small businesses	Concern that small businesses may lose market share and not survive competition; small business sector not benefitting from government support: unable to make sustained contribution to economic development	Develop small business laws and policies to legally support small business; establish a carve out for vulnerable groups, local content, community procurement and women in business, and use them; establish joint bidding facility	2	Small business procurement policies developed and backed up by legislative provisions; small businesses taking up procurement opportunities	Political directorate; private sector
9	Lack of donor coordination for more than diagnostics	Multiple simultaneous initiatives, some of which do not take into account legally binding regional mandates; strain on already limited human capacity	Engage with donors as a region on cross-cutting, common issues; recognize and support regional obligations for a single harmonized procurement system	1	More shared or joint donor-funded projects; harmonized regional public procurement policy implemented with IDP encouragement and support	International development partners; CARICOM Secretariat leadership

(*Continued*)

Table 2.6 (Continued)

#	*Problem*	*Impact*	*Opportunity*	*Priority*	*Indicator*	*Authority and Influence*
10	Limited to no involvement of civil society	Limited accountability to citizens; limited demand for transparency of process and award; lack of commitment to shared responsibility for development	Bring civil society into the fold of discussion and accountability regarding national and regional development and management; conduct country-by-country awareness campaigns	2	Civil society increasingly and actively engaged with demanding transparency and accountability; countries willingly and easily proving access to information	Political directorate; IDP community; CARICOM Secretariat leadership
11	Lack of institutional capacity	Institutional framework inadequate to meet current procurement demands	Institution building/strengthening both at the national and regional level through benchmarking within and outside the region	1	Key institutions established resources and operational at national first then regional level	National governments; CARICOM Secretariat leadership
12	Lack of collection of statistical data	Absence of key economic and planning information decisions not based on empirical evidence; lack of business intelligence	Implement harmonized e-procurement system region-wide; implement other electronic PFM tools that collect data	1	Integrated e-procurement and financial management systems in place; statistical data easily generated; planning based on data analysis	Political directorate; IDP community; CARICOM Secretariat leadership
13	Absence of a unified codification system	Barrier to market access and regional coordinated procurement	Agree and implement common codification system	1	Codification system in use across CARICOM	CARICOM Secretariat leadership

14	Absence of regional monitoring	Lost opportunity for coordinated research, development and innovation; lost opportunity for wider funding beyond traditional donors	Establishment of an observatory	2	More coordinated research, development and innovation = more effective use of multiple donor sources; access to funding from non-traditional donors; involvement from universities	Regional university; CARICOM Secretariat leadership; national governments
15	No use of local preference	Lost opportunity to incubate and encourage growth of sunrise industries	Develop and implement clear harmonized contract value threshold policy for national and regional markets and apply margin of preference to benefit local suppliers when it is economically beneficial to so do	1	Local suppliers, especially sunrise industries, gaining access to more government contracts	CARICOM Secretariat leadership

Applying the idea of a problem-driven approach similar to that discussed by Andrews, Pritchett and Woolcock (2012) and the call by Ruprah (2013) for an examination of the real challenges to growth, Table 2.6 below attempts to capture the direct and indirect procurement-related factors where opportunities of enhancement rest.

Notes

1 See Articles 8 and 9 of the Revised Treaty.
2 The Procurement and Contract Administration Act, 2011.
3 Public Procurement and Contract Administration Act, 2012.
4 Section 1 (2) of the Act states that "the Act shall come into force on such day as the Minister of Finance may, by Order published in the Gazette" while subsection (3) "provides the limitation of the Minister's discretionary privilege to January 21, 2015".
5 Adquisiciones y eficiencia operativa: análisis de la ejecución de proyectos financiados por el BID.
6 Anguilla, Antigua and Barbuda, British Virgin Islands, Dominica, Grenada, Montserrat, St. Kitts and Nevis, St. Lucia and St. Vincent and the Grenadines.
7 www.oecs.org
8 Originally established as the Eastern Caribbean Drug Service with USAID grant of US$3.5 million and counterpart funding of US$0.7 million.
9 The OECS PPS is also currently exploring pooled procurement of dental and laboratory supplies.
10 Obtained from WB presentation "Best Practice Procurement in a Development Environment?" by Christopher Brown, Chief Procurement Officer, WB, February 2014.
11 Millennium Challenge Corporation, USA, Fact Sheet– MCC and Indonesia: Investing in Innovation for Sustainable Economic Growth. November 2011. www.mcc.gov
12 The Lome and Cotonou Conventions were successive non-reciprocal ACP-EU conventions.
13 CARIBCAN granted unilateral duty-free access to eligible goods from beneficiary countries in the English-speaking Caribbean up to 2013.

References

Andrews, M., Pritchett, L., and Woolcock, M. (2012). *Escaping capability traps through problem – driven iterative adaptation*. HSK Faculty Research Working Paper Series, RWP12-036.

Angaladian, H. (2005b). *Government procurement frameworks in the Caribbean community: Towards a regional best practice regime for the CARICOM single market and economy*. Public Procurement in the CARICOM- A Comparative Assessment.

Brown, C. (2014). *Best practice procurement in a development environment*. World Bank, February. Available at www.worldbank.org/en/events/2014/02/04/procurement-delivering-development-outcomes

Caribbean Community (CARICOM) (2001–2005). *Country procurement assessment reports*.

Caribbean Community (CARICOM) (2011). *Framework Regional Integration Policy on public Procurement (FRIP) 2011*.

Navarro, C. (2014). *Presentation "competitiveness and innovation in the Caribbean"*. February. Available at www.iadb.org

Ruprah, I. J. (2013). *Does size matter? Yes, if you are Caribbean!* Inter-American Development Bank Policy Brief, IDB-PB-201.

Woolcock, S. (2008). *Public Procurement and Economic Partnership Agreements: Assessing the Potential Impact on ACP Procurement Policies*. London: London School of Economics; Commonwealth Secretariat.

3 Local preferences as non-discriminatory instrument in public procurement of fresh foods

Why, when and how

Boštjan Ferk and Petra Ferk[*]

1 Introduction

In 2007–2008 the world faced a global food crisis. After 2008, food prices have continued to rise globally due to a number of complex factors, raising concerns on food prices and retail competition also within the European Union (EU). The EU had to respond to this situation, as did the Member States. It was no surprise that various economic protectionist slogans have (re)emerged.

Local (national) preferences within the EU law are considered as an instrument restricting the free movement of goods and freedom to provide services, which are two of the fundamental principles of the EU law. This general observation also refers to the EU public procurement law. Namely, the award of public contracts by or on the behalf of the Member States' authorities has to comply with the general principles of the Treaty on the Functioning of the European Union (TFEU), and in particular with the free movement of goods, freedom of establishment, and the freedom to provide services, as well as the principles deriving therefrom, such as equal treatment, non-discrimination, mutual recognition, proportionality, and transparency. However, in this article, we argue that in some cases in the EU public procurement law the local preferences cannot be regarded as a discriminatory instrument and examine when it can be so and under which conditions. In the assessment, we focus on public procurement of fresh foods, having in mind principally school food. The latter, in particular, is significant for providing nutrition and improving food security. Schools are also an important venue to set an example on healthy food and nutrition behaviours, as many schools provide two to four meals a day.[1]

In the first part of the chapter, we examine the main challenges of the EU food market as well as the theoretical background and the existing case law of the Court of Justice of the European Union (CJEU) on the topic. We analyse the existing case law related to the development of the free movement of goods in the EU and combatting national economic protectionism. We also offer some insight into the existing case law concerning the issue in the field of public procurement and taking into account that procurement procedures were introduced in the EU legal order to eliminate national practices which directly or indirectly restricted access to government contracts for goods, services, and providers originating from another Member State and to establish an internal public procurement market. Deriving from this analysis, it may seem that the principle of non-discrimination is per se violated by introducing local preferences into public procurement. However, as elaborated, local preferences regarding the vicinity factor do not a priori violate the principle of non-discrimination.

In the second part of the article, we present a hypothetical case study of the public procurement model 'Buy Fresh', i.e. procuring fresh food for e.g. public schools, nursery schools, hospitals, and other contracting authorities having an obligation to procure foods. In the first part of the assessment, we present the notions of quality food, healthy food, fresh food, and local food. Also, we present the main benefits of the fresh food consumption, which represent an objective justification for introducing additional requirements, including the vicinity factor, into the tender documentation when procuring fresh foods without violating the principle of equal treatment. We analyse under which conditions could local preferences not only be eligible, but even a required instrument to pursue the objectives of the Directive 2014/24/EU on public procurement as well as some of the EU primary goals, such as protection of public health, protection of the environment, facilitating the participation of small- and medium-sized enterprises (SMEs) in public procurement, and support of common societal goals. We aim to answer the question of how a contracting authority can pursue these goals in practice. Therefore, we identify several possibilities for the quality demands, including the vicinity factor, to be introduced in the contract award procedure to pursue the identified and legitimate goals in a manner that the principle of equal treatment is not violated.

This article aims to demonstrate that, when procuring for foods, the contracting authorities have not only the possibility but also the responsibility to procure for quality food. If it can be stated that the politicians and the policy-makers have in their power to bring the food prices down, but might not use this power and do not respond to the development of the food market (Collier, 2008, p. 67), it can also be stated that the politicians and the policy-makers have in their power to procure for quality foods. However, there is no excuse for the contracting authorities not to procure for quality foods. The 2014 Public Procurement Directives provide for several options, enabling the contracting authorities to pursue common societal goals (Directive 2014/24/EU, Directive 2014/25/EU, and Directive 2014/23/EU). These goals include environmental protection, social responsibility, innovation, combating climate change, employment, public health, and other social and environmental considerations. If the public procurement procedure for quality fresh foods requires the vicinity factor to be introduced, the contracting authorities should have the possibility to do so.

2 Main challenges of the EU food market as part of the global economy

In 2003, the UN Food and Agriculture Organization (FAO) estimated that an additional 120 million hectares – an area twice the size of France or one-third of India – will be needed to support the traditional growth in food production by 2030, without considering the compensation required for certain losses resulting from unsustainable forms of agricultural production (Bruinsma, 2003). Although this expansion will occur mainly in developing countries (De Schutter, 2009, p. 3), this indicates that the food market situation is growing dire and that providing the necessary quantity for feeding the population is going to be a serious challenge, not to mention the quality. If the situation aggravates, we will be left with little room for manoeuvre when it comes to systems of quality food provision. Hence, now is the time to act in this direction and put the ideas into motion.

In the past few years, we have been faced with a global food crisis. In 2008, after many years of stability,[2] the global food prices skyrocketed by 83 percent since 2005, which was a stern warning of a food crisis throughout the world. In the US and Europe, the increase in food prices was not something new and was shaded by the rising prices of energy and the falling prices of real estate. In the developing world, however, this was a major political event (Collier, 2008, p. 67); in some countries, this even resulted in food riots (Shah, 2008). After 2008, the food prices continued to increase globally due to a number of complex factors,[3] raising concerns on food prices and retail competition also within the EU (Ratliff, 2013, p. 150). The EU had to respond to this situation.[4]

In 2008, the Commission adopted the Communication 'Tackling the challenge of rising food prices – Directions for EU action' (COM (2008) 321, final). The Commission assessed that high food prices are not a temporary phenomenon but are likely to persist in the medium term, though most likely not at the record levels that have been recently reached. Nevertheless, these prices are unlikely to fall back to the 2008 pre-crisis level in the short to medium term (COM (2008) 321, final, p. 6). The Commission concluded that it will continue to monitor the evolution of the situation and the reasons behind the rise in food prices. At the EU level, three complementary lines of intervention were identified: actions to address and mitigate the short- and medium-term effects of the food price shock, actions to increase agricultural supply and ensure food security in the longer term, and actions to contribute to the global effort to tackle the effects of the price rises on poor populations (COM (2008) 321, final, pp. 9–13). In terms of competition law, in 2012 the Commission established the EC Task Force on Food within DG COMP with the purpose of coordinating antitrust enforcement in the food sector (Ratliff, 2013, p. 150). In addition to the antitrust practices,[5] the EU also faced food frauds (the most notorious being the horsemeat fraud). Factors contributing to food fraud were identified as the current economic crisis, the austerity measures affecting control agencies, and pressure from retail and others to produce food ever more cheaply (INI (2013) 2091).[6] Nevertheless, on a global level, the 2008 food crisis and the rising prices were seen by the Commission as a new opportunity that could, in the medium to long term, offer new income-generating opportunities for farmers and enhance the contribution of agriculture to economic growth, although several factors may slow down this adjustment and although adjustments of the rural economy, which can create new opportunities, will take time to reach the poor and to increase the agricultural output (COM (2008) 321, final, p. 9).

As observed by *Gouveia*, modern European food supply chains consist of a large number of farmers (around 13 million) connected to the agri-food industry (around 300,000 companies) and retailers (roughly a handful). Among chain members, enormous differences regarding the numbers and economic power exist. This situation is a result of globalisation; the farmers are price-takers rather than price-setters. Recent years have brought about a huge consolidation in processing and the retail sector. This led to ferocious competition amongst retailers and frequent price wars at the expense of those with less negotiating power. This has resulted in unfair and abusive commercial practices. The farming sector is squeezed between the players upstream and downstream, leading to negative results for the agriculture sector. *Gouveia* recalls that a study carried out by FranceAgriMer demonstrates that the margin the farmers get out of €100 of consumer expenditure is €8.10 (much less than the industry or the retail sector). The consequence is a relentless downward pressure on prices. Often, farmers cannot even cover their production costs and hence cannot invest in their businesses. This leads to abandoning the sector, which might restrict the choice and flexibility of supply to consumers. It might also reflect in a distortion of competition and negative impacts on the functioning of the internal market (Gouveia, 2015, p. 12).

3 'Buy local' food campaigns and free movement of goods in the EU

It is no surprise that the times of crisis give rise to greater demand for protection,[7] including for example the plans for public procurement of local foods, as in the case of the UK (Department for Environment, Food & Rural Affairs, A Plan for Public Procurement, 2014).

Many aspects of various 'buy domestic' and 'buy local' campaigns which emerge in times of crisis have already been addressed by *Hojnik* (2012) in an article in which she explores how recent crises challenged the landmark judgement *Buy Irish* (the CJEU Case C-249/81). In *Buy Irish*, the CJEU found that the campaign reflected a national practice intended to check the flow of trade between the Member States by substituting domestic products for imports. 'That the effort was unsuccessful' was held to be irrelevant; the mere possibility that trade could be affected was sufficient to trigger the prohibition of Article 30 EEC Treaty (now Article 34 TFEU), which prohibited not only quantitative restrictions on imports, but also all measures with an equivalent effect. The CJEU also determined it irrelevant that the measures used to implement the campaign were non-binding. Instead, the campaign was held to constitute a prohibited 'measure of equivalent effect' since the potential effect of the campaign was comparable to that of a binding measure (Case C-249/81, para. 28; Williams, 1983, pp. 585–590). The CJEU found that

> Ireland has [. . .] failed to fulfil its obligations under the Treaty by organising a campaign to promote the sale and purchase of Irish goods within its territory, thereby prohibiting State spreading of negative stereotypes against imported goods.
>
> (Case C-249/81, para. 30)

However, as assessed by *Hojnik*, in *Buy Irish*, only national origin of goods was highlighted. Therefore, the decision in *Buy Irish* should be distinguished from the decision in *Apple and Pear Development Council* (Case C-222/82) from which one may conclude that State-sponsored promotion of national goods in general is illegitimate if merely the national origin of goods is highlighted, while on the other hand the promotion of specific goods having distinctive qualities, besides those of national origin, is permissible (Barnard, 2010, p. 83).[8] As noted by *Hojnik*, the line delimiting the two types of promotion is obviously very thin (Hojnik, 2012, p. 306), and since even the two abovementioned Court's cases did not provide answers to the open issues, the Commission in 1986 issued Guidelines for Member States' involvement in promotion of agricultural and fisheries products (COM (1986) 272, final, pp. 3–5). In this document, the Commission emphasised that

> identification of the producing country by word or symbol may be made providing that a reasonable balance between references, on the one hand to the qualities and varieties of the product and, on the other hand, its national origin is kept. The *references to national origin should be subsidiary to the main message* put over to consumers by the campaign and not constitute the principal reason why consumers are being advised to buy the product. [. . .] *Qualities of the products which it is permissible to mention* include taste, aroma, freshness, maturity, value for money, nutritional value, varieties available, usefulness (recipes, etc.). [. . .] References to quality control should only be made where the product is subjected to a genuine and objective system of control of its qualities.
>
> (COM (1986) 272, final, pp. 3–5; emphases added)

As observed by *Hojnik*, although these principles were toughened by the CJEU in 2002 with regard to the German quality label for domestic agricultural produce (Case C-325/00), and although the CJEU in its case law regarding campaigns that boost consumer ethnocentrism did not seriously consider possible justifications, the CJEU might be forced to consider the States' interests in more detail than it has done so far, especially considering the crises (Hojnik, 2012, p. 307). In this respect *Hojnik* identifies and elaborates on the following national interests that could be accepted as a justification for ethnocentric market campaigns by the CJEU in light of its settled case law: public finances' hardships and job preservation, consumer protection, national tradition and culture, national food self-sufficiency and food security, and environmental protection (Hojnik, 2012, pp. 307–320).

Having this in mind, public procurement of foods seems a convenient instrument enabling national governments to support local food production. However, one should recall that coordinated public procurement procedures were introduced in the EU with the similar objective that can be found behind the abovementioned CJEU cases (i.e. combatting national economic protectionism). The difference is that in the case of public procurement the aim was to eliminate national practices which directly or indirectly restrict access to *government contracts* for goods, services, and providers originating from another Member State.[9]

In general, certain provisions of the TFEU prohibit government action which discriminates against companies or products from the other Member States. The most important are Article 34 TFEU on free movement of goods, Article 56 TFEU on freedom to provide services, and Article 49 on freedom of establishment. These principles of the TFEU have a direct effect; that is, they are binding on the Member State governments and enforceable against them. These TFEU provisions apply in principle to all contracts awarded by public bodies. This includes the contracts which are outside the scope of the EU procurement directives, including, for example, because their value is below the financial thresholds for the EU directives to apply (Arrowsmith, 2010, p. 66).

General principles of public procurement are defined in Article 18 of the Directive 2014/24/EU and include: equality, non-discrimination, transparency, proportionality, and the new principle of competition.[10] These principles are grounded in the TFEU. Namely, in recital 1, the Directive 2014/24/EU also clarifies that the award of public contracts by or on the behalf of the Member States' authorities has to comply with the *general principles of the TFEU*, and in particular the free movement of goods, freedom of establishment, and the freedom to provide services, as well as the principles deriving therefrom, such as equal treatment, non-discrimination, mutual recognition, proportionality, and transparency. A special application of the principles of the TFEU in the context of public procurement has been established by the CJEU case law and continuously elaborated in academic literature.[11] It derives from the existing case law of the CJEU that the provisions of public procurement directives are to be interpreted in accordance with the fundamental principles and other rules of the TFEU (Case C-275/98, para. 31; Case C-324/98, para. 61). As observed by *Semple*, it is not to be forgotten that the scope of public procurement rules subject to steady evolution is most often justified on the grounds of one or more principles set out in the TFEU (Semple, 2015, p. 35).

From the viewpoint of the topic of this chapter, the principles non-discrimination and equal treatment are of key importance.

The **principle of non-discrimination** in the EU law derives from the free movement of goods and services within the internal market. Regarding the free movement of products, Article 34 TFEU generally applies, first, to measures that discriminate directly between domestic and imported products and, second, it also covers the measures that apply to domestic and imported products equally, but that have the effect of favouring domestic products. In addition to applying to these measures, Article 34 also applies to some measures that may restrict trade in government markets which are neither directly nor indirectly discriminatory.[12] Although the principle of non-discrimination is stated directly in the Directive 2014/24/EU, this is probably just a specific expression of the more general principle of equal treatment, as observed by *Arrowsmith*, who sees this expression as a reminder that non-discrimination on the grounds of nationality is not permitted, and perhaps also to indicate that the existence of such discrimination is to be judged on the same basis as under the Treaty (Arrowsmith, 2014, p. 261).

As assessed by *Semple*, an early application of this principle in the context of public contracts can be found in the *Beentjes* case, where the CJEU stated that an obligation to employ long-term unemployed persons on a public works contract could infringe the Treaty 'if it became apparent that such a condition could be satisfied only by tenderers from the State concerned or indeed that tenderers from the other Member States would have difficulty in complying with it' (Case 31/87, para. 30). References to the general principle of non-discrimination have, however, become less common in the CJEU judgements, as the procurement directives have grown to encompass a larger number of specific rules which give effect to it (Semple, 2015, p. 42).

The **equal treatment principle** in the procurement directives was first articulated by the CJEU in *Storebaelt* (Case C-243/89, para. 33), seen as the turning point in this regard.[13] Although such a principle was not stated expressly in the public procurement directive at that time, the CJEU held that despite not being explicitly mentioned in the directives, the principle of equal treatment lay at the very heart of them (Case C-243/89, para. 33). In the *Walloon Buses*, the CJEU has ruled that the principle of equal treatment does not simply mean that firms from the other EU Member States and domestic firms must be treated equally by the contracting authority: it means that *all* firms must be treated equally. Thus a domestic firm can complain if it considers, for example, that it has not received equal treatment with other firms in the competition of whatever nationality (Case C-87/94, para. 33). It is submitted that the principle forbids different treatment of entities in a comparable competitive position.[14] Therefore, it is first important to assess whether the economic operators are in a comparable position. Given the nature of the comparator, economic operators are *not* necessarily in a comparable position.[15]

In *Commission v France* (Case C-16/98, paras. 107–110), the CJEU made it clear that this principle – which was originally referred to in the jurisprudence as the principle of equal treatment of tenderers – applies not just to firms that have participated in an award procedure, but also to those that hope to participate. Giving more information to domestic firms than to foreign ones, so the latter are deterred from tendering at all can be a breach of the principle, since 'the contractors from other Member States were not in a position to take a decision in the light of all the relevant information which should have been available to them' (Case C-16/98, paras. 111).

Drawing on definitions of equal treatment in other areas of the EU law,[16] the equal treatment principle under the procurement directives has been defined in the *Fabricom*: 'the equal treatment principle requires that comparable situations must not be treated differently and that different situations must not be treated in the same way, unless such treatment is objectively justified' (Joined Cases C-21/03 and C-34/03, para. 27).

Tridimas explains that once it has been determined whether the economic operators are in a comparable position, then the question arises as to what is different treatment. In most cases this is straightforward, but not always. Differences in treatment between those in a comparable position may, however, be permitted when justified on objective grounds. In other contexts, under the EU law, considerations of administrative convenience have been held to justify different treatment (Tridimas, 2006, para. 2.5.3.4.), and this should also apply under the procurement directives, as assessed by *Arrowsmith*, which further elaborates that a decision to select some firms but not the others to participate based simply on convenience might be permitted under this element. For example, in a negotiated procedure without notice, an entity should be able to approach known reliable suppliers, without opening the opportunity to all who might be interested (Arrowsmith, 2014, p. 616). In our view, *Arrowsmith's* example is quite broad, but nevertheless we support the idea that the Contracting Authority has to have this possibility and that the equal treatment principle does not, in general, preclude a contracting authority from taking account of market advantages enjoyed by one firm above another, such as a superior location, greater experience, or other cost advantages – it is the nature and indeed the very purpose of a competitive market that companies may exploit this kind of advantages to win contracts (Arrowsmith, 2014, pp. 617–618).

As observed by *Arrowsmith*, there is a significant discretion for the CJEU in applying a principle of this kind. Although it will be clear that certain matters violate this principle, in many cases, however, such definitions cannot be applied automatically to give solutions to a problem, but involve the CJEU or other regulator in making policy decisions on how to balance the principle of equality of treatment with other goals of the procurement process when deciding what is a justification/relevant consideration for different treatment.[17]

Having in mind what was said, we can assess that although it might seem that the principle of equal treatment could be violated *per se* by introducing 'local preferences' into public procurement procedure,[18] in our view, introducing 'local preferences' in some cases does not *a priori* violate the principle of equal treatment if introduced and assessed properly and with justified objectives.

4 Eligible objectives justifying introduction of the local preferences in public procurement of fresh foods

Generally, as practices in public procurement that do not allow for free competition from other states to serve the public market are a possible source of distortion in the natural patterns of trade, and thus may be detrimental to maximising national and global economic welfare, Arrowsmith illustratively identifies various types of practices that fall into this category, under which – notably – also the support of social and environmental objectives could belong. As assessed by Arrowsmith, prior to the adoption of the 2014 Public Procurement Directives, striking a balance between the benefits of trade and the legitimate objectives of government in using procurement to promote social and environmental goals is one of the most difficult problems for systems that seek to open up markets in procurement (2010, pp. 44–51).

However, in the last couple of years – although social and environmental policies have played a varying role in the different EU Member States since the onset of the Union in the early 1950s – a widely accepted urge was present to enhance social and environmental policies where this can be done without further drawbacks (Arrowsmith, 2010, p. 298). In the 2010 Monti Report, it was thus made one of the key recommendations to make public procurement work for innovation, green growth, and social inclusion by imposing specific mandatory requirements, and, furthermore, to establish a single market for green products, by developing the EU-wide standards for measuring and auditing carbon footprints and for energy-efficient products, including trade certificates for renewable energy products (Monti, 2010, pp. 47–49).

As emphasised by Advocate General *Trstenjak* in *Commission v. Austria*, in the CJEU's more recent case-law (reference is given to the judgements *Commission v Belgium, Aher-Waggon, PreussenElektra, Commission v Germany*), there are clear indications that public health and environmental protection can be relied on as an overriding reason in the public interest to justify discriminatory measures having an equivalent effect to a quantitative restriction, while the principle of proportionality must naturally always be observed (Case C-28/09 Opinion, para. 83, 84).[19] Some additional well-known CJEU decisions related to green public procurement are e.g. *Concordia Bus* (Case C-513/99, para. 149), the *Wienstrom* case (Case C-448/01) and *Evropaïki Dynamiki* (Case T-331/06). Although these rulings were issued before the 2014 Public Procurement Package, they are still relevant and can impact the way in which procurement is conducted. One is referring to the procurement of food, i.e. *Dutch Coffee* (Case C-368/10).

In *Dutch Coffee*, the disputed tender was for the supply of coffee machines and ingredients in which social and environmental requirements were included. The case focused on two labels, one relating to fair trade aspects of purchasing and the other to the organic agricultural production of ingredients. Regarding organic agricultural production, the ruling confirmed that although it was not possible to set a requirement that the supplied goods need to bear a specific eco-label, it is admissible to do so by using detailed technical specifications defined by that eco-label (Case C-368/10, paras. 61–70).

Following the development in the CJEU public procurement case law, and probably also due to following the path of several social and environmental provisions to be included in the two Treaties of the Lisbon Treaty (Arrowsmith, 2010, p. 298), environmental protection, social responsibility, innovation, combating climate change, employment, public health, and other social and environmental considerations were included in the 2014 Public Procurement Directives (European Commission – Environment, Legal framework for Green Public Procurement). Therefore, the 2014 Public Procurement Directives – even more than its predecessors – encourage a greater quality orientation of public procurement and explicitly provide for the Member States to be permitted to prohibit or restrict the use of price only or cost only to assess the most economically advantageous tender where they deem this appropriate (Directive 2014/24/EU, recital 90). Additionally, one of the goals of the Directive 2014/24/EU on public procurement was to further the possibilities of SMEs to participate in public procurement (recital 3). Therefore, local preferences in procuring food could also be considered in this function, since local micro and SMEs do not have the possibility to compete with the economy of scale of multinational food companies. All of this offers good possibilities for contracting authorities to procure quality food.

If the practice of the CJEU before the adoption of the Directive 2014/24/EU is to be read in light of enabling the contracting authorities the possibility of a green and social procurement, with the 2014 Public Procurement Directives, this possibility has become more mainstream. However, most of the social and environmental provisions remain optional.[20]

Needless to say, however, such *obligations* might derive from other sector-specific EU or national legislation/guidelines. Namely, the Directive 2014/24/EU declares, that

> nothing in this Directive should prevent the imposition or enforcement of measures necessary to protect public policy, public morality, public security, health, human and animal life, the preservation of plant life or other environmental measures, in particular with a view to sustainable development, provided that those measures are in conformity with the TFEU.
>
> (Directive 2014/24/EU, recital 41)

5 Quality food versus healthy food versus fresh food versus local food

In this section, the aim is to estimate what is quality food and what could be the objectives justifying the additional inclusion of a vicinity factor in the public food procurement procedures.

At first glance, 'healthy food', 'quality food', 'fresh food', and 'local food' may seem synonymous, but they are not and should not be considered as such, although there is no clear definition of any of these concepts.

Food quality is a complex notion frequently measured using objective indices related to the nutritional, microbiological or physicochemical characteristics of the food (Cardello, 1995, pp. 163–170). Since the dawn of the information era, the basic characteristics of 'healthy food' are widely known and accessible to the general public. However, there is no single accepted definition of what 'healthy' food refers to. The term is used to refer to food high in nutrients and low in calories, fats, sodium, and additives/processed ingredients – particularly fruits and vegetables.[21]

The EU law prescribes stringent requirements guaranteeing the standards of all European products. Also, the EU quality schemes identify products and foodstuffs farmed and produced following strict specifications. Food quality is an important topic for every farmer and buyer, whether dealing with commodities produced in accordance with basic standards or the high-end quality products in which Europe excels (European Commission, Food Quality Policy; European Commission, EU Agricultural product quality policy). Nevertheless, one has to keep in mind that food standards, as stringent as they might be, provide only minimum requirements for food quality. If pursuing the goal to buy quality food, one has to exceed those standards and require additional requirements that define food quality.

It is commonly known that fresh (whole) food outplays the processed food when it comes to the best nutritional, microbiological and physicochemical characteristics. Therefore, when buying food for domestic consumption, it seems logical to give priority to fresh (whole) food. When dealing with whether the contracting authorities have the possibility to do the same under the public procurement rules, it is important to briefly outline the main advantages of consuming fresh (whole) food in comparison with the processed food. Various studies show multiple significant advantages of consuming fresh food over the processed ones; this is why this fact is so commonly known today and taken as indisputable.

First in the line of advantages of the fresh quality food is **the positive influence on health**, which has been intensively communicated for at least a century.[22] Studies show that increasing consumption of (ultra)processed foods impacts human health, not only from the viewpoint of the nutritional profile (more added sugar, more saturated fats, more sodium, less fibre, and much higher energy density) but also from the viewpoint of the processing process itself (unprocessed/minimally processed foods; processed culinary ingredients; or ultra-processed ready-to-eat or ready-to-heat food products). Additionally, the study from Brazil shows that the high energy density, the unfavourable nutritional profiling of ultra-processed ready-to-eat or ready-to-heat food products, and their potentially harmful effects on eating and drinking behaviours indicate that governments and health authorities should use all possible methods, including legislation and statutory regulation, to halt and reverse the replacement of minimally processed foods and processed culinary ingredients by ultra-processed food products (Monteiro, Bertazzi Levy and Moreira Claro, 2011, pp. 5–13).

One of the major harmful factors of processing is using salt. Traditionally, salt (sodium chloride) has been used as a food preservative that kills or limits the growth of foodborne pathogens and spoilage organisms by decreasing water activity and increasing osmotic pressure on cells' membranes. Salt also performs other important functions in foods by adding flavour and masking bitter tastes, controlling growth of yeast and fermentative bacteria, and promoting binding of proteins and other components in foods to achieve desired textures. Many processed foods contain high levels of salt and several countries have already developed national programs for significantly reducing the sodium chloride content in many processed foods, encouraging a decrease in discretionary salt use. Recent surveys estimate that over 95 percent of men and over 75 percent of women exceed the recommended daily tolerable upper intake of sodium. Since these high levels of dietary sodium are associated with a high prevalence of hypertension, prehypertension and, possibly, other adverse effects on health,[23] many national and international health organisations recommend that sodium intake be significantly decreased (Ellin Doyle and Glass, 2010, pp. 44–56). In terms of fresh food, the nutritional value reaches its peak when harvested and then gradually drops; that is, fruits and vegetables show a gradual decrease in vitamin C content as the storage temperature or duration increases, or if artificially ripened during storage.[24] Needless to note, but still, if quality food has good influence on health, it also has good influence on health expenditure.

Second in the line of advantages of the fresh quality food is **the positive influence on the environment**. In this respect, various 'good agricultural practices' are being developed,[25] and the term 'food miles'[26] has become part of the vernacular among food professionals when describing the farm-to-consumer pathways of food. Food miles are the distance food travels from where it is grown to where it is ultimately purchased or consumed by the end user. A Weighted Average Source Distance (WASD) can be used to calculate food miles by combining information on the distances from production to point of sale and the amount of food product transported. The study from the US shows that the average WASD for locally grown produce to reach institutional markets was 90 km, while the conventional WASD for the produce to reach those same institutional points of sale was 2,404 km, nearly 27 times further. Conventional produce items travelled from eight (pumpkins) to 92 (broccoli) times farther than the local produce to reach the points of sale (Pirog and Benjamin, 2003). Additionally, studies have shown that this distance has been steadily increasing over the last 50 years, and furthermore, that processed food in the US has shorter food miles (over 2,092 km) than fresh food, which travels over 2,414 miles before being consumed (Hill, 2008). Using the same WASD methodology, Canadian researchers Stephen Bentley and Ravenna Barker compared food purchased at a local farmers market and a nearby supermarket. They compared transport distances, energy consumption, and carbon dioxide emissions of seven locally produced items and equivalent imported items. They found, for example, that carrots from California travelled 59 times further to Toronto than carrots sourced from a nearby farm. While half a kilogram of local lamb generated seven grams of carbon dioxide through transportation, the same quantity of fresh New Zealand lamb yielded over eight kilograms (Bentley and Barker, 2005, p. 3). Similar tendencies to lower the food miles for food travels also exist in Europe. For example, consumers in Sweden can choose food according to the impact its production and transport have on the climate, as indicated by a label for climate-friendly foods. The logic behind the measure is that 'it is unlikely that a product that has been transported by plane would be called climate-friendly', as indicated by the Swedish food consumer organisation KRAV (2015) that is behind the scheme. The scheme was introduced since the climate issue is one of the biggest questions when it comes to environmental sustainability (Edie, 2007). The Swedish government even strived for the EU on guidelines for climate-friendly food choices to be adopted, but has at a later stage decided to withdraw the National Food Administration's proposal to the EU on guidelines for climate-friendly food choices since the EU Commission found that the recommendations to eat more locally produced food contradict the EU principles for the free movement of goods, and asked Sweden to revise the guidelines. As seen by Inger Andersson, the Swedish National Food Administration's Director, 'free trade was considered more important than the environment' (Dahlbacka, 2010). In the UK, Tesco wanted to label all its 70,000 products with their carbon footprint, but has in 2012, after five years of trying, abandoned the plan, blaming the amount of work involved and other supermarkets for failing to follow its lead (Vaughan, 2012). The UK Department for Environment, Food and Rural Affairs (DEFRA) released a report in 2005 which determined that food miles alone are not a valid indicator of the sustainability of the food system. In some cases, reducing food miles may reduce energy use, but there may be other social, environmental or economic trade-offs. The consequences of food transport are complex and require a group of indicators to determine the global impact of food miles (Smith et al., 2005). Nevertheless, a study released in the UK in 2005 found that air transport is the fastest growing mode of food distribution, and although air transport accounts for only 1 percent of food transport in the UK, it results in 11 percent of the country's CO2 emissions. The UK report also estimated that the social and economic costs of food transport including accidents, noise, and congestion amount to over £9 billion every year or US$18 billion (Smith et al., 2005). The challenge of transporting fresh food has recently been recognised by the EU and addressed by the INEA action, which is a part of the Global Project whose objective is to achieve a safe, sustainable and efficient fresh food transport system in the Euro-Mediterranean area through long-term effective and sustainable connection between the Trans-Mediterranean Transport Network (TMT-T) and the Trans-European Transport Network (TEN-T). The overall objective of this pilot action is to test and enhance a sustainable inter-modal transport and logistics system for freight movement between Mediterranean and Northern European destinations by rail and sea.[27] Taking into account all that has been said in this section, one can see that the transport of the (ultra)processed food is cheaper since less expensive (and less burdensome for the environment) transport modes can be used.

Third, consuming fresh (unprocessed) food, which is transported in an environmentally friendly manner, has **positive financial influences**. As to some extent already indicated above, the health and environmental aspects of food production and consumption are also closely related to the financial aspects. Additionally, it has been shown that during the 2007–2008 food crisis, the inflation in EU has been higher for processed foods (where raw material prices account for a smaller proportion) than for unprocessed foods (such as fruits and vegetables but also meat). The inflation increase on unprocessed food was more gradual and lower, because raw materials used in processed food were more vulnerable to price increases (in terms of food, but also in terms of other inputs, such as energy), whereas unprocessed food, such as vegetables, fruit, and fish, did not experience price increases. With regard to meat, this can be explained by a time-lag between higher feed costs through increased cereal prices and the resulting higher animal output prices (COM (2008) 321, final, p. 7).

'Healthy food' is often being equalised with 'local food'. However, as explained below, local food is not necessarily more nutritious than non-local food, but additional factors have to be taken into account.

Supporters of local food systems often draw on a standard list of benefits which are assumed to accrue to such systems. The benefits range from reductions in carbon dioxide emissions and energy use, stimulation of local economies and creation of a greater sense of community. Key points and cited references, categorised as benefits to producers, consumers and communities, are the following: economic benefits to producers and communities, economic benefits to consumers, non-economic benefits to individuals and communities, health benefits to consumers and communities, environmental benefits (energy use and reductions in carbon dioxide emissions), stimulation of local economies, creation of a greater sense of community (Dunning, 2011) and other social benefits (Norberg-Hodge, Merrifield and Gorelick, 2002; Morgan, Marsden and Murdoch, 2016; Edwards-Jones, 2010, pp. 588–589). However, the research-based support for those claims is difficult to find (Dunning, 2011), and they are difficult to be conducted (Edwards-Jones, 2010, pp. 588–589). Also in terms of organic food, the European Food Information Council assesses that, in general, organic food and farming benefit from favourable consumer perceptions, some of which cannot be scientifically substantiated, and that further research is needed to strengthen scientific evidence about the relative risks and benefits of organic compared to conventional foods and farming so that consumers can make decisions based on accurate and objective information (EUFIC, 2013). It is probably needless to remark that conducting such a research is expensive and probably not in the interest of big 'players' on the food market, who have sufficient funds to finance the research.

As said, food quality depends on a number of factors, not only on the vicinity of the producer to the consumer. By the time fruits and vegetables reach the consumer – whether from a stall at a local farmers market or the supermarket produce department – several factors determine their nutritional quality: the specific variety chosen, the growing methods used, ripeness when harvested, post-harvest handling, storage, extent and type of processing, and the distance transported. The vitamin and mineral content of fruits and vegetables depends on decisions and practices all along the food system – from seed to table – whether or not that system is local or global. Nevertheless, as assessed by the Center for Health and the Global Environment at the Harvard T.H. Chan School, local food has some distinct advantages. First, even when the highest post-harvest handling standards are met, the foods grown far away must spend a significant time on the road, losing nutrients before reaching the marketplace. Second, farmers growing for a local (and especially a direct) market favour taste, nutrition and diversity over shippability when choosing varieties. Greater crop diversity from the farmer means greater nutritional diversity for the eater. Third, in direct and local marketing strategies, produce is usually sold within 24 hours after harvest, at its peak freshness and ripeness, making consuming them a more attractive prospect. Fourth, during this short time and distance, produce is likely handled by fewer people, decreasing the potential for damage, and typically not harvested with industrial machinery. Minimising transportation and processing can ensure maximum freshness, flavour, and nutrient retention. This seems like an overly simplistic explanation of why local fruits and vegetables are healthier than those from our conventional long-haul agricultural system (Frith, 2007),[28] but nevertheless, the vicinity of the producer to the consumer is an important factor for the quality of food, although not the decisive factor for determining the quality of food. As the quality of food is best assured by fresh food, shorter food supply chains seem a better solution for assuring the freshness of the food products. Positive effects of short supply chains within the EU are recorded and various case studies on the diversity of short food supply chains in Europe have been examined and their contribution to sustainable rural development, economic aspects, environment, health, and well-being (Galli and Brunori, 2013).

As assessed above, the studies show that there are generally positive effects present in promoting and including healthy food (in schools).[29] Therefore, a contracting authority should have the possibility to buy healthy and high-quality fresh foods, like a normal consumer.

It has to be noted that although the comparison of purchasing possibilities of a normal consumer with a contracting authority in this context is in place, it could be treated as a tricky one. Namely, the role of the sponsor is important and is a distinguishing feature if speaking of vertical and horizontal direct effects under Article 34 TFEU.[30] However, this situation must be treated differently from the situation when a contracting authority procures quality foods and includes the vicinity factor in the procurement process, especially if 'local' is not a decisive factor. It has to be taken into account that contracting authorities should have the responsibility to provide quality food. Just because the contracting authority is subject to public procurement rules, this may not be the reason for them to be bound to procure food of a lower quality (i.e. prepacked, precooked, processed convenient food).

It should be in the interest of the contracting authorities as well as the EU, pursuing above all public health objectives, that the food delivered to public schools, kindergartens, hospitals, etc. is delivered *fresh*. This can easily be achieved if harvested and delivered within a supply chain that is as short as possible.

However, if we wish to bring health and environmental aspects into the public procurement of foods at the same time, this might require the introduction of the vicinity factor to the public procurement procedure. Namely, there are two possibilities to keep the food fresh and to achieve the shortest possible time between harvest and consumption (i.e. either to use quick air transport or to shorten the transfer distance). Needless to say, the second is much less environmentally friendly and is more expensive.[31]

From this point of view, local preference seems quite a logical choice when procuring fresh food. However, it has to be noted that 'local' cannot and must not be equated with 'national'. The geographical radius should be considered, regardless of the State borders. Having in mind the CJEU judgement in *Fabricom* and considering the possibilities under the Directive 2014/24/EU, any such measures to be introduced must be objectively justifiable and measurable (e.g. defining the short supply chain, enabling fresh foodstuffs to be delivered from field-to-table in 24 hours with a minimum impact on the environment), and proportionate, i.e. (i) appropriate to achieve the objectives they pursue and (ii) do not go beyond what is needed to attain those objectives.[32]

Here, it is necessary to recall, what was said above in this section – not only the vicinity of the producer to the consumer influences the food quality. Food quality depends on a number of factors. Therefore, it is essential, that also other quality measures, such as labels, apply.[33] In a sea of competing claims about the social and environmental characteristics of products, contracting authorities must find objective and rigorous means of verification. Reference to labels is clearly one of the most common and useful ways of doing this, and can reduce work for both buyers and suppliers (Semple, 2012).

In these circumstances, including the vicinity factor in public food procurement procedures in our view does not violate the Article 34 TFEU or the principle of equal treatment.

6 'Buy fresh' public procurement procedure of fresh foods in practice

For the verification purposes of the abovementioned hypotheses and arguments a hypothetical case study will be presented on the implementation of the procurement procedure for foods faced by many contracting authorities throughout the EU – from nursery schools to hospitals and retirement homes which aim at procuring as fresh and healthy food as possible.

Based on the assumption argued above, namely that fresh food is of better quality than processed food, we are faced with the challenge common to all public procurements in which an element of quality needs to be included, namely how to define, measure, and compare the quality of individual subjects of public procurement. The dilemma will be illustrated in the case of foods procurement. Therefore, we will focus on the criterion of "freshness" as one of the elements by which the quality of certain food products can be defined. Fresh food can be defined as those food products in which the time of their production to the consumption is the shortest, and therefore does not require any special processing procedures, reprocessing, preservation, or other means to maintain their period of use.

Recital 41 in the preamble to Directive 2014/24/EU states that nothing in the Directive should prevent the imposition or enforcement of measures necessary to protect public policy, public morality, public security, health, human and animal life, the preservation of plant life, or other environmental measures, in particular with a view to sustainable development, provided that those measures are in conformity with the TFEU. The cited provision clearly summarises the public interest to be followed in the context of the Directive, namely the implementation of measures that enhance public health and sustainable development, which becomes important when the provisions of the tender documentation with which we pursue those targets need to be defended. In terms of public procurement of foods, the following sections of the Directive 2014/24/EU are also worth mentioning: defining the requirements of a contract,[34] use of labels,[35] lowest price award and life-cycle costing (LCC),[36] and consulting the market.[37]

Here, we wish to answer the question how a contracting authority can pursue these goals in practice. Contracting authorities have several ways for the element of freshness or quality to be effectively included in the contract award procedure.

The first possibility is **defining the subject matter of the contract** when they define the quality standard which they pursue. The contracting authorities must identify the descriptive attributes and characteristics of the subject of the contract, as well as – when dealing with food – its form, manner and type of packaging, production method and processing, the raw materials used, the expiration date, the manner and delivery period, etc. In the same section, they can also define the specific characteristics of the subject of the contract or its method of production as well as technical standards, eco-labels, or other features of the subject of public procurement. From the aspect of measuring the quality in terms of freshness of the food delivered, one could identify the maximum allowable time period from the moment of "harvesting" the crop until its delivery to the end user, or define the concept of short supply chains and in this way define a maximum period of "freshness" still acceptable to the contracting authority. The simplest example is the supply of "fresh" milk, namely non-homogenised milk, or supply of the products made of "fresh" milk, e.g. cheeses, yogurts, cottage cheeses, etc.; therefore, we are dealing with the definition of the procedure of processing non-homogenised raw milk. Consequently, milk must be used in a much shorter period of time than homogenised and pasteurised or otherwise treated milk. To ensure that fresh milk retains its usability it has to be subject to specific terms and conditions of delivery, packaging, and storage. Indeed, the habits of end users have to be adapted as well because the way of using fresh milk is different from the way of using the homogenised one, namely the storage mode, the time to consumption, usage and, last but not least, also its taste. In a similar manner the majority of food products could be described and their properties characteristic of fresh food descriptively defined.

The second possibility is using the **technical specifications**. Recital 90 in the preamble to Directive 2014/24/EU explains that the technical specifications drawn up by public purchasers need to allow public procurement to be open to competition as well as to achieve objectives of sustainability. To that end, it should be possible to submit tenders that reflect the diversity of technical solutions standards and technical specifications in the marketplace, including those drawn up on the basis of performance criteria linked to the life cycle and the sustainability of the production process of the works, supplies and services. Consequently, technical specifications should be drafted in such a way as to avoid artificially narrowing down competition through requirements that favour a specific economic operator by mirroring key characteristics of the supplies, services or works habitually offered by that economic operator. Where reference is made to a European standard or, in the absence thereof, to a national standard, tenders based on equivalent arrangements should be considered by contracting authorities. It should be the responsibility of the economic operator to prove equivalence with the requested label. To prove equivalence, it should be possible to require tenderers to provide third-party verified evidence. However, other appropriate means of proof such as a technical dossier of the manufacturer should also be allowed.[38] Logically, also the provision of Article 42 of the Directive 2014/24/EU reflects a move towards life-cycle thinking, stating that technical specification which lay down the characteristics required of a works, service or supply may also refer to the specific process or method of production or provision of the requested works, supplies or services or to a specific process for another stage of its life cycle even where such factors do not form part of their material substance provided that they are linked to the subject matter of the contract and proportionate to its value and its objectives. This means that also technical specifications for organic food are in principle acceptable.[39]

It has to be noted, however, that **labels** can be used not only to define or to verify the compliance with technical specification, but also to define the award criteria or the contract performance clauses.[40]

The third possibility is **defining the selection criteria** for determining the capability of the tenderer, where the tenderers may be required to provide evidence relating to the compliance of their financial, personnel, technical, organisational and general abilities for the performance of the contract, whereby the stated condition for the recognition of capabilities must be formulated in such a way as to be related to the subject of the contract and, simultaneously, it must also be proportionate. In the case of food products procurement, the condition for the recognition of skills could be defined, for example, in terms of specific production methods or processing or supply of foodstuffs, e.g. by submitting the evidence that the tenderer (the manufacturer) is part of the scheme for production and processing of food using organic methods.[41]

Due to the method of "fresh" foodstuffs supply the tenderers must be, of course, organisationally capable of providing more frequent deliveries of foodstuffs as the contracting authorities cannot store the "fresh" food for longer periods of time, which means that the supply has to be more frequent; therefore, the selection criteria can be defined for the recognition of such capability in a way to verify the ability of the tenderer in terms of technical equipment with delivery vehicles, personnel, participation in joint delivery systems, etc., in order to ensure the delivery within the agreed deadlines and in the manner as defined by the contracting authority. In doing so, the distance to the place of delivery should not be relevant to contracting authorities, but rather the time in which the tenderer can provide the delivery. A characteristic of the conditions for the recognition of capabilities is that they are designed to verify the tenderer's capability, namely its properties, especially its capacity, the level of organisation and performance of the contract. The legal consequence of failure to comply with each selection criterion for the recognition of the capability is the rejection of the tenderer; in practice, the selection criteria for the recognition of the capability are often abused for the purpose when contracting authorities pursue the objective of unjustifiable discrimination or preferential treatment of a particular tenderer or group of tenderers.

As assessed above, in connection with the formulation of the selection criteria for the recognition of the tenderers' capabilities, the contracting authority can easily find itself in a trap when it wants to prefer "local" suppliers solely on the basis of the place of production or processing of a particular food product or on the basis of the distance from the place of delivery. The concept of the supply of fresh food is therefore closely related to the concept of preference for local suppliers; however, such preference can easily become unjustified territorial discrimination, which means that the contracting authority creates a distinction among comparable tenderers based on the place of incorporation, place of establishment of the entity or its distance to the contracting authority.[42]

Territorial discrimination can take the form of a definition of a selection criterion, or as an award criterion (e.g. the contracting authority favourably assesses those tenderers which are closer to its location). On the other hand, when the subject of the contract or the performance of the contract being awarded genuinely objectively justifies the differentiation of tenderers based on their location, such differentiation is permissible (e.g. in cases when providing a short response time is necessary for the purpose of protecting the life, health and property). The contracting authority which because of the nature and specificity of the subject of the contract causes territorial discrimination must clearly demonstrate that the subject of the public supply contract objectively justifies such conduct by the contracting authority. Any departure from the fundamental principles should be applied restrictively and only in objectively justified cases.[43]

The fourth possibility is defining **the award criteria** for selecting the most economically advantageous tender in a manner as to include elements of measuring the quality of the offered subject of the contract. A 2011 European Commission study (p. 146) showed that approximately one-third of all public contracts published on the EU public procurement portal had a sole award criterion 'lowest price', while the remaining two thirds used the award criterion 'most economically advantageous tender', whereby the criterion 'lowest price' was mostly present in low-value contracts.

Recital 89 in the preamble to Directive 2014/24/EU states that the notion of award criteria is central to the Directive. It is therefore important that the relevant provisions be presented in as simple and streamlined a way as possible. This can be obtained by using the terminology 'most economically advantageous tender' as the overriding concept, since all winning tenders should finally be chosen in accordance with what the individual contracting authority considers to be the economically best solution among those offered. In order to avoid confusion with the award criterion that is currently known as the 'most economically advantageous tender' in Directives 2004/17/EC and 2004/18/EC, a different terminology should be used to cover that concept, the 'best price-quality ratio'. Consequently, it should be interpreted in accordance with the CJEU case law relating to those Directives, except where there is a clearly materially different solution in the Directive 2014/24/EU.

Recital 90 in the preamble to Directive 2014/24/EU stresses that the contracts should be awarded on the basis of objective criteria that ensure compliance with the principles of transparency, non-discrimination and equal treatment, with a view to ensuring an objective comparison of the relative value of the tenders in order to determine, in conditions of effective competition, which tender is the most economically advantageous tender. It should be set out explicitly that the most economically advantageous tender should be assessed on the basis of the best price-quality ratio, which should always include a price or cost element. It should equally be clarified that such an assessment of the most economically advantageous tender could also be carried out on the basis of either price or cost effectiveness only. It is furthermore appropriate to recall that contracting authorities are free to set adequate quality standards by using technical specifications or contract performance conditions. In order to encourage a greater quality orientation of public procurement, Member States should be permitted to prohibit or restrict use of price only or cost only to assess the most economically advantageous tender where they deem this appropriate.

The abovementioned recitals clearly indicate the trend of development of the criteria for the award of public contracts, defined by Directive 2014/24/EU currently in force and can be summarised in the following points:

- Each award criterion used by contracting authorities should be related to the subject matter of the contract. The provision stems from the well-known

decision of the CJEU in *Concordia* (Case C-513/99) and is simultaneously stressed in Article 67(3) of Directive 2014/24/EU, and if summarised, it presents a ban on the use of the award criteria which are not related to the subject matter of the public contract or they are not directly connected with it, but could be related to the tenderer itself.
- The award criteria must be objectively defined in advance in the tender notice or in the tender documents presenting the implementation of the principles of transparency and equality of tenderers.
- The 'quality criterion' should supplement the cost criterion.
- The cost criterion arises from the possibility of use of two principles, namely the price or the cost-effectiveness approach, e.g. calculating the life-cycle costing, whereby the methodology for calculating the life-cycle costing must be defined in advance as well as the contracting authority must determine in advance the information that will be required to be submitted from tenderers.
- Member States are permitted to specify the degree of prohibition or restriction of use of price only or cost only criterion to assess the most economically advantageous tender.

The concept of 'quality' criteria is a novelty in the public procurement system and implements the criteria of 'best cost/quality ratio'; however, in the Article 67(2) of the Directive 2014/24/EU it is defined by way of example, and includes:

- quality, including technical merit, aesthetic and functional characteristics, accessibility, design for all users, social, environmental and innovative characteristics, and trading and its conditions;
- organisation, qualification and experience of staff assigned to performing the contract, where the quality of the staff assigned can have a significant impact on the level of the performance of the contract; or
- after-sales service and technical assistance, delivery conditions such as delivery date, delivery process, and delivery period or period of completion.

The purpose of Directive 2014/24/EU is clearly not to define the 'quality' criteria in detail and fill them with substance, but install as clear a framework for national regulators as possible, within which they will be able – depending on the specifics of individual public procurement traditions and practices – to formulate clear national rules concerning the application of the criteria.

Framework within which the contracting authorities can freely operate when setting the quality criteria and the national legislatures when setting national rules in the light of EU law was perfectly summarised by Advocate General Kokott (Case C-368/10, Opinion) in her opinion in *Dutch Coffee*, stating that the contracting authority does not have unrestricted freedom of choice on the award of public contracts.[44] The criteria set by the contracting authority must in fact be linked to the subject matter of the contract.[45] They must be capable of establishing the tender which offers best value for money.[46] Furthermore, contracts should be awarded on the basis of objective criteria that ensure compliance with the principles of transparency, non-discrimination and equal treatment of tenderers, which guarantee the assessment of tenders in conditions of effective competition.[47]

If the above is applied to the measurement of 'freshness' as a quality criterion in the procurement of food, the abovementioned can be used in the context of the criterion with which tenderers that deliver the freshest foodstuffs as soon as possible to the location of the end user would be rewarded. The key distinguishing criterion could have been the time required for the supply of food to the final customer.

Simultaneously, **Environmental Life Cycle Assessment (E-LCA)**, could also be made a part of the criteria. E-LCA is a technique that aims at addressing the economic, social, and environmental aspects of a product and their potential environmental impacts throughout that product's life cycle stages (United Nations, 2009, p. 33): origin of (genetic) resource, agricultural growing and production, food processing, packaging and distribution, preparation and consumption, and end of life. Life cycle evaluation accounts for a matrix of sustainability indicators beyond greenhouse gas emissions, including resource depletion, air and water pollution, human health impacts and waste generation (Heller and Gregory, 2000). The criterion of fresh food could be upgraded in this context in a way to set up the algorithm under which one could financially assess and monitor the distance of the tenderer or producers from the location of the end user, and reward those tenderers that supply the foodstuffs with minimum impact on the costs associated with external environmental factors, such as pollution caused by transport of food to the end user, or use environmentally friendly packaging, recycled packaging, etc.

In this context, the recital 96 of the preamble to the Directive 2014/24/EU provides that all costs over the life cycle of works, supplies or services (i.e. internal costs, such as research to be carried out, development, production, transport, use, maintenance and end-of-life disposal costs but can also include costs imputed to environmental externalities, such as pollution caused by extraction of the raw materials used in the product or caused by the product itself or its manufacturing), provided they can be monetised and monitored. However, the methods which contracting authorities use for assessing costs imputed to environmental externalities should be established in advance in an objective and non-discriminatory manner and be accessible to all interested parties. Such methods can be established at national, regional or local level, but they should, to avoid distortions of competition through tailor-made methodologies, remain general in the sense that they should not be set up specifically for a particular public procurement procedure.

The fifth option is the **contract performance clauses**. The Commission is referring to the contract performance clauses – beside the subject matter, award criteria, selection criteria and technical specifications – in Green Public procurement (GPP) Product Sheet for Catering and Food.[48] As assessed by *Sempl*e, there are two important differences to be noted between technical specifications and contract performance clauses. The first is that technical specifications are much more rigidly defined than contract clauses – a number of rules must be applied to ensure that they afford equal access to all tenderers. The second is that whereas technical specifications act as pass/fail requirements in a tender competition, contract clauses can only be enforced during the performance of the contract.

This difference was pointed out by the CJEU in the *Nord Pas de Calais* (Case C-225/98), and forms an important restriction on the role of contract performance conditions in tender procedures. Otherwise, it would be possible to avoid all the requirements for technical specifications by simply identifying them as contract clauses.[49]

Last but not least we should mention that the use of **the 'modern' electronic procurement techniques as for example electronic Framework Agreements and the Dynamic Purchasing Systems**, shall allow the contracting authorities to procure fresh foodstuffs for their successive current needs more efficiently. One of the features of the Framework Agreements is that they lack one of the essential elements of contracts, e.g. quantity, delivery time, and the like (Directive 2014/24/EU, Article 33). A feature of Dynamic Purchasing Systems is any economic operator that submits a request to participate and meets the selection criteria should be allowed to take part in procurement procedures carried out through the dynamic purchasing system over its period of validity. This purchasing technique allows the contracting authority to have a particularly broad range of tenders, and hence to ensure optimum use of public funds through broad competition in respect of commonly used or off-the-shelf products, works or services which are generally available on the market (Directive 2014/24/EU, Article 34, recital 64). In general, the trend of the supply of goods is moving in the direction of lowering the volume of stocks to contracting authorities to the minimum necessary for normal operation, because stocks on the one hand represent illiquid assets of the contracting authority, and, on the other hand, their storage and management generates additional costs to the contracting authorities. In procurement of foodstuffs, the issue is even more relevant, because usually one has to deal with perishable goods with short expiry dates. An additional advantage of the framework agreements is that they in a transparent and economical way enable the procurement of seasonal foods having two positive effects for contracting authorities; the procurement of fresh seasonal foods usually results in cost savings, because during the season of a particular foodstuff (e.g. a particular fruit or vegetable) its market price is usually lower due to greater supply on the market.

7 Conclusion

A clear trend of promoting sustainable and short food supply chains can be identified in the EU Member States, which is often being wrongly addressed by the contracting authorities which in various forms try to protect local (national) food production. However, the implementation of e-procurement platforms in the near future offers a considerable potential for implementation of modern electronic procurement techniques in a manner that they would facilitate the public procurement of seasonal fresh foods transparently and equitably by using the algorithms for assessment of tenders according to the criteria of freshness of food and the costs arising from external environmental factors and taking into account the criteria as outlined above.

Notes

* We are grateful for the comments received from the conference participants at the 3rd Interdisciplinary Symposium on Public Procurement in Belgrade, 29–30 September 2016. Warm thanks are due to Katja Hodošček for the excellent research and technical assistance.

1 Cf. Story, Nanney and Schwartz, 2009, pp. 71–100.

2 As assessed by the Commission, these followed after food prices both in Europe and globally have for 30 years fallen in real terms. COM (2008) 321, final, p 3.

3 On those factors see Watson, 2013, pp. xi, xii; Weis, 2013, pp. 65–85; COM (2008) 321, final, p 3.

4 For Commission's action on this issue see European Commission, *Agriculture and Food*.

5 For more information, see European Competition Network, *ECN Activities in the Food Sector*, 2012.

6 See also European Commission. *Food and Feed Safety*.

7 Cf. Davis and Pelc, 2017.

8 See also Gormley, 2009, p. 420; Oliver, 2010, p. 168; Hojnik, 2012, p. 305.

9 Our emphasis. On elaboration see Arrowsmith, 2014, p. 180 ff. Cf. Hilson, 2008, pp. 199–200.

10 See Sanchez-Graells, 2015.

11 E.g. Weiss, 1993; Gruber et al., 2006, pp. 79–114; Arrowsmith, 2014, pp. 237–337; Semple, 2015, pp. 35–66.

12 For further elaboration see Arrowsmith, 2014, pp. 253–256.

13 Cf. Arrowsmith, 2014, p. 614; Semple, 2015, p. 42.

14 So Arrowsmith, 2014, p. 615.

15 In *Concordia Bus Finland*, para. 50 of the Opinion, Advocate General Mischo considered that no difference in treatment of comparable situations arose from using award criteria favouring gas-powered buses that only a few operators (including the in-house unit) were able to offer: those able to meet the preferences of the contracting authority were in a different situation from those who could not. His conclusion that there was no violation of equal treatment was endorsed by the CJEU. See Case C-513/99. See Arrowsmith, 2014, p. 616.

16 Cf. Sanchez-Graells, 2015, pp. 227–237.

17 See Arrowsmith, 2010, pp. 129–130.

18 Cf. Case C-315/01, paras. 69 and 70, where the CJEU assessed that the criterion for the award of a public supply contract according to which a tenderer's offer may be favourably assessed only if the product which is the subject of the offer is available for inspection by the contracting authority within a radius of 300 km of the authority cannot constitute a criterion for the award of the contract.

19 For the relevant case law of the CJEU see subsequent paragraphs of the Opinion.

20 Cf. Semple, 2015, p. 171.

21 As foods e.g. encouraged in the Dietary Guidelines for Americans. See The US Department of Health and Human Services and The US Department of Agriculture, 2005; The US Department of Health and Human Services and The US Department of Agriculture, 2015.

22 Cf. Tilden, 1971.

23 It is e.g. estimated by World Health Organisation (WHO) that each 50-gram portion of processed meat eaten daily increases the risk of colorectal cancer by 18 percent. See World Health Organization, 2015.

24 Adopted from Lee and Kader, 2002, p. 212.

25 On 'Good agricultural practices' (GAP), defined as 'practices that address environmental, economic and social sustainability for on-farm processes, and result in safe and quality food and non-food agricultural products' see Burrell, 2011, pp. 251–270. Criteria defining 'good agricultural practice' (GAP) were originally developed for

on-farm production methods and resource use. For a decade, GAP principles have been applied throughout the entire agri-food supply chain by organisations promoting voluntary private standard (PS) schemes.

26 The phrase 'food miles' was first used by Tim Lang in 1992 on a UK television programme but has become widespread since that time. So Edwards-Jones, 2010, pp. 588–589.

27 See Innovation and Networks Executive Agency, 2014.

28 The Center was founded in 1996 to study and promote a wider understanding of the human health consequences of global environmental change. The Center is an official Collaborating Center of the UN Environmental Programme, and is one of the most trusted sources of information on this subject in the world. See www.chgeharvard.org/about-us.

29 See Neff et al., 2009, pp. 282–314. The authors also assess that overall there is a need for more evidence about connections between farm-to-school programs and health.

30 On assessment see Hojnik, 2012, pp. 302–304.

31 Air transport is the least carbon friendly, followed by road and, finally, ship. Vehicle size, loads and other aspects of logistical efficiency can also be expected to make a difference to the overall environmental impact of transport. On this issue see e.g. the Oxford Brookes study prepared for the National Audit Office: Rimmington and Carlton Smith, *Smarter Food Procurement in the Public Sector*.

32 On proportionality see Semple, 2015, pp. 51–56.

33 See Directive 2014/24/EU, Article 43, recital 75. Following the publishing of a feasibility study to evaluate the possibility of including food and feed products in the EU Ecolabel scheme in the future (the EU Ecolabel for food and feed products feasibility study can be found at http://ec.europa.eu/environment/ecolabel/documents/Ecolabel_for_food_final_report.pdf). The EU Ecolabel Board concluded in March 2012 that it would be valuable to extend the EU Ecolabel to food and feed products. Currently, though, the board agreed it was not feasible from a methodological and technical point of view. The board also concluded that synergies with other existing labels (e.g. EU Organic logo) should also be analysed further. See http://ec.europa.eu/environment/ecolabel/faq.html, accessed 7 April 2017.

34 Defining technical specifications is guided through Article 42 and Annex VII of Directive 2014/24/EU; and Article 60 and Annex VIII of Directive 2014/25/EU.

35 Conditions for using labels are laid out in Article 43 of Directive 2014/24/EU and Article 61 of Directive 2014/25/EU.

36 Awarding public contracts on the basis of the most economically advantageous tender is provided as part of Article 67 of Directive 2014/24/EU and Article 82 of Directive 2014/25/EU.

37 The procurement directives specifically allow for preliminary market consultation with suppliers in order to get advice, which may be used in the preparation of the procedure. See Article 40 of Directive 2014/24/EU.

38 See also Article 43 of the Directive 2014/24/EU.

39 Cf Semple, 2015, pp. 200–201.

40 See Semple, 2015, p. 189 ff.

41 As defined by *Council Regulation (EC) No 834/2007, p. 1.*

42 See the judgement of the CJEU in Case C-315/01, para 69–70.

43 Cf Matas, 2016, pp. 64–66.

44 Reference is made to Case C-31/87, para. 26; Case C-19/00, para. 37; Case C-513/99, paras. 61 and 64.

45 In this sense, it refers for example to judgement in Case C-513/99, paras. 59 and 64; Case C-448/01, para. 66, and Case C-331/04, para. 21.

46 Reference is made to the third paragraph of the recital 46 in the preamble to Directive 2004/18; see also recital 5 in the preamble to the Directive.

47 It refers to the first paragraph of the recital 46 and recital 2 in the preamble to Directive 2004/18; see, to that effect, the CJEU judgements in Case C-513/99 and Case C-331/04, para. 21.

48 Available online on http://ec.europa.eu/environment/gpp/eu_gpp_criteria_en.htm. [Accessed at 7 April 2017.] The Guidelines are being under revision. Cf. Galli and Brunori, 2013. The authors assess that in order to facilitate local sourcing in public procurement through more effective communication and sharing of experiences, updating of existing Green Public Procurement criteria for 'food and catering services', and, possibly, introduction of social considerations into public procurement within the broader framework of a socially responsible purchasing policy is required. See p. 29.

49 As assessed by A. Semple under the Directive 2004/18/EC and in reference to the *Dutch Coffee* case. See Semple, 2012.

References

Arrowsmith, S. (ed.) (2010). *EU Public Procurement Law: An Introduction*. Nottingham: University of Nottingham. Available at www.nottingham.ac.uk/pprg/documentsarchive/asialinkmaterials/eupublicprocurementlawintroduction.pdf [accessed 3 April 2017].

Arrowsmith, S. (2014). *The Law of Public and Utilities Procurement: Regulation in the EU and UK*, 3rd ed. London: Sweet & Maxwell.

Barnard, C. (2010). *The Substantive Law of the EU: The Four Freedoms*. Oxford: Oxford University Press.

Bentley, S., and Barker, R. (2005). *Fighting global warming at the farmer's market: The role of local food systems in reducing greenhouse gas emissions*. A Food Share Research in Action Report [Online]. Available at http://foodshare.net/custom/uploads/2015/11/Fighting_Global_Warming_at_the_Farmers_Market.pdf [accessed 3 April 2017].

Bruinsma, J. (ed.) (2003). *World Agriculture: Towards 2015/2030: An FAO Perspective*. Rome: FAO and London: Earthscan.

Burrell, A. (2011). Good agricultural practices' in the agri-food supply chain. *Environmental Law Review*, 13(4), 251–270.

Cardello, A. V. (1995). Food quality: Relativity, context and consumer expectations. *Food Quality and Preference*, 6(1), 163–170.

Case 222/82, *Apple and Pear Development Council v. K.J. Lewis Ltd* [1983] ECR I-4083.

Case 249/81, *Commission v. Ireland* [1982] ECR 4005.

Case 31/87, *Beentjes v. Netherlands State* [1988], ECR 4635.

Case C-16/98, *Commission v. France* [2000] ECR I-8315.

Case C-19/00, *SIAC Construction v. County Mayo, CC* [2001] ECR I-7725.

Case C-225/98, *Commision v. France* [2000] ECR I-7445.

Case C-243/89, *Commission v. Denmark* [1993] ECR 1-3353.

Case C-275/98, *Unitron Scandinavia v. Ministeriet for Fødevarer* [1999], ECR I-8291.

Case C-28/09, *Commission v. Austria* [2011] ECR I-13525, Opinion of AG Trstenjak.

Case C-315/01, *Gesellschaft für Abfallentsorgungs-Technik GmbH (GAT) v. Österreichische Autobahnen und Schnellstraßen AG (ÖSAG)* [2003] ECR I-06351.

Case C-324/98, *Telaustria and Telefonadress v. Telekom Austria* [2000], ECR I-10745.

Case C-325/00, *Commission v. Germany* [2002] ECR I-9977.

Case C-331/04, *ATI EAC e Viaggi di Maio and Others* [2005] ECR I-10109.

Case C-368/10, *Commission v. the Netherlands* [2012] ECR 1-284, Opinion of AG Kokott.

Case C-368/10, *European Commission v. Kingdom of the Netherlands* [2012] ECR 1-284.

Case C-448/01, *EVN AG in Wienstrom GmbH proti Republik Österreich* [2003] ECR I-14527.

Case C-513/99, *Concordia Bus Finland v. Helsinki* [2002] ECR 1-07213.

Case C-8/74, *Procureur du Roi v. Benoît and Gustave Dassonville* [1974] ECR 837.

Case C-87/94, *Commission v. Belgium (Walloon Buses)* [1996] ECR 1-02043.

Case C-95/10, *Strong Segurança SA v. Município de Sintra and Securitas-Serviços e Tecnologia de Segurança* [2011] ECR I-1865.

Case T-331/06, *Evropaïki Dynamiki v. AEE* [2010] ECR II-00136.

Collier, P. (2008). Politics of hunger – how illusion and greed fan the food crisis. *Foreign Affairs*, 87(6).

Commission communication concerning State involvement in the promotion of agricultural and fisheries products, COM (1986), 272, final.

Dahlbacka, B. (2010). *Sweden withdraws proposal on climate friendly food choices*. USDA Foreign Agricultural Service. [Online]. Available at http://gain.fas.usda.gov/Recent%20GAIN%20Publications/Sweden%20Withdraws%20Proposal%20on%20Climate%20Effective%20Food%20Choices_Stockholm_Sweden_12-1-2010.pdf [accessed 3 April 2017].

Davis, L., and Pelc, K. J. (2017). Cooperation in hard times – self-restraint of trade protection. *Journal of Conflict Resolution*, 61(2), 398–429.

De Schutter, O. (2009). *Large-scale land acquisitions and leases: A set of minimum principles and measures to address the human rights challenge*. UN Human Rights Council. [Online]. Available at www.oecd.org/site/swacmali2010/44031283.pdf [accessed 29 March 2017].

Department for Environment, Food and Rural Affairs (2014). *A plan for public procurement*. [Online]. Available at www.gov.uk/government/publications/a-plan-for-public-procurement-food-and-catering [accessed 10 April 2017].

Directive 2014/23/EU of the European Parliament and of the Council of 26 February 2014 on the award of concession contracts [2014] OJ L 94/1.

Directive 2014/24/EU of the European Parliament and of the Council of 26 February 2014 on public procurement and repealing Directive 2004/18/EC [2014] OJ L94/65.

Directive 2014/25/EU of the European Parliament and of the Council of 26 February 2014 on procurement by entities operating in the water, energy, transport and postal services sectors and repealing Directive 2004/17/EC [2014] OJ L 94/243.

Dunning, R. (2011). *Research-based support and extension outreach for local food systems*. North Carolina: Center for Environmental Farming Systems. [Online]. Available at https://cefs.ncsu.edu/wp-content/uploads/research-based-support-for-local-food-systems.pdf?522a23 [accessed 3 April 2017]

Edie (2007). *Sweden to climate-label food*. [Online]. Available at www.edie.net/news/5/Sweden-to-climate-label-food/12960/ [accessed 3 April 2017].

Edwards-Jones, G. (2010). Does eating local food reduce the environmental impact of food production and enhance consumer health? *Proceedings of the Nutrition Society*, 69(4), 582–591.

Ellin Doyle, M., and Glass, K. A. (2010). Sodium reduction and its effect on food safety, food quality, and human health. *Comprehensive Reviews in Food Science and Food Safety*, 9(1), 44–56.

EUFIC (2013). *Organic food and farming: Scientific facts and consumer perceptions*. [Online]. Available at www.eufic.org/article/en/expid/Organic_food_and_farming_scientific_facts_and_consumer_perceptions/ [accessed 3 April 2017].

European Commission (2011). Evaluation report: Impact and effectiveness of EU public procurement legislation. SEC 853 final.

European Commission. *Agriculture and food*. [Online]. Available at http://ec.europa.eu/competition/sectors/agriculture/documents_en.html [accessed 29 March 2017].

European Commission. *EU agricultural product quality policy*. [Online]. Available at http://ec.europa.eu/agriculture/quality/index_en.htm [accessed 3 April 2017]

European Commission. *Food and deed safety: The action plan.* [Online]. Available at http://ec.europa.eu/food/food/horsemeat/plan_en.htm [accessed 29 July 2016].

European Commission. *Food quality policy.* [Online]. Available at http://ec.europa.eu/agriculture/organic/eu-policy/eu-legislation/food-quality-policy/index_en.htm [accessed 3 April 2017].

European Commission. Tackling the challenge of rising food prices – Directions for EU action, COM (2008) 321, final.

European Competition Network (2012). *ECN activities in the food sector: Report on competition law enforcement and market monitoring activities by European competition authorities in the food sector.* [Online]. Available at http://ec.europa.eu/competition/ecn/food_report_en.pdf [accessed 29 March 2017].

Frith, K. (2007). *"Is local more nutritious?" It depends.* Harvard: Center for Health and the Global Environment at the Harvard T.H. Chan School. [Online]. Available at www.chge-harvard.org/sites/default/files/resources/local_nutrition.pdf [accessed 3 April 2017].

Galli, F., and Brunori, G. (eds.) (2013). *Short food supply chains as drivers of sustainable development.* Evidence Document. EU FP7 project FOODLINKS (GA No. 265287).

Gormley, L. W. (2009). *EU Law on Free Movement of Goods and Customs Union.* Oxford: Oxford University Press.

Gouveia, P. (2015). *Unfair trading practices in the business-to-business food supply chain.* [Online]. Study for the IMCO Committee. Available at www.europarl.europa.eu/RegData/etudes/STUD/2015/563438/IPOL_STU(2015)563438_EN.pdf [accessed 29 March 2017].

Gruber, G., Gruber, T., Mile, A., and Sachs, A. (2006). *Public Procurement in the European Union.* Graz: BWV.

Heller, M. C., and Gregory, A. K. (2000). *Life Cycle-Based Sustainability Indicators for Assessment of the U.S. Food System.* Michigan: University of Michigan. [Online]. [Accessed 3 April 2017]. Available at http://css.snre.umich.edu/css_doc/CSS00-04.pdf

Hill, H. (2008). *Food miles: Background and marketing, ATTRA sustainable agriculture program.* [Online]. Available at https://attra.ncat.org/attra-pub/viewhtml.php?id=281 [accessed 3 April 2017].

Hilson, C. (2008). Going local? EU law, localism and climate change. *European Law Review*, 33(2), 194–210.

Hojnik, J. (2012). Free movement of goods in a labyrinth: Can buy Irish survive the crises? *Common Market Law Review*, 49(1), 291.

Innovation and Networks Executive Agency (2014). *Fresh food corridors.* [Online]. Available at https://ec.europa.eu/inea/en/connecting-europe-facility/cef-transport/projects-by-country/multi-country/2014-eu-tm-0531-s [accessed 3 April 2017].

Joined Cases C-21/03 and C-34/03, *Fabricom v. Belgium (Fabricom)* [2005] ECR I-1559.

KRAV (2015). *Buy KRAV-labelled products.* [Online]. Available at www.krav.se/buy-krav-labelled-products [accessed 3 April 2017].

Lee, S. K., and Kader, A. A. (2002). Preharvest and postharvest factors influencing vitamin C content of horticultural crops. *Postharvest Biology and Technology*, 20(3), 207–220.

Matas, S. (ed.) (2016). *Zakon o javnem naročanju (ZJN-3) s komentarjem [A Commentary of Public Procurement Act (ZJN-3)].* Ljubljana: Uradni list RS.

Monteiro, C. A., Bertazzi Levy, R., and Moreira Claro, R. (2011). Increasing consumption of ultra-processed foods and likely impact on human health: Evidence from Brazil. *Public Health Nutrition*, 14(1), 5–13.

Monti, M. (2010). *A new strategy for the single market at the service of Europe's economy and society.* [Online]. Report to the President of the European Commission. Available at http://ec.europa.eu/internal_market/strategy/docs/monti_report_final_10_05_2010_en.pdf [accessed 3 April 2017].

Morgan, K., Marsden, T., and Murdoch, J. (2016). *Worlds of Food: Place, Power and Provenance in the Food Chain*. Oxford: Oxford University Press.

Motion for a European Parliament resolution on the food crisis, fraud in the food chain and the control thereof, INI (2013) 2091.

Neff, R. A., Palmer, A. M., Mckenzie, S. E., and Lawrence, R. S. (2009). Food systems and public health disparities. *Journal of Hunger & Environmental Nutrition*, 4(3–4), 282–314. [Online]. Doi:10.1080/19320240903337041.

Norberg-Hodge, H., Merrifield, T., and Gorelick, S. (2002). *Bringing the Food Economy Home: Local Alternatives to Global Agribusiness*. London: Zed Books.

Oliver, P. J. (ed.) (2010). *Oliver on Free Movement of Goods in the European Union*. London: Hart Publishing.

Pirog, R., and Benjamin, A. (2003). *Checking the Food Odometer: Comparing Food Miles for Local Versus Conventional Produce Sales to Iowa Institutions*. Iowa: Leopold Center for Sustainable Agriculture. [Online]. Available at www.leopold.iastate.edu/files/pubs-and-papers/2003-07-checking-food-odometer-comparing-food-miles-local-versus-conventional-produce-sales-iowa-institution.pdf [accessed 3 April 2017].

Ratliff, J. (2013). Major events and policy issues in EU competition law, 2011–2012 (Part 2). *International Company and Commercial Law Review*, 24(4), 127.

Sanchez-Graells, A. (2015). A deformed principle of competition? – the subjective drafting of article 18(1) of directive 2014/24. In G. S. Olykke and A. Sanchez-Graells (eds.), *Reformation or Deformation of the EU Public Procurement Rules in 2014*. Cheltenham: Edward Elgar Publishing.

Semple, A. (2012). *Grounds for change: ECJ judgment in Dutch coffee case points to need for reform of procurement rules, Case C-368/10 Commission v. Netherlands*. [Online]. Available at file:///C:/Users/Petra/Downloads/Grounds+for+change+-+Case+368+of+2010.pdf [accessed 30 March 2017].

Semple, A. (2015). *A Practical Guide to Public Procurement*. Oxford: Oxford University Press.

Shah, A. (2008). Global food crisis 2008. *Global issues*. [Online]. Available at www.globalissues.org/article/758/global-food-crisis-2008 [accessed 30 March 2017].

Smith, A., Watkiss, P., Tweddle, P., McKinnon, A., Browne, M., Hunt, A., Treleven, C., Nash, C., and Cross, S. (2005). *The validity of food miles as an indicator of sustainable development*. [Online]. Available at http://webarchive.nationalarchives.gov.uk/20130131093910/http:/www.defra.gov.uk/statistics/files/defra-stats-foodfarm-food-transport-foodmiles-050715.pdf [accessed 3 April 2017].

Story, M., Nanney, M. S., and Schwartz, M. B. (2009). Schools and obesity prevention: Creating school environments and policies to promote healthy eating and physical activity. *The Milbank Quarterly*, 87(1), 71–100.

Tilden, J. H. (1971). *Food: Its Influence as a Factor in Disease and Health*, 2nd ed. Pomeroy: Health Research Books.

Tridimas, T. (2006). *The General Principles of EU Law*, 2nd ed. Oxford: Oxford University Press.

United Nations (2009). *Guidelines for Social Life Cycle Assessment of Products*. United Nations Environment Programme.

The US Department of Health and Human Services and the US Department of Agriculture (2005). *Dietary Guidelines for Americans*, 6th ed. [Online]. Available at https://health.gov/dietaryguidelines/dga2005/document/pdf/DGA2005.pdf?_ga=1.181161575.1766187188.1471952207 [accessed 3 April 2017].

The US Department of Health and Human Services and the US Department of Agriculture (2015). *Dietary Guidelines for Americans 2015–2020*, 8th ed. [Online]. Available at https://health.gov/dietaryguidelines/2015/resources/2015-2020_Dietary_Guidelines.pdf [accessed 3 April 2017].

Vaughan, A. (2012). Tesco drops carbon-label pledge. *The Guardian*. [Online]. Available at www.theguardian.com/environment/2012/jan/30/tesco-drops-carbon-labelling [accessed 3 April 2017].

Watson, R. T. (2013). Prologue: Food security. In C. Rosin, P. Stock, and H. Campbell (eds.), *Food Systems Failure: The Global Food Crisis and the Future of Agriculture*. London: Routledge.

Weis, T. (2013). The meat of the global food crisis. *The Journal of Peasant Studies*, 40(19), 65–85.

Weiss, J. F. (1993). *Public Procurement in European Community Law*. London: Athlone Press.

Williams, R. P. (1983). Combatting economic protectionism in the EEC: The buy Irish decision. *Georgia Journal of International and Comparative Law*, 13(2), 585.

World Health Organization (2015). *IARC Monographs evaluate consumption of red meat and processed meat*. [Online]. Available at www.iarc.fr/en/media-centre/pr/2015/pdfs/pr240_E.pdf [accessed 3 April 2017].

Part 2

Joint public procurement

4 Colloquium

Nicola Dimitri and Tünde Tátrai

1 Tünde Tátrai – inconsistent regulatory interpretation of joint public procurement

It can be observed that joint procurement and the new European procurement directives conceptually converge. The new rules do not only support aggressive centralization, but are likewise supportive of voluntary common purchasing of contracting authorities. In the following I put forth some excerpts of Directive 24/2014/EU, formulating the view that a fundamental misunderstanding regarding joint public procurement stems from the public procurement directive, which leads to the opposite of its original purpose, as described in the Preamble of the Directive. I also assume that by joint procurement we mean the one of contracting authorities, entities that work together, thus I do not deal with in-house collaborations of public procurements (Art. 12(4)).

Let's start with the Preamble. The Preamble (71) clearly favors joint procurement to centralized public procurement. It prefers the less institutionalized solution, namely the voluntary joint procurement, to artificially centralized solutions. It is important that the term "occasional joint procurement", appears only this once in the text of the Preamble. Consequently it appears that the Directive envisages joint solutions as only occasional ones.

"*(71) Strengthening the provisions concerning central purchasing bodies should in no way prevent the current practices of occasional joint procurement, i.e. less institutionalised and systematic common purchasing or the established practice of having recourse to service providers that prepare and manage procurement procedures on behalf and for the account of a contracting authority and under its instructions.*"

Moreover, the innovative aspects of cooperation, of course, are also highlighted in the Preamble.

"*(71) On the contrary, certain features of joint procurement should be clarified because of the important role joint procurement may play, not least in connection with innovative projects.*"

For the better understanding of common public procurement, the legislation also determines the distinction between different forms of joint public procurement:

> "*(71) Joint procurement can take many different forms, ranging from coordinated procurement through the preparation of common technical*

specifications for works, supplies or services that will be procured by a number of contracting authorities, each conducting a separate procurement procedure, to situations where the contracting authorities concerned jointly conduct one procurement procedure either by acting together or by entrusting one contracting authority with the management of the procurement procedure on behalf of all contracting authorities."

Three joint procurement models are thus formed depending on the level of coordination:

1 separate purchases following a joint preparation phase or
2 joint arrangement procedures or
3 giving one contracting authority mandate to conduct the procurement process.

While apparently technical, in fact this distinction does not primarily emphasize taking advantage of economies of scale or exploiting the benefits of joint procurement but is guided by practical considerations. The distinction is clearly on administering the process in a legal procedural sense where responsibility issues arise as follows:

> *(71) Where several contracting authorities are jointly conducting a procurement procedure, they should be jointly responsible for fulfilling their obligations under this Directive. However, where only parts of the procurement procedure are jointly conducted by the contracting authorities, joint responsibility should apply only to those parts of the procedure that have been carried out together. Each contracting authority should be solely responsible in respect of procedures or parts of procedures it conducts on its own, such as the awarding of a contract, the conclusion of a framework agreement, the operation of a dynamic purchasing system, the reopening of competition under a framework agreement or the determination of which of the economic operators party to a framework agreement shall perform a given task.*

The joint procurement conditions of liability are important if within a framework agreement or a Dynamic Purchasing System certain procedural actions can be clearly separated and, indeed, within the framework of the joint procurement, the needs of each organization are separately, individually catered for.

It is important to mention cross-border joint purchasing. In this context economies of scale and risk-benefit sharing arise that are or at least would have been relevant in general terms, not only in cross-border aspects.

"*(73) Joint awarding of public contracts by contracting authorities from different Member States currently encounters specific legal difficulties concerning conflicts of national laws. Despite the fact that Directive 2004/18/EC implicitly allowed for cross-border joint public procurement, contracting authorities are still facing considerable legal and practical difficulties in purchasing from central purchasing bodies in other Member States or jointly awarding public contracts.*

In order to allow contracting authorities to derive maximum benefit from the potential of the internal market in terms of economies of scale and risk-benefit sharing, not least for innovative projects involving a greater amount of risk than reasonably bearable by a single contracting authority, those difficulties should be remedied."

It is interesting that the Directive considers cross-border joint procurement explicitly as an area for regulation in order to make clear applicable rules for the stakeholders. Centralized procurement and joint public procurement rules have been mixed in the Preamble (72)–(73), in particular those that arise in the application of centralized procurement of another Member State. The focus thus shifts towards centralization.

"*(73) Therefore new rules on cross-border joint procurement should be established in order to facilitate cooperation between contracting authorities and enhancing the benefits of the internal market by creating cross-border business opportunities for suppliers and service providers.*"

Art. 38 about joint purchasing focuses on voluntary joint procurement and on responsibility terms. Hence it does not confirm the rule that seeks solution in voluntary common solution instead of centralization. The normative text is more focused on practical issues. Accordingly, joint procurement on achieved on a by-case basis; therefore the title became "Occasional joint procurement".

Art. 38

1. *Two or more contracting authorities may agree to perform certain specific procurements jointly.*
2. *Where the conduct of a procurement procedure in its entirety is carried out jointly in the name and on behalf of all the contracting authorities concerned, they shall be jointly responsible for fulfilling their obligations pursuant to this Directive. This applies also in cases where one contracting authority manages the procedure, acting on its own behalf and on the behalf of the other contracting authorities concerned.*

   Where the conduct of a procurement procedure is not in its entirety carried out in the name and on behalf of the contracting authorities concerned, they shall be jointly responsible only for those parts carried out jointly. Each contracting authority shall have sole responsibility for fulfilling its obligations pursuant to this Directive in respect of the parts it conducts in its own name and on its own behalf.

Art. 39 is about "Procurement involving contracting Authorities from different Member States", which is based on Preamble (72)–(73) that focus mainly on centralized public procurement dealing with different co-operations of contracting authorities from different Member States. Related to this interesting thought – as in ANNEX V – Centralized Purchasing body appears as a form of a joint procurement.

"*Where appropriate, indication that the contracting authority is a centralised purchasing body; or that any other form of joint procurement is or may be involved.*"

Based on what is written above, the main rule is that joint procurement appears on an ad hoc basis and is not protected against centralized public procurement. The Preamble sets out in general terms the primacy of joint purchasing, but focuses on the conditions of liability regarding cross-border and domestic procurement.

Joint procurement is therefore less about economies of scale but rather about clarifying the responsibility issues in domestic and cross-border procurements. It appears that the Directive missed an opportunity as a result of which voluntary joint procurement cannot resist aggressive centralization even if there would be demand for it.

2 Nicola Dimitri – some economics of joint procurement

The 2014 EU Directive on Public Procurement (JP) focuses on a number of interesting issues. One of them is certainly joint procurement, the possibility for a number of institutions to purchase as a single subject. The EU interest was further manifested in the 2014 EU Agreement on JP for medicines against pandemics. This last agreement is based on voluntary decisions by the EU states, and indeed after its inception, with seven signing countries, gradually several other Member States entered the agreement which is now covering almost 450 million EU inhabitants. The 2014 EU Directive explicitly allows JP to take different forms; for example, in the case of medications JP could concern Member States, groups of hospitals, geographical regions, etc.

Although JPs may take alternative configurations they could share common traits and raise similar economic issues. In what follows I aim to discuss some of them.

Price For standardized goods and services, such as medical drugs or medical devices, in a JP it is likely that firms would compete on a single unit price, the same for all the institutions behind the JP. This would be fine as long as the cost (standard) of living is similar across the JP institutions. For example, suppose countries A and B decide to perform a JP to purchase *n* units of a vaccine, and suppose country A has a meaningfully higher average income than country B. How should such procurement be designed? Should there be the same unit price for a single vaccine dose, valid for both countries, or should the unit price be differentiated according to the different average income? In the former case the price may turn out to be too high for citizens in country B, to the extent that unless they are subsidized by their own State or other institutions they could not afford buying it. Alternatively, if citizens in B are not subsidized and the price turns out to be affordable by people in both countries, perhaps those in country A would pay much less than they could and were willing to, with the supplier losing potential profits. The lower-than-potential earnings by the contractor in this case could be interpreted as the implicit cost paid by the supplier for the right to execute the contract for both countries. In this sense, it could be seen as a form of cross subsidy to citizens of country B, giving up some profits that could have been obtained by selling to citizens of country A only, at a higher price.

A possible solution to the above concerns may be to differentiate the price between the two countries; however it is not clear whether this should be done by setting up two different lots, one for each country, or by setting up a single lot. In the former case, allowing for combinatorial offers (which is when a firm could submit a price for country A only, alternatively for country B only or for both A and B) would probably be a flexible and appropriate procurement design.

Savings A main advantage induced by JP could be monetary savings, since contracts would have larger size and bigger firms could exhibit their economies of scale. Savings in a procurement could be an unconditional advantage for contracting authorities if quality delivered by the supplier would be as promised, and if larger contracts in JP would not create the conditions for the emergence of dominant market positions in the future. Given the contract size, for the procurer it will be even more important in this case to make sure that possible low prices would not induce strategic behavior by the contractor in the attempt to renegotiate more favorable conditions during contract execution.

Skills Closely related to the issue of savings and contract size is that of procurers' skills. Indeed, the larger the contract the more skilful buyers should be, as mistakes in procurement design and management may have serious negative effects on the relevant organizations. This is because larger contracts typically exhibit higher complexity in design and management. Buyers' competence is also needed to avoid strong risk aversion by the officers in charge prevailing and making procurements economically less effective than they could be, even if legally impeccable. Therefore, JP requires the due expertise, which of course would need relatively high rewards. Yet, high pay to the officers could be more than compensated by the savings enhanced through effective procurements as well as by the lack of cost duplications induced by JP.

Lots Whether JP procurements being tendered as a single large contract or split into more than one lot could be an issue. As above, if international JP would concern countries with meaningful differences in average income and standards of living, then choosing to procure a single lot, with uniform award conditions across the consortium parties, may induce unbalances among the purchasing subjects. Furthermore, single large contracts would make it more difficult for SMEs to compete, or even access, procurements. Therefore, multiple lots setting a JP would mostly be justified by concentration of competence and/or sensitivity to SMEs and/or market structure-related concerns.

Quality A JP can have an effect on various aspects concerning quality. First the JP could serve as a quality control device, notably for those subjects who would lack the needed internal competence and expertise to perform and enforce the right quality check. Furthermore, tailor-made procurements for specific needs would be difficult to implement in a JP, which would turn out suitable mostly for shared, standardized needs.

3 Tünde Tátrai – response to paper 2

Obligation or free choice?

I agree with the importance of issues such as price savings, lots or quality, all of which are main priorities from an economic perspective. In my opinion these priorities should be completed with a "structure" that largely determines the various alternative forms of joint procurement.

It is possible that the "structure's" role is undervalued from the legal and procedural point of view. The same procedure is after all to be conducted anyhow – regardless of how many contracting authorities are involved in the public procurement procedure. In fact, it is legally irrelevant after all that joint purchasing is voluntarily assumed by the parties or that it is prescribed to them to join up or perhaps that they have the obligation to do purchasing through a central purchasing entity.

When it comes to joint procurement, discussion is about a certain type of centralized model; for instance when a legislator determines whether it is mandatory for contracting authorities to stand together in procurements or which organization to mandate with purchasing on behalf of other contracting authorities. From my point of view one of the most common forms of the latter is when procurement entities are obliged to submit their procurement requests to a central purchasing organization entity which delivers the orders based on the contracts it has entered into beforehand.

The use of compulsory joint procurement legally simplifies the procurement process; however, legal options of central purchasing organizations are far from being exhausted. Further legal options are available for contracting authorities that are obliged to act in groups. Naturally, risk aversion exists in these cases too.

I would like to bring up some examples to demonstrate why it is very dangerous to enforce joint public procurement by the legal means:

- Using a model framework agreement, the parties have an interest in reducing risk wherever possible and admitting all potential suppliers; therefore in the first part of a framework agreement procedure there will be no real competition and the price will remain high.
- The coordinating function of an external body is enough to interfere unethically and has the ability to achieve its goals by misconduct without liability.
- In the cases of joint purchasing it is common that lack of flexibility can be perceived when determining needs. Such controversies stem from conflicting institutional interests.
- During the joint procurement the different actors call for solutions that ultimately lead to the selection of their preferred suppliers through the composition of buyers baskets assembling individual consultations.
- When designing the union electronic catalog, particular aspects come to the fore in the absence of relevant skills and knowledge. Weak catalog management leads to poor-quality suppliers and growing vulnerability.

If the legislature structurally determines everyone's role, responsibility and authority in centralization and determines contracting for themselves in exchange for a more comfortable purchasing, the distinction between the operational and strategic purchasing is terminated – a result of a highly questionable and dubious nature.

The aspects highlighted by Dimitri on joint procurement are very realistic starting points in my opinion. Still, it would have been necessary to examine the structural background of this market, namely who is responsible and who does what in joint acquisition processes and which conclusions to draw. It is interesting that from the legal point of view this matter is simply treated in the procedural sense because after the clarification of liability issues it is easy to see who does what, what are the role and the mandate of the players.

The legislative background focuses on the form of centralization and thus masks the real problem that scientific discussion is about a flexible, market-demands, costs—-and-savings-oriented model.

I would like to formulate criticism regarding joint procurement because when we do not limit accurately the degree of freedom of the individual players and, instead, we consider various solutions of centralization to be having equal value, we make a mistake.

It is therefore necessary to emphasize the importance of the new rules on central purchasing bodies in the directives which are trying – although only mildly – to establish specific rules in this area as well. But centralization faces the same problem because there is a separate answer when organizations voluntarily join central purchasing systems, to be differentiated from when a single central purchasing body is responsible to procure certain products for certain central government bodies. The price-savings-skills-lots-quality contexts prevail in the same way, only the structural frames are different.

I see an overlap when, for example, a law obliges operators to conduct joint procurement, because in this case it is practically a form of centralization achieved by a kind of common procurement. Temporary solutions are especially interesting at institutions where the affected establishments – such as a centralized procurement organization – do not have the expertise or the legislature did not consider the conditions that should have been created for a smooth organizational centralization. In the economic sense, in my opinion, joint procurement is a useful instrument; however, it is vulnerable to become equal to centralization, and thus the desirable results of Price-Savings-Skills-Lots-Quality can be fragile.

When Dimitri writes that joint procurement is "the possibility for a number of Institutions to purchase as a single subject," in my opinion, this is formulated very well. The importance of the structural background should be however emphasized within this framework and a unique definition of joint procurement should be created on this basis.

Nicola Dimitri – response to paper 1

I found the issues raised by Tünde extremely interesting and much to the point for an appropriate application of joint procurement. In what follows I will focus on what in my view are the two main ones, concluding their discussion by posing a main question.

1 Inconsistency

Potential inconsistency of the rules may induce problems and is therefore undesirable for the relevant parties, and the legislation in general. Indeed, in the Preamble, the 2014 EC Directive on Public Procurement seems to be pursuing two apparently conflicting goals. First, due to their increased use and popularity, it reinforces the provisions for possible top-down type of central purchasing bodies and activities while, at the same time, making sure that "spontaneous", bottom-up kind of joint procurement would not be discouraged by this operation. As a matter of fact, what the EC seems to be concerned about is that aggregation behind joint procurement should be voluntary.

The two potentially conflicting perspectives could however be reconciled and made consistent, as long as resorting to (and existence of) central purchasing bodies is voluntary, rather than mandatory, for contracting authorities. However, one should be aware that when access to contracts awarded by central purchasing bodies is purely voluntary then some possible advantages of centralization, as those due to aggregation and economies of scale, may fail to materialize.

Even when contracting authorities are mandated to resort to central purchasing bodies, there could be sufficient underlying consensus within the authorities. This is for instance when central purchasing bodies may have been set up under the initiative of contracting authorities themselves. If not, then some kind of superior, system-wise reason should justify so, such as: public debt mitigation, centralized payments, increased professionalism, curbing of corruption and others.

The Directive is perhaps encompassing all this, as leaving joint procurement to be completely voluntary may not always originate desirable outcomes.

Therefore, to summarize the first part, a main question could be: should joint procurement be always purely voluntary and, if not, to what degree could it be?

2 *Liability*

The second important point I want to discuss is liability of the relevant authorities raised by joint procurement. The Directive seems clear in imputing joint, rather than limited, responsibility for joint procurement. Leaving aside for a moment the problem of the prevailing legislation, in case of cross-border procurement, from an economic perspective the rule introduces interesting elements for possible opportunistic behavior by contracting authorities. To discuss this, consider two authorities *A* and *B* who jointly procured a number of laptops. Based on the award conditions, authority *A* has to pay €100,000 while *B* pays €300,000. Then suppose that for some reason authority *A* breaches the contract paying less than agreed in the contract, say, €70,000. Then under joint liability it seems like that *B* too is responsible for compensating the supplier of the unpaid €30,000. This formalizes the idea that *B* should have an incentive to monitor *A*, to make sure it will comply with contract conditions, and vice versa. On the other hand, precisely because of joint liability, sharing the punishment may provide an incentive to *A* to free ride and breach the contract. In the example, if the unpaid €30,000 are equally split then *A* will only have to pay €15,000 while *B* the remaining €15,000.

Moreover, how liabilities would be shared is also very important. Penalties should be equally shared among the relevant authorities or, alternatively, distributed according to their "relative weight" in the contract, if a criterion to set a weight could at all be identified and agreed upon. Indeed if *B* were to breach the contract paying, say, €200,000 under an equally shared liability, then *A* will have to pay €50,000, that is, 50 percent additional costs with respect to its own expenses. If assigned with respect to a relative weight established in terms of their own procurement costs, then *A* should pay of the penalty of *B*'s missing payment, that is €25,000. These simple considerations should have pointed out that the definition of joint liability, which is somewhat left open by the Directive, should be carefully specified to discourage opportunistic behavior by the contracting authorities and take care of possible asymmetries across them.

Therefore, a second main question that joint procurement may raise is: how should joint liability for contract non-compliance be set up to prevent possible opportunistic behavior by the contracting authorities?

4 Tünde Tátrai – conclusions

In my opinion it is a very good approach to grasp the issue by dividing joint procurement types between top-down and bottom-up kinds of joint procurement. It appears that these are the two ends of the spectrum, for there are completely mixed solutions which belong to the same centralized procurement system but where – for instance – the central purchasing bodies are not able to perform their duties, thus stakeholders join up for purchasing.

I noticed a new phenomenon, namely that institutions such as municipalities or universities realized that they can promote cooperation if they act together within the framework of centralized procurement so they take advantage of economies of scale and exploit competition over the products available in the framework of the mandatory centralized procurement. Of course, this may be due to a more general modernization of the market when available sufficient resources are able to renew institutional integrated information system.

Similarly it is a kind of hybrid solution that is provided by the same centralized public procurement systems, but this sort of hybrid solution only increases the contracting authorities' administrative burden so the contracting authorities tend to bypass centralized systems when cooperating with each other and adopting creative solutions with their counterparts.

I would like to emphasize that cooperation itself can be directed to many goals and it might be unclear what kind of purpose centralization actually serves. For example, if the government wants to obtain government communications through one channel and would have the ambition to centralize the procurement of communication services, it effectively curtailed the freedom of decision of contracting authorities. Institutions would like to make their own decisions about the content of contracts and subject matters regarding the procurement of communication and advertising. In such situations governments often tend to centralize procurement partly in order to create a certain right of approval to control and direct procurements of communication services. All this is so because they primarily want to establish control while efficient procurement is only a secondary priority.

I agree with the opinion of Dimitri, who explains joint procurement's voluntary versus non-voluntary nature and approaches the issue from a liability perspective. All this is to be completed with a question to which I did not get a response by reading the European Public Procurement Directive. What is joint procurement for – if not for better service and better quality of spending public money? Does joint procurement contribute to more professional procurement and does it offer better economies of scale in procurements? However, when there are so many hybrid solutions between the top-down and bottom-up joint procurement types, joint procurement distorts the original purpose. We do not get an answer on what purpose is served when joint procurement is advertised in Europe. Is this interesting from a legal point of view because there is an agreement between parties regarding cooperation? If this is so, then we have really lost the essence of the joint procurement.

6 Conclusions – Nicola Dimitri

One size does not fit all

I would like to thank Tünde Tátrai for focusing on a very important issue related to joint procurement, which she refers to as a structural problem. Indeed, in principle, whether the centralization process is top down or bottom up should not make a major difference. Those in charge of the joint purchasing should simply execute the procurements pursuing best value for money for the stakeholders.

However, in reality, the way centralized purchasing is put in place and officers in charge come to be chosen may have major implications on joint procurement success. This is certainly related to people skills but may go beyond professional abilities. Though true in general, as Tünde Tátrai points out this is particularly important when enforcing a top down model, since centralization may be perceived as an imposition and requisition of functions by the relevant administrations, creating discontent at a decentralized level. This might be due to a loss of direct control by the administrations on the own procurements, but also to the fact that centralized purchasing may be unable to fulfil their desiderata. In this case, precisely because of the top down approach, officers working in the centralized authority should be carefully chosen in so far as their skills and moral integrity are concerned. Indeed, if gains from centralization are not evident, the project may be liable to find resistance in the public sector and fail. This is also because top down decisions are often presented and justified as institutional mechanisms supporting rationalization of public expenditure, which, if not delivered, could endanger the whole project.

When a joint procurement initiative emerges spontaneously as a bottom up approach, originally perhaps only to the benefit of those who promoted the initiative, acceptance would not be an issue as well as the attitude towards officers in charge, who are now chosen by the stakeholders, rather than being imposed by law. Yet failure to deliver effective procurements is always possible for a variety of reasons, such as incompetence or low moral integrity by the officers.

Yet, at least in principle, in this second case of spontaneous joint purchasing initiative the likelihood of dissatisfaction by the stakeholders should be lower. Therefore, as typical in procurement, one size does not fit all; that is, depending upon how it was formed, centralized procurement may receive different degrees of acceptance by the stakeholders and have different levels of intrinsic motivation by the officers in charge. As a result, the final outcome may be affected by how the decision to centralize emerged.

5 Addressing in part market imbalances in the pharmaceutical sector through voluntary joint public procurement

Antoinette Calleja

1 Introduction

Medicines play a vital role in the delivery of quality health care. The world pharmaceutical market was worth an estimated €651,500 million at ex-factory prices in 2014 (European Federation of Pharmaceutical Industries and Associations, 2015). The North American market (the US and Canada) comprised 44.5 percent and Europe 25.3 percent of the market share (European Federation of Pharmaceutical Industries and Associations, 2015). According to a recent report by OECD (2015) pharmaceuticals (pharmaceutical expenditure covers prescription medicines and medicines procured over the counter, i.e. not requiring a prescription) comprise the third largest health care expenditure item after inpatient and outpatient care, representing approximately 1.4 percent of GDP across OECD countries (OECD, 2015, p. 180). In year 2013 such costs were estimated at 17 percent of the total health care budget. This estimate did not take into account the expenditure of medicines in hospitals in which case if included would amount to an estimated 20 percent of total health care budget across OECD countries. Wide variations in retail pharmaceutical spending per capita across OECD countries reflect differences in volume, consumption patterns and prices. It appears that in 2013, the US spent double the average – US$ PPP 1,026 per capita on pharmaceuticals, OECD average stood at US$ PPP 515 with Denmark spending the least – US$ PPP 240 (OECD, 2015, p. 179). When it comes to public expenditure on pharmaceuticals across OECD countries, expenditure dropped on average by 3.2 percent between 2009–2013 (OECD, 2015, p. 180). This comes in response to various policy measures that have sought to shift the burden of expenditure from the public purse to private payers.

Across the 34 high-income countries in the WHO European Region, public spending on health ranges from 3.3 percent to 10.0 percent of GDP. In the EU, health care is publicly financed on the basis of solidarity and universal access allowing entitlement to a wide range of medicines. Total health care expenditure in the EU is estimated at €1 300 billion per year (10 percent of GDP) of which an estimated €220 billion (23 percent) are spent on pharmaceuticals and €100 billion (11 percent) for medical devices. The figures are forecasted to increase.

There appears to be a positive relationship between pharmaceutical expenditure per capita and GDP per capita (European Commission, Directorate-General for Internal Policies, 2011, p. 12). Member State expenditures per capita on pharmaceuticals vary greatly with a more than three-fold difference in per capita pharmaceutical spending being reported – Greece with €682 per capita and Poland with €127 per capita (European Commission, Directorate-General for Internal Policies, 2011, p. 12). The cost drivers in the pharmaceutical industry are mainly influenced by the entrance of new branded products into the market and products going off-patent (Urbinati et al., 2014). The rising trend of an ageing population with a growing prevalence of chronic diseases expands further the use of new medical technologies and biologic drugs, which in turn further increase pharmaceutical expenditure (Urbinati et al., 2014). The development of personalized medicine further poses health systems with new challenges.[1] All this needs to be seen within a scenario where health care budgets are experiencing significant constraints in view of the ever-increasing health care demands, escalating costs and concurrent health care budget cuts as part of the austerity measures in response to the economic downturn.

Presently, major and rapid developments are occurring within the field of medicines. While on one hand the development of new drugs offers new prospects for people confronted with otherwise untreatable diseases (as in certain cases of lung cancer, cystic fibrosis, HIV and hepatitis C), on the other hand we are confronted with a situation where the very high costs of new medicines are hindering access to such innovations. *'Sovaldi'* intended for the treatment of hepatitis is a point in case, where its launch price was set at $1,000-a-pill, in effect making its treatment out of reach for patients (Loftus, 2015).[2] Another example demonstrating how certain medicines end up out of reach for patients is the case of a wide range of injected generic medicines, such as Phenytoin, where it was reported that despite their clinical need, manufactures decided that their profit margin did not justify their continued manufacture (Fox, Sweet and Jensen, 2014).

Further, the issue of drug shortages of various medicines effective for a range of conditions is another matter of concern. The World Health Organisation recognises drug shortages as a global problem (Gray and Manasse, 2012). While the causes for drug shortages are largely under-reported, production problems have been identified as the leading cause for shortages in European countries and the US (Pauwels et al., 2014). However, it has also been observed that were there to be improved reporting systems, this would allow for better insights to the reasons behind such shortages.

Notwithstanding the fact that the pharmaceutical industry is strongly regulated[3], the presence of asymmetrical information gives pharmaceutical suppliers a high degree of leverage in the market. In year 2008 the European Commission launched a sector inquiry into pharmaceuticals given that, "competition in the pharmaceutical market in the European Union might not be working well" (European Commission, Competition DG, 2009). The inquiry sought to examine the reasons for observed delays in the entry of generic medicines to the market and the apparent decline in innovation as measured by the number of new medicines coming to the market. The results suggested that the behaviour of originator companies[4] contributed to the obstacles for generic[5] and originator[6] entry, while acknowledging that other factors such as the regulatory framework might also play an important role.

During the Employment, Social Policy, Health and Consumer Affairs Council meeting on 17 June 2016, EU health Ministers adopted Council conclusions that were presented by the Dutch Presidency of the Council, on strengthening the balance in the pharmaceutical system in the EU and its Member States (Council Conclusions, 2016). Health ministers acknowledged market failure in a number of Member States and claimed that,

> patients' access to effective and affordable essential medicines is endangered by very high and unsustainable price levels, market withdrawal of products that are out-of-patent, or when new products are not introduced to national markets for business economic strategies and that individual governments have sometimes limited influence in such circumstances.
>
> (Para. 16, pg. 5)

Further, Member States were invited to explore ways of cooperation on a voluntary basis while ascribing full respect to Member States' competencies. Such cooperation is to include the proactive exchange of information between Member States (e.g. national pricing and reimbursement authorities), particularly in the pre-launch phase. In addition, Member States were also urged to explore the possibility of strategies on voluntary joint price negotiations in coalitions of Member States.

Given the various complexities ingrained within the pharmaceutical industry the following section (Section 2) will attempt to assess the potential for voluntary joint public procurement of medicines first by presenting a discussion that seeks to capture a general understanding of the structures underpinning the pharmaceutical market both from the supply and the demand side. Section 3 provides a glimpse on the cross-border efforts for joint procurement while Section 4 discusses the type of set up that is needed for developing an effective and efficient joint procurement model. Section 5 presents concluding remarks highlighting scope for developing joint innovation partnerships.

2 Overview of the structures underpinning the pharmaceutical market

2.1 On the supply side

The pharmaceutical industry is a complex and highly sensitive sector. It directly employs 707,000 people across Europe and generates three to four times more employment indirectly (European Federation of Pharmaceutical Industries and Associations, 2015). In 2014 it invested an estimated

€30,500 million in R&D in Europe (European Federation of Pharmaceutical Industries and Associations, 2015). Around a quarter of all pharmaceutical sales globally are from the EU (European Commission, 2015). Production takes place in several Member States, but the bulk of manufacturing is mainly located in France, Germany, Ireland, Italy, Spain and the UK (European Commission,

2015). In general two main types of companies characterize the sector – originator companies and generic companies.

Originator companies range from large multinationals to SMEs. The latter tends to focus on niche areas. Their innovations are later either out-licensed or sold to the larger pharmaceutical companies because of their lack of resources to perform the necessary clinical trials and subsequent marketing (European Commission, Competition DG, 2009). The life cycle of an originator product is divided into three distinct phases: the pre-launch period, where R&D as well as regulatory approval takes place; the marketing and sales period, during which the product benefits from exclusivity; and a later period when the patent expires and generic competition is possible (Vancell, 2012).

Competition between originator companies tends to focus on therapeutic innovations, their relative efficacy and absence of side-effects rather than on price. Notwithstanding such, in view that R&D costs need to be recouped through medicine prices, pharmaceutical companies tend to focus their innovations on areas that are most profitable. The so-called blockbusters[7] form the backbone of their company strategies which in effect may not necessarily mean that they are tapping on unmet health care needs. Biopharmaceuticals[8] and personalized medicines appear to be paving the future for these companies.

Generic companies sell generics which basically contain the same active pharmaceutical ingredients as the originators, but they are usually sold at a much lower price. Generic manufacturers also need to prove the quality, efficacy and safety of their products though they do not need to provide details on pre-clinical tests and clinical trials if there is sufficient proof that the product in question is equivalent to the originator product. Most generic companies are SMEs, some of which have managed to penetrate the global market with a turnover exceeding €1 billion per year (European Commission, Competition DG, 2009).

Generic products authorised pursuant to Directive 2004/27/EC (Council Directive 2004/27/EC, 2004) cannot be placed on the market until 10 years have elapsed from the initial authorisation of the originator product. However, it is worth noting other extended patent protections enjoyed by originator products. The *Supplementary Protection Certificate* by way of regulation (EC) No 469/2009 extends further the protection period because it was deemed that the period of effective protection under the patent was insufficient to cover the investment put into research by the originator companies. Therefore, following the expiry period of the basic patent protection the Supplementary Protection Certificate provides protection for an additional five years. Thus, the holder of both a patent and a certificate are able to enjoy an overall maximum of 15 years of exclusivity from the time the medicinal product in question first obtained authorisation for its placing on the market.

Regulation (EC) 141/2000 seeks to encourage the development and authorisation of medicinal products for rare diseases. It establishes a regime of incentives and rewards for orphan drug development. It is estimated that 5 000 to 8 000 distinct rare diseases exist in the EU (Commission Staff Working Document, 2015). Although their prevalence is low, rare diseases affect 27 to 36 million people in the EU (6–8 percent of the population). Therefore, the development of orphan medicinal products is an important consideration to ensure that people suffering from rare disease also have access to medicinal products. Thus, by way of Regulation (EC) 141/2000 in addition to the usual patent protection, manufacturers also receive up to ten years of market exclusivity for designated orphan medicinal products. It has been argued that the loosely applied definition attached to the concept of 'orphan drug' and the length of market exclusivity appear to have contributed towards an upsurge of these new products with resultant monopolies and their associated prices (Dearson, 2011).

Under Article 37 of Regulation (EC) 1901/2006 on medicinal products for paediatric use, market exclusivity may be extended to 12 years if a paediatric investigation plan is completed. This regulation establishes a regime that seeks to reward and provides incentives for pharmaceutical companies to develop medicines appropriately tested, authorised, and formulated for use in children. It also harmonizes the manner of how clinical studies are to be conducted on children.

Availability of some generics depends on the geographical size of the market or the product market. In small national markets or in the case of a small product market sales of generics may not exceed the entry costs and thus are not made available, with consequent more expensive choices for patients and health systems (European Commission, Directorate-General for Internal Policies, 2011).

2.2 On the demand side

Notwithstanding the various specificities characterising the supply side, the demand side is also characterised by unique features. Across the EU health care is publicly financed on the basis of solidarity and universal access. The State or health insurance funds are major purchasers for pharmaceutical products. Article 168 (1) TFEU, holds that, "[T]he Union shall complement the Member States' action in reducing drugs-related health damage, including information and prevention." In addition,

> The Commission may, in close contact with the Member States, take any useful initiative to promote such coordination, in particular initiatives aiming at the establishment of guidelines and indicators, the organisation of exchange of best practice, and the preparation of the necessary elements for periodic monitoring and evaluation.
>
> (Article 168 (2) TFEU)

However, it is not within the competence of the EU to regulate the market after market authorisation of medicines is obtained. According to Article 168 (7) TFEU,

> Union action shall respect the responsibilities of the Member States for the definition of their health policy and for the organisation and delivery of health services and medical care. The responsibilities of the Member States shall include the management of health services and medical care and the allocation of the resources assigned to them.

It is up to Member States to decide which benefits are to be included in their health care package, including the range of medicines that are to be funded through public funds. Medicines represent the third most important cost component in health care budgets (European Commission, Directorate-General for Internal Policies, 2011). Considerable price differences between Member States exist. Such differences have been mainly attributed to differing pricing policies and regulations and differences in total health expenditure and expenditure associated with per capita GDP levels across Member States. For instance when comparing retail prices for patent drugs across Germany, UK, France, Italy and Spain, Germany was found to have the highest retail price – 23 percent higher than the average, followed by the UK (exactly at the 5-country average), Spain (5 percent lower), Italy (6 percent lower) and France (14 percent lower) (Kanavos et al., 2011). Greater differences across Member States have been found for drugs no longer covered by patents. For instance the evolution of prices for generics increase from 12 months to 24 months following patent expiry of the originator in France, Italy, Spain, the Netherlands and Portugal and was reported to decrease in the UK, Germany and Austria in particular and to a lesser extent in Sweden, Greece and Finland (European Commission, Directorate-General for Internal Policies, 2011).

Governments in their role as both regulators and purchasers influence the pharmaceutical market in three major ways (European Commission, Directorate-General for Internal Policies, 2011, p. 34).

** First by way of the methods they employ to determine prices, for instance through:

External price referencing (EPR). This is the most common pricing policy that is used in European countries. The prices of medicine in one or several countries are used as a reference or benchmark in order to set or negotiate prices;
Negotiations with manufacturers holding a patent where the price agreed upon seeks to be not unreasonably too low or too high;
Issuing of tenders for off-patent products;
Price capping where price ceilings on generic and originator products following originator patent expiry is set;
Different taxation of pharmaceuticals influences pharmaceutical companies' pricing strategies.

** Second through pharmaceutical reimbursement policies – governments make use of regulatory mechanisms to determine which pharmaceuticals are covered and at what price, such as through national formularies, health technology assessment (HTA) and internal reference pricing.
** Third through policies affecting physicians, pharmacies and patients – given that patients or consumers rely on the prescribing practitioner, different regulatory mechanisms have been introduced aiming to ensure more efficient use when purchasing pharmaceuticals, such as by prescribing the cheaper but equally effective alternatives.

As mentioned above Member States are responsible for regulating pricing and reimbursement of medicines pursuant to Article 168 (7) TFEU. However, compliance with the Transparency Directive needs to be respected (Council Directive 89/105/EEC, 1988). As stipulated by the Courts, any national measure to control the prices of medicinal products for human use or to restrict the range of medicinal products covered by their national health insurance systems needs to comply with the requirements of the directive (Case C-424/99, 2001; Case C-229/00, 2003; Case C-311/07, 2008). Such a requirement does not affect Member States' competencies for determining the pricing and reimbursement schemes of medicinal products in so far that it is necessary to attain transparency for the purposes of that Directive. Thus, in the Duphar case (Case 238/82, 1984) the court held that,

> Community law does not detract from the powers of Member States to organize their social security systems and to adopt, in particular, provisions intended to govern the consumption of pharmaceutical preparations in order to promote the financial stability of their health-care insurance schemes.
> (para. 16.)

In the Roussel case the Court held that although price control systems do not in themselves constitute measures having an effect equivalent to a quantitative restriction, they may have such an effect when the prices are fixed at a level such that the sale of imported products becomes either impossible or more difficult than that of domestic products (Case C-181/82, 1983).

In its attempt to outline an industrial policy for the pharmaceutical sector the European Commission in 1994 issued a communication recognising the industry as a substantial asset for growth and employment. However, at the time it also noted weaknesses in its ability to finance research and development of new therapeutically innovative medicines and thus called for a better integrated European market with more open competition in order for the industry to regain its competitiveness. Although the EU strives for a free internal market in the pharmaceutical sector, it is not within its remit to regulate the market following the market authorisation of medicines. Nonetheless, the pharmaceutical market needs to respect the four freedoms including the free movement of goods and to a certain extent the EU competition rules. This hence leads to a rather complicated system where the principle of subsidiarity enabling Member States to determine the manner by which they organize their health care services runs counter to the single European market.

3 Stepping up efforts for the joint procurement of medicines

In a scenario where asymmetrical information together with other market imbalances predominate the pharmaceutical market, public purchasers are faced with a relatively unusually low degree of bargaining power when it comes to the purchasing of essential health commodities. Joint procurement for pharmaceuticals can help offset such imbalances. Indeed, while there are apparent opportunities one should not lose sight of potential barriers, especially when it comes to cross-border collaboration between countries or regions. For instance, one may encounter hurdles in view of differences in reimbursement processes between collaborating countries, differences in labelling and indications for use, differences in currencies, and recognition of applicable legislation including that relating to remedies. However, this in no way should hinder proactive collaboration for the joint procurement of medicines.

Indeed, there is a growing interest across Europe where Member States are teaming up to collaborate in the procurement of medicines. The outbreak in 2009 of H1N1 pandemic influenza highlighted various weaknesses where Member States ended up competing with one another to get hold of medicinal supplies that were set at high prices and which at the end were hardly needed, with critics maintaining that they did not work that well after all (PharmExec.com, 2015). In 2010, the Council requested the Commission to start preparations for joint procurement of vaccines in the frame of a future pandemic in order to ensure proper preparedness in the case of serious cross-border threats to health. Article 5 of Decision 1082/2013/EU empowers the institutions of the Union and any Member State on a voluntary basis to engage in a joint procurement procedure for the advance purchase of medical countermeasures for serious cross-border threats to health. This with a view to ensure that participating Member States are guaranteed equal access to timely and sufficient quantities of pandemic vaccines and other medical countermeasures.

As an implementing action of the decision, the Joint Procurement Agreement, which precedes the joint procurement procedure, determines the practical arrangements governing that procedure; defines the decision-making process with regard to the choice of the procedure; and organizes the assessment of the tenders and the award of the contract. The Joint Procurement Agreement (JPA) was adopted on 10 April 2014. To date, the JPA has been signed by 23 EU countries. The JPA has been put to use for the first time where it is envisaged that by the first half of July 2016 a contract is to be signed off by five EU participating countries – Belgium, Croatia, Cyprus, Italy and Malta, who have joined forces to jointly purchase personal protective equipment. The JPA cannot be used for the procurement of innovative medicines for use against, for instance, cancer or orphan medicines given that its scope for use concerns the procurement of medical countermeasures against serious cross-border threats to health.

In April of 2015, it was announced that as of 2016, Belgium and the Netherlands will work together to negotiate prices of orphan medicines with pharmaceutical companies (EHC Quarterly Health Policy Update, 2015). The two countries intend to exchange information, share registries and coordinate evaluation methods. In doing so it is expected that they will be in a better position to negotiate prices and that other countries will also join up. In September 2015, the Grand Duchy of Luxemburg joined Belgium and the Netherlands in their cooperation on orphan drugs to jointly negotiate with pharmaceutical companies to moderate the price of orphan drugs (Communiqué de presse, 2015).

4 What type of set up is needed for developing an efficient and effective joint procurement model?

A functioning pharmaceutical market needs to ensure the availability, accessibility and affordability of medicinal products including innovative treatment solutions for the benefit of patients and consumers. It clearly calls for a model that embraces at its core the social dimension.[9] The social dimension needs to be clearly driven by a *public interest function*[10] where patients and consumers are seen as an end in themselves and not as the means towards an end or more specifically the means for simply balancing the supply and demand equation. An effective and efficient joint public procurement model recognises public procurement contracts as a,

> [s]pecial category of contracts wherein one of the parties represents the public interest and is manifest through complex exchanges that occur in social relationships and which in the process are separated in part by the passage of time.
>
> (Calleja, 2015, p. 159)

Joint procurement can take many different forms. According to Directive 2014/24/EU on public procurement, this could range from coordinated procurement by way of preparation of common technical specifications following which contracting authorities conduct their procurement separately, to situations where contracting authorities procure collectively either by entrusting one contracting authority with the management of the procurement procedure on behalf of all contracting authorities or by acting together. The World Health Organisation (2007) identifies four levels of collaboration ranging from information sharing to collective purchasing, elaborating as follows:

- Informed buying – defined as information sharing, in which purchasers or countries share information on prices and suppliers but procurement is done individually.
- Coordinated informed buying – is also defined as information sharing, whereby purchasers or countries conduct joint market research, share information on supplier performance and prices, but procurement is done individually.
- Group contracting – member countries negotiate prices collectively and select suppliers based on the agreement that procurement will be from the selected suppliers, while the actual purchase can be conducted individually.
- Central contracting and procurement – this generally involves a central buying unit established by the member countries to act as their procurement agent in the tendering and award of contracts.

WHO, 2007, p. 9

When it comes to considering joint procurement models for the purchase of medicines, customised strategies targeted to meet specific needs so as to help mitigate the diverse challenges that are to be taken into consideration as opposed to a one size fits all approach. Different buyer and supplier groups have different motivations depending upon their perceived level of risk, opportunities and expectations. Therefore, a better understanding of the underlying motivations for collaboration is essential and this needs to form part of the discussions initiating the joint procurement. As was previously highlighted there appears to be a positive relationship between pharmaceutical expenditure per capita and GDP per capita. This thus points in the direction that there is scope for countries with quasi-similar levels of GDP per capita to team up for the purposes of joint procurement, as their underlying motivations are more likely to be compatible with one another.

The following lists key elements for facilitating successful joint procurement:

i Strong political commitment;[11]
ii Trust – partners who collaborate through a sense of mutual trust develop a commitment to succeed;[12]
iii Good governance and transparency in the procurement process;[13]
iv Effective communications with internal and external stakeholders;
v Procurement tailored to meet the needs of the collaborating countries possibly initiated with a limited list of products;
vi Continuity with expectations for future collaborations. Multi-year contracting has been regarded as an important aspect to ensure stable sources of supply and for bringing about closer ties. Nearly 25 percent of all joint purchasing is done using framework agreements;[14]
vii Clarity as to who will be responsible for managing the joint procurement procedure and against what remuneration;[15]
viii Clarity as to applicable public procurement legislation, including the applicable legislation on remedies and the modus operandi of the joint procurement;[16]
ix Efficient payment mechanisms;
x Ensuring sufficient capacity with the relative skills and expertise leading the public procurement process;
xi Sharing of information and experiences;
xii Developing databases on key issues such as prices, patent status, prequalification of suppliers and medicines registration.

While the above lists key elements for consideration by public purchasers prior to engaging in public procurement strategies, equally important is the need for pharmaceutical companies to proactively engage with key stakeholders. Worth noting is a recent announcement by the European Federation of Pharmaceutical Industries and Associations (EFPIA) claiming that the European Pharmaceutical industry leaders were considering a radical shift in their approach to the way it prices drugs in Europe by basing such pricing on the basis of the clinical benefit of treatments as opposed to negotiating on the basis of the volumes sold (Hirschler, 2016). This comes in reaction to the high prices that health care systems are facing and signifies industry's readiness to negotiate a new pricing framework that is based on an outcomes-based reward system. Such a system although attractive has been argued to face practical hurdles inhibiting its widespread adoption (Eichler et al., 2016). There appears to be difficulties in collecting and interpreting patient-level data in a given health care system, a matter which has been argued could be reversed were regulators to facilitate data collection. All this further reflects the complexities involved and that it is worth bearing in mind that ultimately any public procurement contract arrived at will explicate the public interest through such complex social exchanges across a wide range of stakeholders.[17]

5 Concluding remarks

The special nature of the pharmaceutical market, the existing asymmetries in information, the varying bargaining powers that Member States have towards industry and industry's relatively high bargaining leverage all make the adoption of joint public procurement initiatives on a voluntary basis the logical choice. Joint public procurement of medicines on a voluntary basis offers a potentially viable option for public purchasers which could help off-set the powerful influences that the pharmaceutical industry enjoys while better serving public health care needs. However, if one were to take this line of thinking further, could it be argued that, as a consequence, consolidation on the demand side in certain market segments can shift the scenario altogether where prices are lowered to such an extent that it diminishes the suppliers' interest to invest further in research and development? This appears to have been the argument put forth particularly by US industry (Huff-Rousselle, 2012) and therefore merits further research.

This also draws our attention to a very crucial aspect, as most of the value of new medicines is related to research and development. It is a known fact that research and development costs are factored into medicine prices. Joint public procurement of innovation could serve the needs of research and development and also very importantly be the means for separating the research and development costs from medicine prices, making such prices more transparent. Article 31 of Directive 2004/27/EC on innovation partnership allows for the combination of developing innovative products and their subsequent purchase while putting in place legislative requirements that mandate equal treatment and transparency of the economic operators during the procurement process. Thus, public purchasers may decide to set up the innovation partnership with one partner or with several partners conducting separate research and development activities. Indeed, by aggregating demand through innovation partnerships, risks, linked with the innovations, could be shared. This also makes risk capital easier to attract while potentially encouraging the participation by small- and medium-sized enterprises (SMEs). According to a study by the Office for Harmonization in the Internal Market only 9 percent of SMEs in Europe own intellectual property rights, but on average for those SMEs that do own such rights these generate 32 percent more revenue per employee than those that do not (OHIM, 2015).

Thus, voluntary joint public procurement in the area of medicines by way of joint innovation partnerships and other joint public procurement formats tailored to meet the specified needs of the collaborating countries or regions presents one of the solutions that can help in part offset imbalances in the pharmaceutical market as well as better serve the goals of public health.

Notes

1 Although there is no universally accepted definition, the Horizon 2020 Advisory Group has defined personalised medicine as "a medical model using characterization of individuals' phenotypes and genotypes (e.g. molecular profiling, medical imaging, lifestyle data) for tailoring the right therapeutic strategy for the right person at the right time, and/or to determine the predisposition to disease and/or to deliver timely and

targeted prevention". European Commission, *Research and innovation, health*. Available at http://ec.europa.eu/research/health/index.cfm?pg=policy&policyname=personalised [accessed July 2016].

2 Controversy about impaired access to innovative medicines on grounds of cost has been reignited by the case of *Sofosbuvir*, a treatment for Hepatitis C that is highly effective in eliminating infection and preventing progress to cirrhosis. In some European countries it is sold for about €25,000 per course (prices have been negotiated under confidentiality clauses). This means that it is, in effect, unaffordable for most of those affected in several European countries. Generic versions of Sofosbuvir can be produced for under $300 per course.

3 The structure of the pharmaceutical sector has been described as unique, as various stakeholders are involved with significant involvement of the state and a high degree of regulation which aim to achieve different objectives – "*These objectives range from supporting innovation to ensuring a high degree of public health and keeping public expenditure under control. The sector itself is R&D-driven and continued innovation is only possible when the protection of intellectual property rights (primarily patents) is adequately ensured.*" See European Commission, Competition DG (2009). *Pharmaceutical sector inquiry*. Final Report, 19. Available at http://ec.europa.eu/competition/sectors/pharmaceuticals/inquiry/staff_working_paper_part1.pdf [accessed July 2016].

4 An "Originator company" is defined as a company that sells originators.
See European Commission, Competition DG (2009). *Pharmaceutical sector inquiry*. Final Report, ibid., 9.

5 *"Generic" is defined as a medicinal product which has the same qualitative and quantitative composition in active substances and the same pharmaceutical form as a reference (originator) medicinal product and whose bioequivalence with the reference medicinal product has been demonstrated. If these conditions are met, a generic applicant for marketing authorisation is exempted from the requirement to prove safety and efficacy through pre-clinical tests and clinical trials, and the competent authority relies on the proof of safety and efficacy provided by the reference product. The term "generic*" also includes biosimilars, unless otherwise specified.* See European Commission, Competition DG (2009). *Pharmaceutical sector inquiry*. Final Report, 7, 9. Available at http://ec.europa.eu/competition/sectors/pharmaceuticals/inquiry/staff_working_paper_part1.pdf [accessed July 2016].

6 *"Originator" is defined as a novel drug that was under patent protection when launched onto the market.*
See European Commission, Competition DG (2009). *Pharmaceutical sector inquiry*. Final Report, 9. Available at http://ec.europa.eu/competition/sectors/pharmaceuticals/inquiry/staff_working_paper_part1.pdf [accessed July 2016].

7 *"Blockbuster medicine" is defined as being one which achieves annual revenues of over US$1 billion at global level.*
See European Commission, Competition DG (2009). *Pharmaceutical sector inquiry*. Final Report, 6.

8 *"Biopharmaceutical" is defined as a biological medicinal product in particular when produced by using biotechnology.*
See European Commission, Competition DG (2009). *Pharmaceutical sector inquiry*. Final Report, 6.

9 For a more detailed account on *the social dimension* vis-à-vis public procurement, refer to, Calleja, A. (2015). *Unleashing Social Justice Through EU Public Procurement*, Vol. 3. Routledge.

10 For a discussion on the *public interest*, see Calleja, A., 2015. *Unleashing Social Justice Through EU Public Procurement* (Vol. 3). Routledge, pp. 150–158.

11 See Directorate of Social and Human Development and Special Programs SADC Secretariat (2011). *Strategy for Pooled Procurement of Essential Medicines and Health Commodities, 2013–2017*. Gaborone, Botswana.

World Health Organization (2007). *Multi-Country Regional Pooled Procurement of Medicines*. Geneva, Switzerland: World Health Organization.

12 See Eriksson, P. E., and Westerberg, M. (2011). Effects of cooperative procurement procedures on construction project performance: A conceptual framework. *International Journal of Project Management*, 29(2), 197–208; Kim, K. K., Umanath, N. S., Kim, J. Y., Ahrens, F., and Kim, B. (2012). Knowledge complementarity and knowledge exchange in supply channel relationships. *International Journal of Information Management*, 32(1), 35–49.

13 See World Health Organization (2007). *Multi-Country Regional Pooled Procurement of Medicines*. Geneva, Switzerland: World Health Organization.
Directorate of Social and Human Development and Special Programs SADC Secretariat (2011). *Strategy for Pooled Procurement of Essential Medicines and Health Commodities, 2013–2017*. Gaborone, Botswana.
O'Neil, M. M. (2010). *Regional Pooled Procurement of Essential Medicines in the Western Pacific Region: An Asset or a Liability?* New Zealand: The University of Auckland Centre for Development Studies.

14 See World Health Organization (2007). *Multi-Country Regional Pooled Procurement of Medicines*. Geneva, Switzerland: World Health Organization.
Kelley, H. H., et al. (1983). *Close Relationships*. New York: W. H. Freeman and Company.
Framework Agreements are particularly common in the Nordics, Slovakia and the Netherlands. Some countries such as Portugal and the Czech Republic have a high degree of co-variation – but have very little use of frameworks overall. See PWC, London Economic, Ecorys (2011). *Public procurement in Europe – cost and effectiveness, a study on procurement regulation*. Prepared for the European Commission. Available at www.eipa.eu/files/topics/public_procurement/cost_effectiveness_en.pdf [accessed March 2017].

15 Tátrai, T. (2015). Joint public procurement. *ERA Forum*, 16, July, 7–24, Springer Berlin Heidelberg.
World Health Organization (2007). *Multi-Country Regional Pooled Procurement of Medicines*. Geneva, Switzerland: World Health Organization.

16 See Recital 73 of Directive 2014/24/EU of the European Parliament and of the Council of 26 February 2014 on public procurement and repealing Directive 2004/18/EC, Official Journal of the European Union, L 94/65.

17 Calleja, A. (2015) defines public procurement contracts as a special category of contracts wherein one of the parties represents the public interest and is manifest through complex exchanges that occur in social relationships and which in the process are separated in part by the passage of time. See Calleja, A. (2015). *Unleashing Social Justice Through EU Public Procurement*, Vol. 3. Routledge.

References

Calleja, A. (2015). *Unleashing Social Justice Through EU Public Procurement*, Vol. 3. Abingdon: Routledge.

Case 238/82, *Duphar and Others* [1984] ECR 523, para 16.

Case C-181/82, *Roussel Laboratory v. Netherlands* [1983] ECR 3849, para. 17.

Case C-229/00, *Commission v. Finland* [2003] ECR I-5727, para 37.

Case C-311/07, *Commission v. Austria* [2008] ECR I-0000, para 29.

Case C-424/99, *Commission v. Austria* [2001] ECR I-9285, para 30.

Commission Staff Working Document, SWD (2015). 13final, 26.1.2016, *Inventory of union and member state incentives to support research into, and the development and availability of, orphan medicinal products – state of play 2015*, Brussels.

Communiqué de presse (2015). *The grand duchy of luxembourg joins Belgium-Netherlands initiative on orphan drugs*. 24 Septembre. Available at www.deblock.

belgium.be/fr/grand-duchy-luxemburg-joins-belgium-netherlands-initiative-orphan-drugs [accessed March 2017].

Council conclusions on, strengthening the balance in the pharmaceutical system in the EU and its member states. (2016), June. Available at www.consilium.europa.eu/register/en/content/out/?&typ=ENTRY&i=ADV&DOC_ID=ST-10315-2016-INIT [accessed July 2016]

Council Directive 2014/24/EU of the European Parliament and of the Council of 26 February 2014 on public procurement and repealing Directive 2004/18/EC, Official Journal of the European Union, L 94/65.

Council Directive 2004/27/EC of 31 March 2004 amending Directive 2001/83/EC on the Community code relating to medicinal products for human use [2004] OJ L 136/34.

Council Directive 89/105/EEC of 21 December 1988 relating to the transparency of measures regulating the prices of medicinal products for human use and their inclusion in the scope of national health insurance systems [1988] OJ L040/8.

Dearson, V. (2011). *Orphan Drug Protection in Guide to EU Pharmaceutical Regulatory Law*, Sally Shorthose (ed.), 2nd ed. Kluwer Law International.

Directorate of Social and Human Development and Special Programs SADC Secretariat (2011). *Strategy for Pooled Procurement of Essential Medicines and Health Commodities, 2013–2017*. Gaborone, Botswana.

EHC Quarterly Health Policy Update (2015). *Belgium and the Netherlands announce joint procurement of medicines for rare diseases*. Available at www.ehc.eu/belgium-and-the-netherlands-to-team-up-for-joint-procurement-of-medicines-for-rare-diseases/ [accessed March 2017].

Eichler, H. G., Hurts, H., Broich, K., and Rasi, G. (2016). Drug regulation and pricing – can regulators influence affordability? *New England Journal of Medicine*, 374(19), 1807–1809.

European Commission (2015). *Expert panel on effective ways on investing in health*. Access to health services in the European Union, Brussels, 76.

European Commission. *Research and innovation, health*. Available at http://ec.europa.eu/research/health/index.cfm?pg=policy&policyname=personalised [accessed July 2016].

European Commission, Competition DG (2009). *Pharmaceutical sector inquiry*. Final Report, 13. Available at http://ec.europa.eu/competition/sectors/pharmaceuticals/inquiry/staff_working_paper_part1.pdf [accessed July 2016].

European Commission, Directorate-General for Internal Policies (2011). *Executive Summary: Differences in Costs and Access to Pharmaceutical Products in the EU*. Brussels: European Commission. Available at europarl.europa.eu/document/activities/cont/201201/20120130ATT36575/20120130ATT36575EN.pdf [accessed July 2016].

European Federation of Pharmaceutical Industries and Associations (EFPIA) (2015). *The pharmaceutical industry in figures*. Available at www.efpia.eu/uploads/EFPIA-statistic_leaflet_january2016_V13.pdf [accessed July 2016].

European Parliament and Council Regulation (EC) 141/2000 of 16 December 1999 on orphan medicinal products [2000] OJ L18/1.

European Parliament and Council Regulation (EC) 1901/2006 of 12 December 2006 on medicinal products for paediatric use and amending Regulation (EEC) 1768/92, Directive 2001/20/EC, Directive 2001/83/EC and Regulation (EC) No 726/2004 [2006] OJ L 378/1.

European Parliament and Council Regulation (EC) no 469/2009 of 6 May 2009 concerning the supplementary protection certificate for medicinal products.

Fox, E. R., Sweet, B. V., and Jensen, V. (eds.) (2014). *Drug shortages: A complex health care crisis*. Mayo Clinic Proceedings, Elsevier in European Commission, Expert panel on effective ways on investing in health, 2015. Access to Health Services in the European Union, Brussels, 76.

Gray, A., and Manasse Jr., H. R. (2012). Shortages of medicines: A complex global challenge. *Bulletin of the World Health Organization*, 90(3), 158.

Hill, A., Khoos, F. J., Simmons, B., and Ford, N. (2014). Minimum costs for providing Hepatitis C direct acting antivirus for use in large-scale treatment access programs in developing countries. *Clinical Infectious Diseases*, Advance Access publication, 13, February, 2014.

Hirschler, B. (2016). *Industry weighs radical shake-up of European drug pricing*. Reuters, June. Available at www.reuters.com/article/us-pharmaceuticals-europe-idUSKCN0YV0V5 [accessed March 2017].

Huff-Rousselle, M. (2012). The logical underpinnings and benefits of pooled pharmaceutical procurement: A pragmatic role for our public institutions? *Social Science & Medicine*, 75(9), 1572–1580.

Joint procurement agreement to procure medical countermeasures. Available at http://ec.europa.eu/health/preparedness_response/docs/jpa_agreement_medical countermeasures_en.pdf [accessed March 2017].

Kanavos, P., Vandoros, S., Irwin, R., Nicod, E., & Casson, M. (2011). *Differences in costs of and access to pharmaceutical products in the EU*. IP/A/ENVI/ST/2010-12. European Parliament, Brussels.

Kelley, H. H., et al. (1983). *Close Relationships*. New York: W. H. Freeman and Company.

Loftus, P. (2015). Gilead knew hepatitis drug price was high, Senate says. *The Wall Street Journal*. Available at www.wsj.com/articles/gilead-knew-hepatitis-drug-price-was-high-senate-says-1449004771 [accessed July 2016].

O'Neil, M. M. (2010). *Regional Pooled Procurement of Essential Medicines in the Western Pacific Region: An Asset or a Liability?* New Zealand: The University of Auckland Centre for Development Studies.

OECD (2015). *Health at a Glance, 2015: OECD Indicators*. Paris: OECD Publishing. Available at http://dx.doi.org/10.1787/health_glance-2015-en

OHIM (2015). *Intellectual property rights and firm performance in Europe: An economic analysis*. Firm-Level Analysis Report.

Pauwels, K., Huys, I., Casteels, M., and Simoens, S. (2014). Drug shortages in European countries: A trade-off between market attractiveness and cost containment? *BMC Health Services Research*, 14(1). Available at www.biomedcentral.com/1472-6963/14/438, [accessed July 2016].

PharmExec.com (2015). *Joint procurement moves up the agenda*. Available at www.pharmexec.com/joint-procurement-moves-eu-agenda [accessed March 2017].

Urbinati, D., Rémuzat, C., Kornfeld, Å., Vataire, A. L., Cetinsoy, L., Aballéa, S., Mzoughi, O., and Toumi, M. (2014). EU pharmaceutical expenditure forecast. *Journal of Market Access & Health Policy*, 2, 1–9.

Vancell, A. (2012). *Harmonized Internal Market in the EU – Reality, Rhetoric or a Possibility*. Malta: University of Malta.

World Health Organization (2007). *Multi-Country Regional Pooled Procurement of Medicines*. Geneva, Switzerland: World Health Organization.

6 Joint procurement and the EU perspective

Francesco Saverio Mennini, Nicola Dimitri, Lara Gitto, Francois Lichere and Gustavo Piga

1 Introduction

Health systems are globally facing an urgent need for the control of drug expenditure to decrease pressure on health care financial resources (Milovanovic et al., 2004). Hence, when striving for cost-efficiency, health care purchasers may experiment new ways of organizing health services.

Joint Procurement (JP) is argued to be one such way to respond to this need (European Commission, 2008).

This innovative procedure can take several forms (Tátrai, 2015). There might be a coordinated purchase through the preparation of common technical specifications for services that will be procured by a number of contracting authorities from the same or different countries, each conducting a separate procurement procedure. Alternatively, the joining authorities, from the same or different countries, may carry out procurement procedures either acting together or by entrusting another subject (Bovaird, 2006; Kuiper, Meijer and Van Dam, 2015).

There are potential advantages arising from bundling public purchases of two or more contracting authorities. It could be possible to exploit economies of scale; to reduce administrative costs (Odagiri, 2003); or to share knowledge and expertise, as contracting authorities may better pool their skills and best practices (Fernie et al., 2003). Moreover, it could be easier to develop new products and technologies since, if a large volume of production is guaranteed, suppliers are more encouraged to engage themselves in innovative activities as compared to the situation when procurements are run by individual investors, who may not be willing to bear high costs (Rönnberg Sjödin, 2013).

However, together with advantages, costs and risks may arise: for example, there could be the creation of a monopoly-monopsony at the EU level, if this purchasing mechanism would not ensure the presence of multiple providers in the market (Wilkinson, 2014).

In the economic literature there are still few contributions that have been aimed at describing the implementation and the impact of JP. Dimitri, Piga and Spagnolo have examined different kinds of procurement; numerous examples of JP concern the pharmaceutical market and the production of drugs (Dimitri, Piga and Spagnolo, 2006).

The production of vaccines, their costs and benefits and the identification of the subject who should pay for them has been an issue widely debated in the economic literature and may well be invested by the implementation of JP schemes (Grabowski, 2005; Pauly, 2005; Bärnighausen et al., 2014).

As of now, many developing-country governments and other stakeholders have been thinking of vaccines as donor-supplied commodities: Woodle outlines how, for the most part, low-income and some middle-income countries do not even include them in annual health budgets (Woodle, 2000). Donor organizations provided, in the past, programs related to immunization, vaccines and related commodities from their own sources or arranged with international organizations, such as UNICEF or the Pan American Health Organization (PAHO): in this way it was possible to purchase and deliver vaccines from a pool of prequalified manufacturers assessed by the World Health Organization (The World Bank and GAVI alliance, 2010). At the same time, UNICEF and PAHO offered procurement services to many low- and middle-income countries, although they may lack the skills and/or infrastructure needed for obtaining safe, effective and reasonably priced vaccines from the international market (Di Fabio and de Quadros, 2001; Velandia-González et al., 2015).

Foreign experiences of JP have concerned drugs for HIV-AIDS, TB and malaria (Danzon, Mulcahy and Towse, 2015) and have revealed success in lowering prices. Danzon, Mulcahy and Towse, in a study carried out for 37 countries, observed how procurement was able to reduce originator and generic prices by 42.4 percent and 35 percent, as compared to their respective retail pharmacy prices, and allowed to reduce quality uncertainty as well by imposing minimum quality standards.

Other applications of JP schemes have regarded developing and transition countries as the Caribbean, Serbia and Jordan (Huff-Rousselle and Burnett, 1996; Milovanovic et al., 2004; Al-Abbadi et al., 2009). In particular, the Organization of East Caribbean States achieved overall savings of ~44 percent when it started to apply JP for purchasing drugs. Furthermore, other groups of countries enjoyed a remarkable increase in savings on pharmaceuticals with JP. The Group of Central American countries and Panama registered 64 percent savings, the West Arab Union recorded 15 percent to 20 percent savings while the Pacific Islands noted total annual savings of 10 percent to 96 percent. Gulf Cooperation Council countries are considered the earliest successful countries that applied JP and achieved an average annual total savings of 30 percent. The pharmaceutical sector in Jordan suffered from several inefficiencies, among which there were the purchasing by the government of the same drug in the same year at different prices, the irrational use of medical drugs and the absence of planning for the needed quantities of medicines.

The goals of centralized procurements were to unify the purchase of drugs and medical supplies among the participating parties, to reduce the cost of purchased drugs by buying large quantities, to minimize wastes and to optimize the allocation of scarce resources for health services (DeRoeck et al., 2006). In Serbia, the procurement experience has seen first the identification of precise steps in the drug procurement process, starting from the establishment of a drug tender list, followed by the selection of the most appropriate offers and the analysis of the results (Milovanovic et al., 2004).

Most cases described in the literature share one key element: the aggregation of needs and the related centralized procurements took place within a given cultural/nationwide territorial entity.

The features of the JP scheme introduced in the EU through the new Procurement Directive make it one of the first in its kind (Glinos, 2010; Sanchez Graells, 2012; Ponzio, 2014; Azzopardi-Muscat, Schröder-Bäck and Brand, 2017): here, different countries, characterized by cultural heterogeneity on the purchaser side, may decide to embark in a common procurement procedure, therefore increasing the degree of integration within Europe itself.

However, this top-down approach to integration may reveal itself to be overly difficult and ambitious to succeed, and a more minimalistic approach, bottom-up, starting from cross-border regional procurement among entities that share several cultural and economic traits (especially, though not necessarily due to geographic proximity to a border), might prove to be in the long run a more successful endeavour.

The chapter is aimed at outlining some critical issues related to JP, both from a legal and economic perspective. The next section will describe the European legislation that has introduced the possibility to set up JP agreements. The economic consequences and the market modifications that may derive will be then examined. Many aspects present some criticisms that will call for further normative interventions in the next years. Some economic issues and open questions raised by JP will conclude the chapter.

2 Methods: the legal and the economic analysis

2.1 The legal perspective

Legal and practical aspects of JP schemes have been developed at the European level. There have been some European Commission initiatives to favor cross-border JP initiatives in the fields of vaccines and drugs, followed by the Decision N° 1082/2013/EU of 22 October 2013 on serious cross-border threats to health (Riccardo et al., 2015). As a consequence, the institutions of the Union and Member States may now engage in a JP procedure: the Directive 2014/18/EU explicitly introduces the possibility for contracting authorities from different Member States to proceed with JP, in order to facilitate cooperation between contracting authorities of different nations and to enhance the benefits of the internal market by creating wider cross-border business opportunities.

The JP procedure has to be preceded by a Joint Procurement Agreement between the parties, determining the operational arrangements and the decision-making process (choice of the procedure, assessment of the tenders and the award of the contract – Article 39 of the Directive).

Three types of cross-border JP contracts are envisaged in the Directive: the use of a foreign Central Purchasing Body, a temporary alliance (called in the Directive "occasional joint procurement" between contracting authorities from different Member States) or a consortium/corporation of contracting authorities from different Member States (joint entities).

The reasons for favoring cross-border JP are stated in Recital 73 of the Directive 2004/18/EC. The participating contracting authorities may allocate specific responsibilities among them and determine the applicable provisions of the national laws of any involved Member State. The agreement shall regulate each single stage of the procurement procedure, as well as its management; the distribution of the works, goods or services to be procured; and the termination of the contracts.

Specific legal restrictions on joint agreements could be represented by the national legislation of each Member State in relation to: (a) access to the procurement procedure (the requirements for participation may be related to the possession of specific qualifications); (b) evaluation of offers (goods and services may need a prior authorization by a competent internal body); (c) execution of the contract (there might be possible restrictions due to national legislation, reducing the organization and management capabilities of the economic operator).

Two main issues arise with regard to the law applicable to cross-border JP: they are related to which law should be applicable to the award phase and which rules should regard the contract itself.

The law applicable to a contract of transnational nature set in Regulation No. 593/2008 does not regard the award phase, since Directive 2014/24 deals only with the award of public procurement contracts and Article 3 of the Regulation explicitly excludes from its scope "*obligations arising out of dealings prior to the conclusion of a contract*" (Article 1.2 (i)).

Recital 73 of the Directive states that the same Directive should adopt new rules and that

> Those rules should determine the conditions for cross-border utilization of CPB and designate the applicable public procurement legislation, including the applicable legislation on remedies, in cases of cross-border joint procedures, complementing the conflict of law rules of Regulation (EC) No 593/2008 of the European Parliament and the Council.

Hence, the Directive does not disregard the rules, but it only complements them, since the Regulation deals with the law applicable to the contract itself and not with the award phase.

About the procurement procedure that should be adopted to award the contract in a JP, competitive tendering (open or restricted procedures, i.e. without negotiation), forms of negotiations (competitive dialogue or negotiated procedures) or a mix of the two (a preliminary market consultation followed by an open or restricted procedure) may be adopted, although it is not clear which would be most recommendable and in what cases.

However, in spite of the clear-cut scope of the two European texts – Article 39 of the Directive for the award phase, the Regulation for the performance – all uncertainties surrounding the two phases of a contract prepared and concluded by a cross-border JP are not removed.

Other aspects need to be analyzed from an economic perspective.

2.2 The economic perspective

The major questions arising from the implementation of JP agreements are mainly related to price, to the number of subjects joining the agreement and the modifications likely to occur in the market and to the quality standards that should be satisfied.

The issue has been examined considering the pharmaceutical market.

Concerning prices, for the same drug, they may vary across different EU countries (Espin and Rovira, 2007): with a JP mechanism the crucial question is at what price the drug will be sold.

The contracting authorities may ask for the same price across all countries adhering to a JP, or for different prices to take account of possible different standards and cost of living in such countries. It could introduce a maximum unit price in the competition, say p_m, such that any price offer above it would not be accepted.

How should P_M be chosen? This price could be set at the minimum of the prices in the countries considered. However, though apparently natural, this answer may be unsatisfactory. Indeed, the difference between the two prices for the same drug could be due to three main reasons, not mutually exclusive: (i) procurement or government negotiation could be more effective in one country; (ii) there could be transaction costs to keep into account; (iii) the price index (or other standard of living indicators, such as the average real income), which includes all consumption goods and not just pharmaceuticals, could be lower in one country and, as a result, the price of the drug could be lower, too.

Faced with the difficulty of separating the three effects, a possible solution to the question on how to set the maximum price, as well as how to design the competitive tendering, may be to ask bidders to compete on the ratio γ

$$r = \frac{p}{P}$$

between the drug price p and the price index P, where the company bidding the lowest ratio would be awarded the JP contract.

Price differentiation across countries, if existing without JP, may be kept under JP. Whether this would occur depends on JPs' choice: the consequences would be for both the countries and the contractor. In this framework, the country with the lower price index level (i.e. with the lower standard of living) would be the one to enjoy higher benefits from price differentiation.

The possibility to purchase drugs through JP schemes in principle raises the question on how many countries and/or public authorities may aggregate to perform a JP. Since a JP is formed on a voluntary basis, it is not possible to know in advance which countries will join a particular agreement, and whether there would be more than one JP for a specific product. With one, or multiple procurers, will there be just one supplier or would it be preferable to have more than one?

The question on how many JPs would be desirable to have and for which drugs cannot have a clear answer and needs to be discussed case by case, possibly in a coordinated setting of procurers, depending on the number of patients, seriousness of the illness and other elements.

JPs schemes can induce significant consequences on the market architecture and the level of R&D investments. Once again, the number of JPs come into consideration.

With a single subject, the contractor could enjoy the major advantage of supplying to a large market for some time. Likewise, this may represent a disadvantage for other companies producing the same or similar drug, since they could not serve the same market. Therefore, at least in principle, a single large JP may facilitate the conditions for some degree of market power by the contractor: a company enjoying some market power should have the needed resources to invest in innovative solutions, especially in those sectors where innovation is very expensive, as it is the pharmaceutical industry.

However whether or not, and to what extent, this would indeed occur depends on the relevant market contestability, i.e. on the presence of barriers to entry to potential competitors, and how much pressure such potential entrance may exert on the incumbent contractor. Potential competition may in turn be negatively affected by the reduced revenues of the tender losers, due to lack of access in the JP market. Additionally, if the contractor believes that the JP would lead to high profit margins for a sufficiently long time, then he may also decide not to invest on innovation since he can perceive a low risk of losing profits for a long enough period. On the other hand, companies other than the contractor may also decide to increase effort to become more competitive in the future, in the same or in other markets, and in so doing, they might invest in innovation.

Which forces would prevail and to what degree it is difficult to say in general, and would very much depend upon the specific market cases.

Moreover, under JPs schemes, the bidding strategies of suppliers may change.

If the size of JP contracts is expected to be large then, because of their attractiveness, some pharmaceutical companies may choose to focus their development and bidding activities on the drugs which would likely be the object of such procurements. Anticipating so, other firms may decide to focus on different markets, in which case a JP may lead to a possible polarization of the industry, with few firms mostly competing for JP contracts while others are in non-JP contracts.

Another crucial issue relates to the challenges to overall quality of the procured good. Contract awards in procurement are often based upon two main components of an offer: the economic component, typically hinging on the price to be paid by the contracting authority, and the quality component. In principle, JP should not affect the quality of the procured good, unless the purchased treatment does not exist yet in the market; some health emergency, such as the sudden outbreak of a pandemic disease, may justify a faster than normal track to approval.

According to the above considerations, if product quality is given, contract award is based mostly on the economic component of an offer. Yet, in case of possible multiple treatments for a disease, where such treatments have different degrees of effectiveness, quality could vary depending upon the resources available to the contracting authorities.

In particular, if more effective treatments are also the most expensive ones, then in large contracts, such as possibly the JP contracts, as long as these generate higher savings than non-JPs, countries adhering to a JP could afford having a better quality treatment.

Other considerations regard the circumstance if the procured drug is already available or not. A main idea inspiring JP is just to coordinate actions, among EU Member States, to tackle pandemic outbreaks. In this case, procurement of a treatment, when the infective agent behind the potential pandemic has already been identified, may differ from when the agent is not yet known.

If the treatment is already available in the market, then the main decision for the JP is whether to procure it and stockpile it, or undertake a prevention campaign, or to procure only the right of having the treatment available at an agreed-upon price, if the pandemic starts, within a specified deadline. In this last case, procurement would be based on a conditional contract, akin to an option contract. Such option contract may also have a cost for the JP, since the contractor would have to manage manufacturing of the treatment to be available in due time. Payment by the JP for the option contract would be justified when there is some risk for the contractor, such as to produce units of the medication which will not be used because the pandemic does not take place.

If the treatment is not available, then JP will first have to decide whether to procure development of the treatment and fund it, or whether to commit to buying the treatment once developed. Alternatively, JP countries may decide to wait and see if the pandemic takes place and then push the pharmaceutical industry for developing a treatment, though in this case timing may be inappropriate as coverage of the population with the medication could be delayed. This last possibility however would not seem to be part of the JP spirit.

Finally, if the infective agent for a potential pandemic is not yet known, then the only procurement a JP can make is again an option contract, which has to manage an even higher degree of uncertainty. In fact, not only would there be uncertainty on whether a drug will be available, and in due time, but there will also be uncertainty on what drug to develop. It seems that the only purchase JP can make in this case concerns the commitment of a firm to try developing a drug in case of a potential pandemic caused by a yet-to-be-identified agent. However, it would be difficult, if not impossible, to define a price for the treatment at that stage with such a deep degree of uncertainty.

Some further issues related to the mechanism through which lots of drugs are awarded to JPs are described in the Appendix.

3 Conclusions

The purpose of the chapter was to summarize the main features of JP as an innovative contracting scheme in pharmaceutical markets: some critical aspects related both to the legal and to the economic perspective have been described.

Although this has been the object of recent legislation, a comprehensive normative framework for JP in Europe has still to be developed. The Directive 2014/18/EU says that it is now possible to set out JP agreements, although it does not go further in drawing a taxonomy of JP contracts that include central purchasing bodies, alliances and consortia.

However, the rules that should apply for each of these organisms are not evidently distinguished. It is not clear which national law would regulate the agreements: would it be preferable to apply the supplier's national law? What would happen in case of more countries joining the procurement? Opting for a mixture of rules implies other problems, related to procurers' willingness to agree on all the aspects considered within the rules.

The economic analysis discussed some aspects related to price, quality and market structure.

Currently, for the same drug, prices may vary across different EU countries. Price differentiation may be kept under JP agreements, but this would imply that the country with the lower price index level might enjoy higher benefits from the agreement.

The possibility to purchase drugs through JP raises the question of how many countries and/or public authorities should aggregate to perform a JP. Here, there is not a predetermined solution, as the price might be the outcome of a negotiation between the procurers and the suppliers and the number of subjects involved in this procedure may depend on various factors, including also the countries' well-being and health policy choices.

Regarding market structure and innovation, once again the question remains open. In fact, scenarios might be different according to market contestability, the presence of barriers to entry and the number of procurers together with the willingness to invest in innovation.

Other aspects examined concern the issue of quality of the procured good and the modifications that might occur in the market: the bidding strategies of suppliers are likely to be modified but the potentially larger size of procurement tenders might also have the effect to reduce the participation of the SMEs.

Hence, there is currently a promising stream of legislation that needs to be refined and tested, and that has to be monitored in the next years.

References

Al-Abbadi, I., Qawwas, A., Jaafreh, M., Abosamen, T., and Saket, M. (2009). One-year assessment of joint procurement of pharmaceuticals in the public health sector in Jordan. *Clinical Therapeutics*, 31(6), 1335–1344.

Azzopardi-Muscat, N., Schröder-Bäck, P., and Brand, H. (2017). The European Union joint procurement agreement for cross-border health threats: What is the potential for this new mechanism of health system collaboration? *Health Economics, Policy and Law*, 12(1), 43–59.

Bärnighausen, T., Bloom, D. E., Cafiero-Fonseca, E. T., and Carroll O'Brien, J. (2014). Valuing vaccination. *Proceedings of the National Academy of Sciences*, 111(34), 12313–12319.

Bovaird, T. (2006). Developing new forms of partnership with the 'Market' in the procurement of public services. *Public Administration*, 84(1), 81–102. doi:10.1111/j.0033-3298.2006.00494.x

Danzon, P. M., Mulcahy, A. W., and Towse, A. H. (2015). Pharmaceutical pricing in emerging markets: Effects of income, competition, and procurement. *Health Economics*, 24(2), 68–77.

DeRoeck, D., Bawazir, S. A., Carrasco, P., Kaddar, M., Brooks, A, Fitzsimmons, J., and Andrus, J. (2006). Regional group purchasing of vaccines: Review of the Pan-American Health Organization EPI revolving fund and the Gulf Cooperation Council group purchasing program. *International Journal of Health Planning and Management*, 21(1), 23–43.

Di Fabio, J. L., and de Quadros, C. (2001). Considerations for combination vaccine development and use in the developing. *World Clinical Infectious Diseases*, 33(4), S340–S345. doi:https://doi.org/10.1086/322571

Dimitri, N., Piga, G., and Spagnolo, G. (2006). *The Handbook of Procurement*. Cambridge: Cambridge University Press.

Espin, J., and Rovira, J. (2007). *Analysis of differences and commonalities in pricing and reimbursement systems in Europe*. European Commission Report. Available at file:///C:/Users/user/Downloads/andalusian_school_public_health_report_pricing_2007_en.pdf

European Commission, DG Environment-G2, B-1049, Bruxelles (2008). Available at http://ec.europa.eu/environment/gpp/pdf/toolkit/module1_factsheet_joint_procurement.pdf

European Commission Green Public Procurement (GPP) Training Toolkit – Module 1: Managing GPP Implementation (2008). Joint procurement Fact Sheet. Toolkit developed for the European Commission by ICLEI – Local Governments for Sustainability.

European Parliament and Council Decision 1082/2013/EU of 22 October 2013 on Serious Cross-Border Threats to Health Official Journal of the European Union L. 293. Available at http://eur-lex.europa.eu/LexUriServ/LexUriServ.do?uri=OJ:L:2013:293:0001:0015:EN:PDF

European Union. Commission Directive 2014/18/EU of 29 January 2014 amending Directive 2009/43/EC of the European Parliament and of the Council as regards the list of defence-related products. Available at http://eur-lex.europa.eu/legal-content/EN/TXT/?uri=CELEX%3A32014L0018

Glinos, I. A., Baeten, R., and Maarse, H. (2010). Purchasing health services abroad: Practices of cross-border contracting and patient mobility in six European countries. *Health Policy*, 95(2–3), 103–112.

Grabowski, H. (2005). Encouraging the development of new vaccines. *Health Affairs*, 24(3), 697–700.

Huff-Rousselle, M., and Burnett, F. (1996). Cost containment through pharmaceutical procurement: A Caribbean case study. *International Journal of Health Planning and Management*, 11(2), 135–157.

Kuiper, E., Meijer, S., and Van Dam, F. (2015). Lessons learnt from a joint EC Co-funded PCP – cloud for Europe eChallenges e-2015. In P. Cunningham and M. Cunningham (eds.), *Conference Proceedings*. IIMC International Information Management Corporation. ISBN:978-1-905824-52-6.

Milovanovic, D. R., Pavlovic, R., Folic, M., and Jankovic, S. M. (2004). Public drug procurement: The lessons from a drug tender in a teaching hospital of a transition country. *European Journal of Clinical Pharmacology*, 60(3), 149–153.

Odagiri, H. (2003). Transaction costs and capabilities as determinants of the R&D boundaries of the firm: A case study of the ten largest pharmaceutical firms in Japan. *Managerial and Decision Economics, special issue: Research Alliances and Collaborations*, 24(2), 187–211.

Pauly, M. V. (2005). Improving vaccine supply and development: Who needs what? *Health Affairs*, 24(3), 680–689.

Ponzio, S. (2014). Joint procurement and innovation in the new EU Directive and in dome EU-funded projects. *Ius Publicum Network Review*. Available at www.ius-publicum.com/repository/uploads/20_03_2015_13_12-Ponzio_IusPub_JointProc_def.pdf.

Riccardo, F., Dente, M. G., Kärki, T., Fabiani, M., Napoli, C., Chiarenza, A., Giorgi Rossi, P., Velasco Munoz, C., Noori, T., and Declich, S. (2015). Towards a European framework to monitor infectious diseases among migrant populations: Design and applicability. *International Journal of Environmental Research and Public Health*, 12(9), 11640–11661.

Rönnberg Sjödin, D. (2013). *Managing Joint Development of Process Technologies Empirical Studies of Interorganizational Collaboration Within the Process Industries*. Luleå University of Technology, Department of Economy, Technology and Society Entrepreneurship and Innovation Centre for Management of Innovation and Technology in Process Industry. ISBN: 978-91-7439-625-6. Available at www.ltu.se

Sanchez Graells, A. (2012). *Competitive neutrality in public procurement and competition policy: An ongoing challenge analysed in view of the proposed new directive*. Social Science Research Network (SSRN). Available at https://papers.ssrn.com/sol3/papers2.cfm?abstract_id=1991302

Tátrai, T. (2015). Joint public procurement. *ERA Forum*, 16, 7. doi:10.1007/s12027-015-0374-3.

Velandia-González, M., Trumbo, S. P., Díaz-Ortega, J. L., Bravo-Alcántara, P., Danovaro-Holliday, M. C., Dietz, V., and Ruiz-Matus, C. (2015). Lessons learned from the development of a new methodology to assess missed opportunities for vaccination in Latin America and the Caribbean. *BMC International Health and Human Rights*, 15(5), 5. doi:10.1186/s12914-015-0043-1

Wilkinson, L. (2014). *Forming buying groups that comply with the antitrust laws: Raising some safeguards that may mitigate potential antitrust concerns*. Available at www.insidecounsel.com/2014/03/24/forming-buying-groups-that-comply-with-the-antitrust

Woodle, D. (2000). Vaccine procurement and self-sufficiency in developing countries. *Health Policy Planning*, 15(2), 121–129.

The World Bank and GAVI Alliance (2010). *The vaccine market pooled procurement*. Available at www.who.int/immunization/programmes_systems/financing/analyses/Brief_12_Pooled_Prourement.pdf

Part 3

Big Data in public procurement

7 Colloquium

Mihály Fazekas and Stéphane Saussier

1 Mihály Fazekas – Big Data in public procurement: great opportunities – mediocre results

This short memo exposes the enormous opportunities presented by the emergence of Big Data in public procurement and the lack of investment and effort for exploiting these opportunities. Big Data in public procurement holds the promise of fundamentally transforming how procurement performance is understood and it can provide a vastly superior guide to effective policy decisions and implementation compared to our current knowledge. However, Big Data implies large structured and high quality datasets which are typically not available in spite of extensive transparency regulations. Successfully harnessing Big Data also requires valid and easy-to-understand indicators to make sense of the enormous diversity revealed by it. In addition, making Big Data analytics part of daily research and policy-making practice requires new skills and a change of culture (Fazekas, 2014).

Due to extensive regulations, the presence of multiple actors, and a demand for public scrutiny, public procurement has long been a data-rich area of public spending. However, with the increasing use of electronic and online procurement tools, this rich set of administrative records has become more readily and more extensively available – giving rise to a data revolution experienced across many other domains of social life (UN Global Pulse, 2012). This enables real-time data analysis using datasets tracking individual behavior such as bids submitted to a tender, evaluation scores assigned, or invoices paid.

1.1 The opportunity

What fundamentally reconfigures our capacity to understand and govern public procurement systems is the move from reviewing individual records to analyzing a structured database. This means that on top of the ability to identify and analyze a small set of public procurement documents and participating organizations, governments, businesses, citizens, and researchers are becoming increasingly capable of systematically analyzing large swaths of procurement activities on a real-time basis.

Big Data in public procurement drastically reduces the cost of obtaining information for the kinds of analyses which were possible without such data. For example, accessing all the contracts and payments related to any particular project is a matter of seconds in an integrated public procurement database regardless of where the project is taking place. This used to be a quite laborious task requiring a journey to the document archive of the procuring body overseeing the project, gathering the contracts and invoices in hardcopy, and manually summarizing information found in individual documents. In addition, databases allow for quick and complex analysis and queries previously simply not possible. For example, a public procurement database can rank all tenders according to their number of bidders in a given market all across a large geographical area while also listing contract values, delays in delivery, etc.

Such analytical possibilities give rise to a range of opportunities for harnessing Big Data in public procurement. Without being exhaustive:

1 Daily spend monitoring;
2 Risk-based audit;
3 Supporting system-wide policy decisions; and
4 Supporting government accountability through, for example, watchdog portals.

1.2 The challenge

In spite of the obvious informational needs and wide-ranging benefits, making the move to a data-rich approach has proven to be surprisingly challenging with some governments and international organizations even decreasing their 'Big Data readiness' rather than improving it (e.g. World Bank procurement reform of the mid 2000s disconnecting administrative systems and removing a number of key structured data fields in pursuance of administrative simplification).

First, building high-quality integrated data systems, even if they only encompass the already collected information, requires considerable investment. Linking disparate procurement data systems, standardizing data formats, and delivering reliable data management infrastructures are typically far from straightforward exercises, with many frontline civil servants opposing change. Crucially, building public procurement data systems require in-depth collaboration across disciplines such as law, political science, economics, and IT.

Capturing past data, typically recorded in semi-structured text files, and building state-of-the-art data infrastructures going forward both require IT expertise and the understanding of complex data systems typically lacking in public sectors. As a result and quite unsurprisingly, most European Big Data systems for public procurement publish data in non or only partially machine-readable format making database construction very difficult: only Belgium, the European Commission, Italy, Norway, Poland, and the UK publish fully machine-readable public procurement data (Cingolani et al., 2015).

Systematizing data collection and publication had frequently revealed that reporting requirements are grossly neglected, making the most essential bits of data missing or incomprehensible. Interestingly, many well-governed countries such as Sweden or the UK extensively fail to report complete information in line with legal prescriptions (Figure 7.1). Improving data quality is a challenge on its own, as examples from Canada,[1] the Czech Republic,[2] the EU,[3] and Hungary reveal (Czibik, Tóth and Fazekas, 2015).

In addition, linking contracts data to databases holding related information is also challenging, even though it promises considerable benefits, most notably the ability to trace investment outcomes back to procurement performance. Potentially linked databases are, for example, public financial management systems, treasury accounts of public bodies, company registry, financial and ownership data, and information on sectoral outcomes such as student achievement or mortality (Fazekas and Tóth, 2014). However, the generally lacking organizational ID

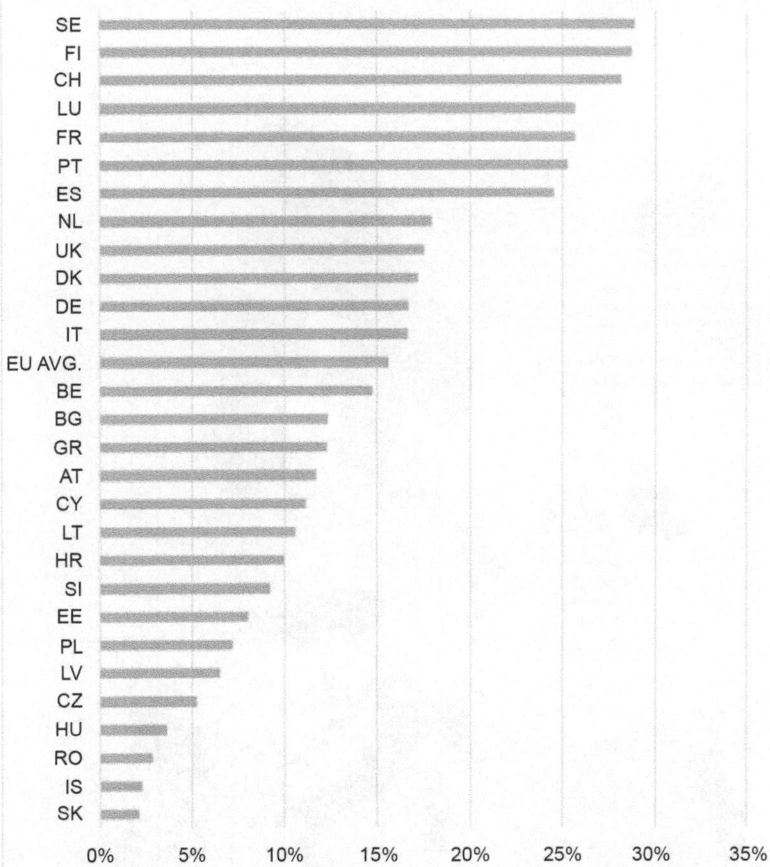

Figure 7.1 Average percentage of missing information among mandatory fields.[4] 2009–2015 (missing or erroneous data, based on TED data)

Source: Own calculations based on Tenders Electronic Daily data (https://open-data.europa.eu/en/data/dataset/ted-1)

numbers make any linking a highly labour-intensive task at best and hopelessly impossible at worst (Figure 7.2).

Second, Big Data in public procurement also gives rise to the need for new, more advanced indicators which help diverse users in making sense of the often-daunting diversity of data; recall that public procurement includes purchases for anything ranging from nuclear power plants to school meals. Such new indicators of value for money and open access to public resources can potentially complement or in some cases replace traditional indicators of governance by providing actionable and more objective insights (Knack, Kugler and Manning, 2003). While there is a long way to go, there is already an emerging literature which develops, tests, and applies objective proxies of open access, corruption, and favouritism around the globe (Trapnell, 2015). These initial innovations nevertheless already amply demonstrate the increasing capacity of indicators and impact evaluations to inform policy decisions and the wider public.

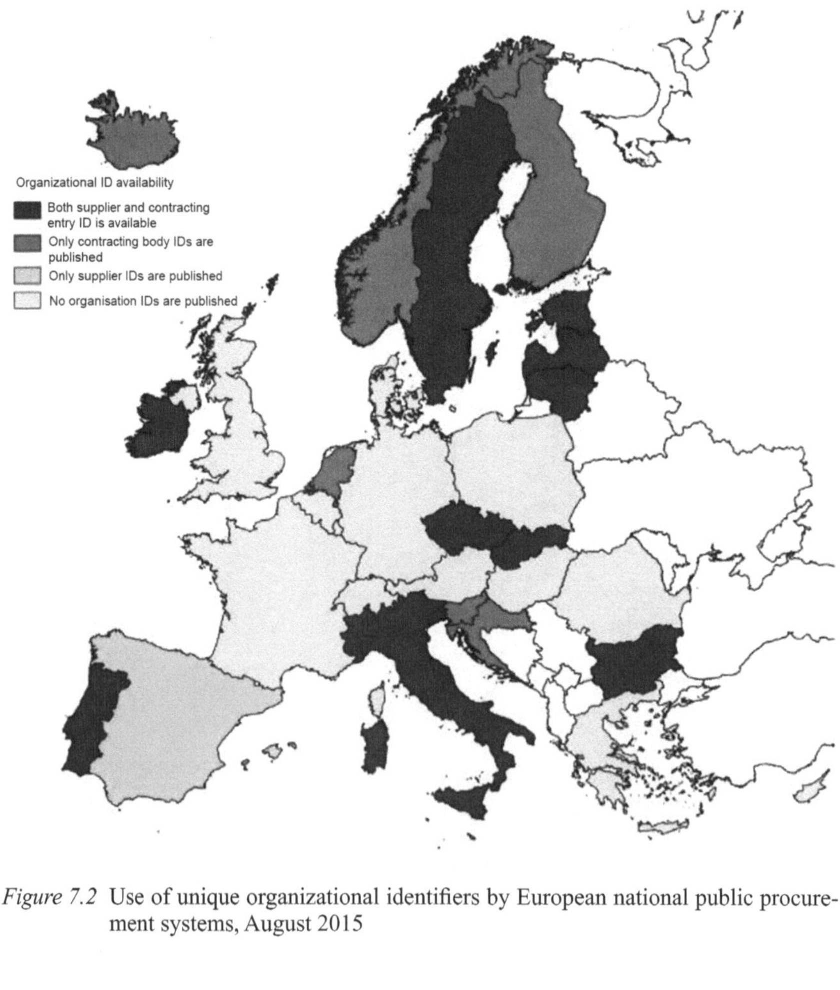

Figure 7.2 Use of unique organizational identifiers by European national public procurement systems, August 2015

Third, parallel to the challenges of data and indicator development, users have to adapt their expectations and skills in order to effectively navigate in the new information landscape. High-frequency, rich datasets can become part of daily practice right across the public sector, businesses, and civil society if a new data culture is accommodated. Given the complex reality captured by Big Data, it requires careful thinking about and experimenting with different information systems in order to avoid information overload while keeping precise and interpretable information readily available to every level of decision-making.

2 Stéphane Saussier – Big and Open Data: a new era for public procurement?

Big Data is a term describing the large amount of data that inundates a business on a day-to-day basis. What matters is what organizations do with those data, not the volume itself. Nowadays, European countries are challenged by a turbulent economic situation, tightening their budget constraints and making the need for the reorganization of the public sector administration stronger than ever. There is also a huge defiance from citizens concerning public administrations. Faced with these challenges, the use of Big Data may give a fresh boost to the public sector, in particular. Its place in society is so important today that Big Data is considered as a key factor for improving future productivity. A McKinsey Global Institute (2011) study indicates that the use of Big Data may reduce the public administration's costs by potentially 15 percent to 20 percent (representing about €150 billion to €300 billion). This cost reduction would result from the generation of efficiency gains often through benchmarking and a reduction between the potential and actual collection of tax revenues.

In this short note we review what are the potential benefits of Big and Open Data for economic actors involved in public procurement in particular as well as for the society as a whole. Big Data may help at reducing contractual issues through several avenues well identified by contract theory and research on asymmetric information as well as incomplete contracting.

2.1 Interest for the public administration

- *Reducing asymmetric information issues*

By allowing the public authorities to observe the agent's behaviour on other attributed markets, Big and Open Data could diminish adverse selection issues (i.e. it would be more difficult for inefficient firms to behave in such a way to be considered as potentially efficient). In addition, this would also present the advantage of disciplining the private operators by giving them incentives to respect the (often-incomplete) contract and implicit rules.

Moral hazard could also be limited by giving tools to the public administration for using data as a benchmark (Shleifer, 1985; Auriol, 2000). Commonly named yardstick competition, this deals with the exploitation of the correlation between operators producing the same goods or services for reducing the asymmetry of information between the principal and the agent, assuming that the compared operators have identical cost structure. This allows for comparing the performance and efficiency of the private operators by introducing a virtual competition with other operators considered as basically similar.

- *Detecting aggressive bidding*

In order to win a public bid, a private operator might get incentives to bid aggressively while anticipating that he may be able to renegotiate the contract (Guasch, 2004; Estache and Saussier, 2014). Some studies show that the more likely a contract is to be renegotiated, the lower the bid will be. In that case, the utility of yardstick competition is also strong. Indeed, by getting access to bid data in a related market with similar characteristics, the public entity may be able to detect unreasonable offers. In addition, by fixing a minimum price based on what data on previous deals provide, it might help to deter cartels (Chassang and Ortner, 2016).

- *Increasing stakeholders' participation*

Stakeholders, especially users as well as consumer associations, are pushing for more involvement in the way public procurement are organized. Collecting, structuring, and providing to stakeholders adequate data about public procurement issues is a way for public authorities to increase citizens' involvement in public affairs (Spiller, 2013).

2.2 Interest for the private operator

- ***Enjoy a reputational effect***

When companies respect their contractual agreements and the related implicit rules, they may be rewarded by benefiting from a reputational effect being more frequently renewed (especially when award procedures let some discretionary power to the public authority as in concession contracts – see Beuve and Saussier, 2017). Indeed, data about a market attribution outcome may indicate the behavior and efficiency of the operator. Therefore, it would give more incentives to build a good reputation and preserve it, and avoid opportunistic renegotiation. In that case, both private operators and public entities may benefit from a winner-winner situation in which the former might be more likely to win a public market and the latter to get the job well done.

2.3 Interest for regulators and academics

- ***Analysis of the competitive environment***

Systematically getting information such as the number of bidders and their identity would be very interesting for assessing the competitiveness of the bidding process. In particular, it would be useful to detect whether large firms blockade entry.

It would then be informative in terms of public policy to implement measures to improve competition in a market, if needed. For example, opening competition to small operators would improve the competitive process and the diversification of operators using the allotment. Amaral et al. (2013) analyzed calls for tender for the bus transportation in London, and concluded that the greater the actual or anticipated number of bidders, the lower the bids. On the reverse, in some specific sectors, some public authorities are restricting competition. Without any proper data it is not possible to assess the efficiency of such restrictions (Chever and Saussier, 2017).

- *Detecting potential collusion*

So far, there is no direct and clear way of detecting collusion, but some suspicious pattern might be detected and should be considered carefully using data (Kaway and Nakabayashi, 2014; Clark et al., 2016). In that case, it would be important to get accurate information with the publication of market attribution such as the number of bidders, their identity and their bids. This would help to detect patterns of bidding such as bid rotation. Using yardstick competition is also a common way to assess the but-for world in a collusion setting. However, as stated by the OECD in the Competition and Procurement report (2011), there is a clear trade-off between collusion and corruption when dealing with transparency. Indeed, too much transparency may facilitate collusion, depending on the characteristics of the market.

2.4 Conclusion

By increasing transparency, Big and Open Data are definitely two key factors that may help public procurement to be more efficient. The society in its entirety could benefit from it by procuring tools for detecting corruption, using statistical and econometric methods, and analyzing public policies implemented through public calls for tender. The first two principles stated in the *OECD Principles for Integrity in Public Procurement* Report (2009) emphasize the importance of transparency in the process of public procurement.[5] Corruption may take on many forms since it can occur before (exchange of confidential information), during (modification of the public offer), or after the call for tender (risk sharing between public and private entities as well as renegotiation issues). Big and Open Data is an opportunity to bring more transparency and integrity in the procurement process. A study led by the World Bank (2014) suggests several avenues for how Big Data can help to assess corruption in public procurement by detecting in official public records and documents rather than the commonly used perceived amount of corruption. Issues at stake are huge: a study performed for the European Commission (2013) evaluated the overall direct cost of corruption in public procurement in five sectors[6] and eight country members[7] to an estimated range between €1.4 billion and €2.2 billion.

Using to their advantage Big and Open Data, public authorities may be more efficient by reducing the asymmetry of information as well as detecting more easily aggressive bids. On the other side, private operators may enjoy a reputational effect tracked down by data and avoid the common trap of bidding too optimistically. Finally, Big and Open Data would be useful for regulators and academics for giving them tools to assess the competitive environment of market as well as detecting patterns for potential cartels and bid riggings.

3 Mihály Fazekas – response to paper 2

3.1 Introduction

This short memo briefly recaps the main arguments presented by the essay of Dr Stéphane Saussier: "Big and Open Data: a new era for public procurement?"; then it raises a number of issues and points worthy of further discussion. In particular, it exposes three main discussion points: 1) Is there Big and Open Data in public procurement?; 2) How to avoid data overload and over-reliance on data analytics; and 3) How does Big and Open Data change power relations in society?

The essay "Big and Open Data: a new era for public procurement?" succinctly enumerates a wide range of potential benefits Big and Open Data in public procurement promises for governments, bidding firms, civil societies, and users of public services more broadly. Most opportunities associated with Big and Open Data stem from our supposedly increasing capacity to detect wrongdoing such as public corruption or inter-bidder collusion, and to identify best practices such as ways to run tenders better or select better suppliers. Almost every promised benefit assumes that it is the lack of information and insight which limits societies in doing better public procurement. However, acting on better analytics is only warranted if motivational structures are right. My below commentary explores all three steps of this impact mechanism: information, insight, and action. The issues raised point at potential harmful effects of Big and Open Data in public procurement.

3.2 Three fundamental challenges

Is there Big and Open Data in public procurement?

Big and Open Data in public procurement is far from being a reality even in countries running well-developed public procurement data systems. Data needs to be comprehensive, encompassing the full tender cycle from needs assessment to contract completion. This wide scope exists in only rare cases in Europe and beyond. Even the most encompassing public procurement data system is of limited use if it is not structured (i.e. information captured and stored in a database format) and it doesn't come with a clear data structure comprehensible for stakeholders and stable enough over time to use past data for informing future transactions. This, again, is far from reality in most countries; think, for example, about frequent legal changes modifying expectations towards procurement actors, data reporting requirements, and variable definitions. Finally, data has to be open, meaning that it is machine readable, and accessible free of charge. Unfortunately, lot of times even structured data is published in a non-machine-readable format or a fee is payable for data download and search. These deficiencies of the underlying information systems are sufficient to demonstrate the point that Big and Open Data in public procurement is more a potentiality than reality even at its most basic level.

How to avoid data overload and over-reliance on data analytics

Even if data was perfect, using it to generate actionable insights is far from warranted. Among the numerous challenges this presents, I will expose only two: data overload and misinterpreting analytical findings, thus overly relying on them. Big Data by definition implies a wealth of extremely detailed information on public procurement tenders, contracts, and payments. For public administrations, bidding firms, and civil societies used to a 'data-poor' debate and action, the new Big Data era can be overwhelming, posing daunting challenges. If there is so much data and so many performance indicators that one doesn't even know where to start, they are actually of very little use. Unfortunately, such Big Data confusion and the investments made to achieve it can cause considerable harm to society.

Furthermore, and probably much more worrisome, lack of experience with Big Data can lead to unrealistic expectations of what it can and cannot reveal. Without the necessary critical appraisal of analytical insights, over-reliance on data ensues diminishing expert judgement and ultimately efficient decision-making. While big and open public procurement data can clearly produce a step change in our capacity to understand public procurement markets, it typically results in probabilistic statements with considerable margin of error, and often lacking the holistic understanding experts develop over the course of their professional careers. In an ideal scenario Big Data analytics complements expert judgement by allowing to exploit the best of both worlds. This however requires knowing the limitations of such analytical tools at the very minimum. Crucially, if some markets are volatile, full of outliers, and disruptive change is frequent, Big Data analytics might not be up to the task.

How does Big and Open Data change power relations in society?

The very notion that it is the lack of knowledge of the best course of action which we lack is called into question by many scholars. If public procurement outcomes reflect entrenched interests, say rewarding loyal business groups for supporting political leaders, improved insights achieve close to nothing other than allowing the informal group to better govern its internal matters. Hence, assuming that governments will act on better evidence, or that bidding firms will improve their performance based on better data are wishful thinking in many contexts.

In reality Big and Open Data allows better decision-making for those who lack public procurement insights and want to and can act on it; while it also has the capacity to fundamentally alter power relations. New information is never power-neutral in a context such as public procurement which lies at the intersection of powerful interests and technical complexities. Think about voters learning from publicly available public procurement databases about public investment projects and the excessive successes of companies with personal ties to the prime minister or a mayor. Such information has led to the demise of a number of governments across the world from Italy to Brazil. Or take, for example, collusive bidders using big, open public procurement data for monitoring each other and hence increasing the stability of their cartel. This latter case again highlights the potential harmful results of big, open public procurement data. Crucially, it is the ability to use Big and Open Data in public procurement and to act on it which determines the changing power relations – those who can harness it better can gain an advantage either for the public's good or harm.

4 Stéphane Saussier – response to paper 1

Big Data is obviously opening the road to great opportunities for improving the efficiency of public procurement. However, I believe that several important steps have not been made in order to realize those opportunities. More precisely, I believe we have to carefully think about 1) What are the exact data needed to improve public procurement efficiency; 2) the potential limit of making such information public; and 3) a clear analysis of what stakeholders have to win in this process. Those three questions are of course interrelated.

Without clear answers, available data will not be easy to use, it will not be easy to manage indicators, and no political willingness will emerge; as a consequence, Big Data in public procurement will only lead to mediocre results.

4.1 What are the exact data needed?

The new European Directives are pushing for more transparency (Directives 2014/24/EU): it will be compulsory for the information exchanged in public procurement procedures to be made paperless as of 18 October 2018. Furthermore, information has to be published concerning the award procedures and the bidders, but also concerning renegotiations. However, it is not clear how far each country should go. For example, do public authorities have only to publish information about the fact that a procurement contract is renegotiated? Do the exact terms of the renegotiations have to be published as well? Should public authorities publish information about bidders? Bids? Should the marks received by every bidder on each criterion be published? As academics, we should say more about what information is needed to improve public procurement without hampering competition.

4.2 When more information hurts?

We should keep in mind that more public information is not always good for competition, as more information may help sustain cartels. For example, the new European Directives are pushing for public authorities to publish their expected price before contract award. Such new information is interesting for academics in order to evaluate how aggressive are bids compared to what was expected by the public authorities. However, such information may also help companies to sustain cartels. As academics, we should say more about what information is needed to improve public procurement without hampering competition and favouring corruption.

4.3 What public officials have to win?

Big Data in public procurement is a revolution. It does not come without any cost. Public authorities need to develop new capabilities that they do not possess yet. As such, it can be analyzed as an organizational innovation for which reluctances exist. What are the gains of more transparency and more scrutiny for public officials? This question should be addressed carefully. The less that is known about public procurement practices, the less public official are challenged. The more is known, the more public officials are susceptible of being challenged by stakeholders who are not necessarily interested in the success of public procurement (e.g. political contesters – (Beuve, Moszoro and Saussier, 2015; Spiller, 2013)). More transparency induced by Big Data might then reduce public officials' discretion that is potentially part of public procurement efficiency (Coviello, Guglielmo and Spagnolo, 2016; Chever and Moore, 2012; Saussier and Tirole, 2015).

In conclusion Big Data in public procurement comes with many promises at a moment when citizens are pushing for more transparency and more involvement in public decisions. Fazekas's note is rightly pointing out the many difficulties that still exist and that are ahead. Those difficulties are somewhat linked with how much transparency is really needed in public procurement. Academics, working on public procurement issues for many years with often very limited data, should now be more explicit about what data they need and what they expect from it, taking into account risks of corruption and cartels as well as political agendas.

5 Mihály Fazekas – conclusions

The two sets of memos agree on a wide range of points giving rise to a narrative which can be further explored in detail. Big Data in public procurement brings enormous opportunities, but just what Big Data means, to whom, how those opportunities are realized, and how some are negatively affected by such developments are questions which require a lot more thinking. Setting the right policies going forward requires explicitly recognizing trade-offs between different aspects of the Big Data revolution and balancing the costs and benefits. This final note will briefly expose some trade-offs lying ahead.

5.1 Big Data brings transparency but not to the benefit of all

Transparency of bidding and contract implementation is generally welcome, but it may well also produce adverse consequences. As Stéphane Saussier pointed out, transparency can also support the maintenance of collusive rings or cartels (unless cartels have monitored each other effectively already before Big Data!). Hence, public demands for transparency supporting government accountability need to be balanced with a potentially increasing risk of collusion. Similarly, increased transparency may increase government accountability by increasing society's capacity to monitor civil servants, which can also cripple innovation and push civil servants to opt for risk-averse strategies rather than pursuing value for money.

5.2 Costly investments draw on scarce public resources

Government austerity implies that the resources to invest in public procurement data systems and train stakeholders to intelligently use the resulting rich datasets are scarce. Such scarce resources could be spent on fixing schools or employment programmes to the long term unemployed. Demonstrating value for money for IT systems enhancements, hiring data scientists into the civil service, and training ordinary civil servants in data use is essential if the Big Data revolution is to be realized.

5.3 More data changes the relationship between state and society

More information on how governments spend public money is never neutral to state-society relationships. More information on the machinery of the state can create more demands on civil servants, which can in a worst-case scenario distract the balanced functioning of the state (i.e. focus on what is measured and transparent to the neglect of those which are less visible, but potentially more important). Moreover, more information can, as expected by many, reveal wrongdoing which if at a large scale can bring complete governments to a halt (e.g. Petrobras in Brazil). Managing the changing state-society relationships and the demands on governments is more of an art than a science, while it certainly plays a crucial role in deciding on the success of public procurement Big Data reforms.

6 Stéphane Saussier – conclusions

I believe that the above memos agree on many points. Maybe the only partial disagreement comes from what are the main difficulties associated with Big Data for public procurement. As Mihály's notes insist on technical difficulties, I believe they might not be the main brakes of the Big Data adventure.

I certainly agree with the statement that Big and Open Data in public procurement is far from being a reality. As an academic, much information I think is relevant for an economic analysis of public procurement efficiency in Europe is missing. However, I would not stress so much technical difficulties (data has to be open, machine readable) as in Mihály Fazekas's note to explain this shortage of data. My feeling is that technical limits that exist today might be overcome as soon as new business models will be identified, producing new services/innovations of value for stakeholders.

I stated in my previous notes that I believe the main challenge are coming more certainly from the fact that

1 Many stakeholders are potentially interested in the Big Data adventure when public procurement is concerned but their objectives are not necessarily aligned in the short term.

2 What is the exact information needed to help academics, firms, public authorities, and more broadly stakeholders is not clear.
3 Even more unclear, as soon as you recognize that it is not true that the more information there are, the better it is.

Those three challenges might necessitate at some point some regulation concerning the way Big Data is produced and used. Raw information is not (or is rarely) sufficient to inform stakeholders and more especially citizens, and might even be misleading. As an example, the right2water European Citizen Initiative provoked discussion between stakeholders concerning who is willing to open their data at what condition, for what kind of benchmarking exercises. Very soon the discussion was turning around the fact that it might not be to the advantage of private water companies to open their data and to let them open to the public without any "treatment": some econometric studies showed that on average private companies are pricing water at a higher price than municipalities that decided not to go private but that this difference does not exist anymore as soon as you compare public and private prices, all things being equal (Chong, Saussier and Silverman, 2015). Raw data might thus be misleading if no explanation or statistical analysis is provided together with the data.

Notes

1 https://sites.google.com/site/do101mtl/seao/iqd-1
2 www.profily.info/
3 www.open-contracting.org/digiwhist_big_data_meets_the_concerned_citizen and http://ec.europa.eu/internal_market/scoreboard/performance_per_policy_area/public_procurement/index_en.htm
4 Nineteen mandatory fields were checked for missing information: contracting body name, contracting body address, contracting body settlement name, contracting body postcode, winner name, winner address, winner settlement name, winner postcode, winner country, procedure type, main CPV code, NUTS code, use of EU Funds, type of assessment criteria used, contract award date, number of bids, contract value, and use of subcontracting.
5 The first principle states that the public entity should "provide an adequate degree of transparency in the entire procurement cycle in order to promote fair and equitable treatment for potential suppliers" and the second one that it should "maximize transparency in competitive tendering and take precautionary measures to enhance integrity, in particular for exceptions to competitive tendering".
6 Road and rail, water and waste, urban or utility construction, training, and research and development.
7 France, Hungary, Italy, Lithuania, the Netherlands, Poland, Romania, and Spain.

References

Amaral, M., Saussier, S., and Yvrande-Billon, A. (2013). Expected number of bidders and winning bids: Evidence from the London bus tendering model. *Journal of Transport Economics and Policy*, 47(1), 17–34.

Auriol, E. (2000). Concurrence par comparaison. *Un Point de Vue Normatif, Revue économique*, 51(3), 621–634.

Beuve, J., Moszoro, M. W., and Saussier, S. (2015). *Political Contestability and Contract Rigidity: An Analysis of Procurement Contracts*. Rochester, NY: Social Science Research Network. SSRN Scholarly Paper. Available at http://papers.ssrn.com/abstract=2475164

Beuve, J., and Saussier, S. (2017). *Renegotiations, discretion and renewals of public-private contracts*. Working paper.

Chassang, S., and Ortner, J. (2016). *Collusion in auctions with constrained bids: Theory and evidence from public procurement*. Unpublished Manuscript.

Chever, L., and Moore, J. (2012). Negotiated procedures overrated? Evidence from France questions the commission's approach in the latest procurement reforms. *European Procurement & Public Private Partnership Law Review*, 7(4), 228–241.

Chever, L., and Saussier, S. (2017). The law of small numbers: Investigating the benefits of restricted auctions for public procurement. *Applied Economics*, 49(42), 4241–4260.

Chong, E., Saussier, S., and Silverman, B. (2015). Water under the bridge: Cith size, bargaining power, price and Franchise renewals in the provision of water. *Journal of Law, Economics and Organization*, 31(1), 3–39.

Cingolani, L., Fazekas, M., Kukutschka, R. M. B., and Tóth, B. (2015). *Towards a Comprehensive Mapping of Information on Public Procurement Tendering and Its Actors Across Europe*. Cambridge.

Clark et al. (2016). *Bid rigging and entry deterrence: Evidence from an anti-collusion investigation in Quebec*. Available at www.economics.utoronto.ca/index.php/index/research/downloadSeminarPaper/63908.

Coviello, D., Guglielmo, A., and Spagnolo, G. (2016). *The effect of discretion on procurement performance*. CEP Discussion Paper, No. 1427, Centre for Economic Performance, London School of Economics and Political Science, London.

Czibik, Á., Tóth, B., and Fazekas, M. (2015). *How to construct a public procurement database from administrative records? With examples from the Hungarian public procurement system of 2009–2012*, Budapest.

Estache, A., and Saussier, S. (2014). Public-private partnerships and efficiency: A short assessment. *CESifo DICE Report*, 12(3), 8–13.

European Commission (2013). *Public procurement: Costs we pay for corruption*. Available at http://ec.europa.eu/anti_fraud/documents/anti-fraud-policy/research-and-studies/pwc_olaf_study_en.pdf.

Fazekas, M. (2014). *The Use of "Big Data" for Social Sciences Research – An Application to Corruption Research*. London: Sage Publications Ltd.

Fazekas, M., and Tóth, I. J. (2014). *New Ways to Measure Institutionalised Grand Corruption in Public Procurement* (No. 2014: 9). Bergen, Norway: U4 Anti-Corruption Resource Centre.

Guasch, J. (2004). *Granting and Renegotiating Infrastructure Concession: Doing It Right*. Washington, DC: World Bank Institute.

Kaway, K., and Nakabayashi, J. (2014). *Detecting large-scale collusion in procurement auctions*. Available at http://isites.harvard.edu/fs/docs/icb.topic1465230.files/Kawai-Kei.pdf.

Knack, S., Kugler, M., and Manning, N. (2003). Second-generation governance indicators. *International Review of Administrative Sciences*, 69, 345–364.

McKinsey Global Institute (2011). *Big data: The next frontier for innovation, competition, and productivity*. Available at www.mckinsey.com/business-functions/business-technology/our-insights/big-data-the-next-frontier-for-innovation.

OECD (2009). *OECD principles for integrity in public procurement*. Available at www.oecd.org/gov/ethics/48994520.pdf.

OECD (2011). *Competition and procurement*. Available at www.oecd.org/regreform/sectors/competitionandprocurement-2011.htm.

Saussier, S., and Tirole, J. (2015). *Strengthening the efficiency of public procurement, report for the French council of economic analysis*. April. Available at www.cae-eco.fr/IMG/pdf/cae-note022-env2.pdf.

Shleifer, A. (1985). A theory of Yardstick competition. *Rand Journal of Economics*, 16(3), 319–327.

Spiller, P. (2013). Transaction cost regulation. *Journal of Economic Behavior & Organization*, 89, 232–242.

Trapnell, S. (2015). *User's Guide to Measuring Corruption and Anti-Corruption*. New York: United Nations Development Programme.

UN Global Pulse (2012). *Big Data for Development: Challenges and Opportunities*. New York: UN Global Pulse.

The WorldBank (2014). *Measuring corruption risk using 'Big' public procurement data in central & eastern Europe*. Available at http://blogs.worldbank.org/governance/measuring-corruption-risk-using-big-public-procurement-data-central-eastern-europe.

8 Open Data and procurement

Bernardo Nicoletti

1 Introduction

Digital transformation refers to the changes associated with the application of digital technology in all aspects of human society. The digital transformation in a specific function or organization implies that digital usages enable new types of innovation and creativity in a particular domain, rather than simply enhance and support the traditional methods. Digital transformation is the use of advanced technologies in support of the management. Digital transformation is impacting all sectors and all functions (da Rosa and Almeida, 2017).

Out of the five major trends in technology (Cloud computing, Mobile, Artificial intelligence, Social Networks, Big Data Analytics), the latter, Big Data Analytics, is the most interesting for improving the procurement function both in the private companies and in the public administration. On the other side, it is also true that the five technologies mentioned before can be much more effective working together.

Traditionally, organizations have used Big Data Analytics to increase spend visibility (Morabito, 2015). It could do much more in support of procurement. This chapter aims to introduce a generalized business model on how to use Big Data in procurement using the so-called Open Data. Open Data is data that is held openly and is free to access, use, re-use, re-distribute, and so on (Benenson, 2016). There are many sources of Open Data, such as public administration data, contracts, weather reports, and social networks.

The Open Data movement to make available the access to public (and other) information is relatively new. It is acting as a powerful, emerging force. The overall intention is to make local, regional, national, international, and even personal (not sensitive) data (and particularly publicly acquired data) available in a form that allows for direct processing using software tools. Such tools make possible, for example, cross-tabulation, visualization, mapping, and so on.

Open Data can be profitably used also in support of procurement, especially by the public administrations but also by private organizations. This is the subject of this chapter. It analyzes both the release of procurement information in the Open Data and their uses.

2 Literature

There are not many papers describing the potential use of Open Data in procurement. Almost all of them refer to public procurement.

Ubaldi (2013, 2015) reviews the international state of the all on the design and implementation of digital services based on Open Data – in particular, those running over Open Government Data (OGD). Drawing from a large set of OECD countries, the author highlights how OGD can become a driver of pervasive change, spurring innovation and promoting efficiency and effectiveness within the public administrations.

This requires setting the appropriate institutional conditions. It requires reforming the status and the norms of civil servants. It should activate a various and heterogeneous network of agents (including citizens and other external stakeholders) in a process that should become self-governed and sustainable, because it is centered on collective learning and feedback, Ubaldi reviews the implications for the development of new methodologies of data collection and monitoring.

Nugroho et al. (2015) found two waves of policy-making. The first wave of policy focuses on stimulating the release of data. The second wave of policy aims at stimulating their use. It concentrates on how Open Data can be used to learn from other policies. It helps to improve open data policies. A third wave of open data policy is expected, focusing on realizing benefits from using Open Data.

Alvarez et al. (2012) described a public procurement information platform that provides a unified pan-European system that exploits the aggregation of tender notices linking Open Data and semantic web technologies. This platform requires a step-based method to deal with the requirements of the public procurement sector and the Open Government Data initiative:

1 modeling the unstructured information included in public procurement notices (contracting authorities, organizations, contracts awarded, and so on);
2 enriching that information with the existing product classification systems and the linked data vocabularies;
3 publishing relevant information extracted out of the notices following the linking Open Data approach;
4 Implementing enhanced services based on advanced algorithms and techniques such as query-expansion methods to exploit the information in a semantic way.

Taking into account that public procurement notices contain variables such as type of contract, region, duration, total amount, target enterprise, and so on, different methods can be applied to expand user queries, easing the access to the information and providing a more accurate information retrieval system. Nevertheless expanded user queries can involve an extra time in the process of retrieving notices. That is why these authors outline a performance evaluation to tune up the semantic methods and the generated queries, providing a scalable and time-efficient system. This platform is supposed to be especially relevant for SMEs that want to tender in the European Union (EU). This platform can ease their access to the information of the notices and fostering their participation in cross-border public procurement processes across Europe. Finally, these authors provide an example of the potential use in evaluating and comparing the goodness and the improvement of the proposed platform regarding to the existing ones.

3 Open Data

3.1 The Open Data movement

The Open Data, literally "open data," is the school of thought (and its "movement") that aims to address the need to be legally entitled to have data "open" or freely (re)usable by any user, for any reason (Kitchin, 2014). The goal of Open Data can be achieved by law, as in the US where the information generated by the federal public sector is in the public domain, or by choice of the right holders, through appropriate decisions (Bizer et al., 2007). The use of Open Data for any purpose implies compatibility with the regulations in force (for example, a list of email addresses will never be used for sending spam). They may provide for a right of attribution to the author or the source is acknowledged. Possibly, there might be an obligation to use the same license of the original dataset for the publication of any modified dataset (so-called viral or copyleft clause) (Monino and Sedkaoui, 2016).

3.2 Diffusion of Open Data

There are many sources of Open Data, such as public administration data, weather reports, social networks, reports on news services, and in general data on the web. The Open Data movement to make available the access to public (and other) information is relatively new. It is acting as a powerful, emerging force. The overall intention is to make personal, local, regional, and national data (and particularly publicly acquired data) available in a form that allows for direct processing using software tools, such as for the purposes of cross-tabulation, visualization, mapping, and so on (Gurstein, 2011).

The idea is that public (and other) data, whether collected directly as part of a census collection or indirectly as a secondary output of other activities (crime or accident statistics, for example, but also social networks or similar) should be available in electronic form and accessible via the web. There are significant initiatives in this area underway all over the world and as part of a wide variety of not-for-profit initiatives.

A certain number of governments have agreed to commit to moving towards Open Data as a matter of policy. For example, all data collected by the British government, not considered essential to national or public security, must be open.

4 Open Data in procurement

4.1 Use of Open Data in procurement

The procurement organizations are at the verge of some dramatic changes in their characteristics (Nicoletti, 2013). In a more competitive market, companies are relying more and more on innovation as a competitive advantage.

Worldwide, there are millions of publicly available databases and sites. They are open for use. Other companies can tap on the same data. It is essential to have the capability to select the appropriate data and use them in a timely, efficient, effective, economic, and ethical way.

Procurement organizations need to consider possible ecosystems suitable to today's markets. In this model, multiple players collaborate. Collaboration, in the meaning of "working together," is necessary in modern times. It is necessary to work with different vendors, partners, outsourcers, fintech, and so on.

Procurement can exploit Open Data in order to provide more tailored services to their organizations and to estimate risk with greater accuracy. The innovation can be of many types.

In procurement, innovation creates the basis for alliance or partnerships between different financial and non-financial institutions. Procurement organizations will need to agree or extend, for instance, on partnerships with the entities providing Open Data and/or technology vendors that can supply and service-connected devices that can support other channels. They will also need to set up broader partnerships to secure direct access to vendors' data and valuable information. New players could also take control of these ecosystems – potentially leveraging far more detailed vendor insights than the ones available to the procurement organizations without accessing Open Data. The long-term result could be lower effectiveness for the procurement organizations if they lose control of the relationships with the customer. As mentioned before, Open Data Analytics can help on this respect.

In order to analyze in a systematic way the possible support of Open Data in procurement, it is interesting to consider the various activities in the procurement process (see also Figure 8.1).

- Demand Analysis and Sourcing Marketing. Choosing the right vendor involves much more than scanning a series of price lists. A correct choice will depend on a wide range of factors such as value for money, quality, reliability, and service. How you weigh up the importance of these different factors should be based on the specific organization's priorities and strategy.
- RfX and Shortlisting. One of the crucial requirements in procurement is matchmaking demand with supply. Open Data can help in finding a vendor with a previous successful history of contracts similar to a current call for support.
- Negotiations, Assignment, and Contractualization. Negotiation can be effected by mere delivery or endorsement followed by delivery. Mode of transfer is not so undemanding. Assignment is done by writing, usually by executing a separate document signed by the transferor. Open Data can help in getting information on contracts.
- Vendor Management and Rating. Vendor rating is the result of a formal vendor evaluation system. Vendors get standing, status, or title according to their attainment of some levels of performance, such as delivery, lead-time, quality, price, or some combination of variables. Open Data can help greatly in doing a comparison with performance of the vendors in the market

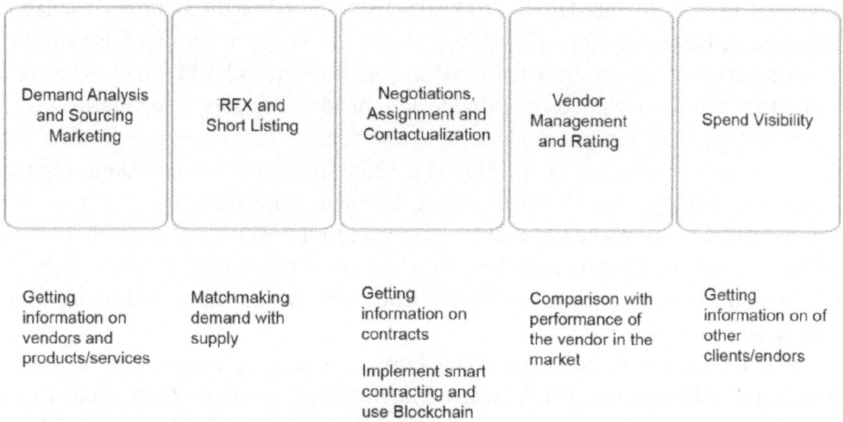

Figure 8.1 The procurement process and Open Data

- Spend Visibility or Analysis. This is the process of collecting, cleansing, classifying, and analyzing expenditure data with the purpose of decreasing procurement costs, improving efficiency, and monitoring compliance. It can also be leveraged in other areas of business such as inventory management, budgeting and planning, and product development. Open Data can help in getting data on the performance of other vendors and customers, but also on other customers' performance.

4.2 Critical success factors to use Open Data in procurement

Data quality is an important factor in using Open Data for procurement. The provision of publicly available Open Data can help in the exchanges, spending, and decisions. This information is served massively and heterogeneously – mostly due to different bureaucratic procedures, systems, and paperwork formats.

Data is considered of high quality if it correctly represents the real-world construct to which it refers (Baškarada and Koronios, 2014). As data volume increases, the question of internal consistency within data becomes significant, regardless of fitness for use for any particular purpose. The main concern is that organizations making available for free Open Data might not invest too much on their accuracy.

Open Data updates do not occur always at regular or at least generally predictable time intervals. Even though the data are available by the providers, users might be overwhelmed from the size/inconsistency of the information they deal with.

Vafopoulos et al. (2012) aimed to promote clarity and enhance user awareness regarding public spending in Greece through easily consumed visualization diagrams. Information provision is based on semantic processing of real-time Open Data provided by Greek government ('Diavgia') and the Greek Taxation

Information System. Second, a proposed ontology for public spending in Greece functions in two distinct levels. It checks the validity of the publicly available data accessed by the system, cleaning, and reconstructing in parallel false entries, while it can interconnect the data to existing ontological and data schemes derived from other similar initiatives worldwide and, in addition, core vocabularies.

To use Open Data in procurement it is essential to have access to the data but also to be able to process them. This is possible thanks to Linked Data. Linked Data is a technology that allows to aggregate and to collect data coming from distributed sources. To make accessible these data to the web (Rizzo, Morando and De Martin, 2009), the data must be published under the condition of use "open." This would allow to consult and to navigate (with any means and through deep linking and aggregation).

The Open Data is at the Linked Data, how the Internet is at the web. The Open Data is the infrastructure (or "platform") of which the Linked Data needs to be able to create the inference network between various data distributed around the web. The Linked Data is a fairly mature technology with great potential. It needs large masses of data linked together that is "linked" to become useful in practice. This is possible with a large amount of Open Data. Ideally, Open Data should already be linked by the same institutions or otherwise made available in a structured way. The Linked Data can provide a powerful representation of the Open Data, in terms of relationships (links): in this sense, Linked Data and Open Data converge and reach their full realization in the approach Linked Open Data (Yu, 2011).

There are claims about the potential of opening data to drive service innovation (Kuk and Davies, 2011). Little is known about the detailed processes of how hackers create or reshape services out of new releases of open datasets, and the conditions for the move from data release to service innovation. Kuk and Davies (2011) argued that the utility of Open Data is accrued through the creation of new artifacts with enhanced performativity transformed by human and material agency. The roles of agency and artifacts in assembling Open Data are complementarities. These Authors found that few of the "rapid prototypes" developed through hack day events are maintained or sustained as service innovations beyond those events. Five artifacts provided the value stack of complementarities: cleaned data available through APIs or bulk downloads, linkable data, shared source code and configuration, source code repositories, and web technologies. Their findings also suggest that only a few open datasets induce the process of change. Initial contributions are driven by the use values but can only be sustained through an open innovative approach to induce further collaboration within a wider Open Data community.

4.3 Limitations of Open Data

There are a certain number of limitations in the use of Open Data (Cole, 2012).

The main difficulty is the fact that there is no central repository from which to select the Open Data useful to the procurement organization. Each party, be it a central or local government entity or a private association, can decide its own format and its own way to organize data. It is also necessary to govern the process and evaluate the benefits of investing resources and time to use Open Data. The business case is not easy to prepare, especially on the side of the benefits. This will be another aspect discussed later in this chapter.

In order to commit to Open Data most data sources must be anonymized. That means any personal identifiable information should be masked or scrambled (Vassiliadis, Simitsis and Skiadopoulos, 2002). This may become problematic in the long term. As more and more people put their personal data in the web or mobile sites, there might be the possibility to rebuild the anonymized parts of the data by comparing the datasets to other sources. With this precaution in mind, there are many data available to procurement organizations that are freely available. Examples are statistics relating to contracts, vendors, technical specifications, and the similar.

Freely available does not mean that they are ready to be used. It is necessary to select them, extract, transform, and load them into a private repository. This is not an easy task. It requires resources and special skills. We refer to specific literature that deals in detail with this subject (Kimball and Ross, 2011).

Open Data governance is part of a broader information governance program that formulates policy relating to the optimization, quality, security, compliance, and monetization of Open Data by aligning the objectives of multiple functions involved, such as strategy, marketing, sales, operations, and so on. Organizations need to create and follow appropriate policies and procedures to prevent the misuse of Open Data, considering regulatory and legal risks when handling social media, geolocation, biometrics, and other forms of personally identifiable information. Organizations should define the governance of power users of Open Data, such as the data scientists (Soares, 2013; Davenport, 2012, Profile Sheet Wsp). An Open Data governance policy should obey the organization's legal and regulatory requirements. An Open Data governance policy might state that an organization will not integrate a customer's personal identifiable information into his or her master data record without the respect of the appropriate compliance. Organizations need to optimize and improve the quality of their Open Data in the following areas:

- Metadata: to build information about inventories of Open Data;
- Data quality management: to cleanse, whenever possible, normalize, and finally manage Open Data;
- Information lifecycle management: to archive and sunset Open Data when it does not make any more sense to retain their massive volumes in internal files.

Open Data must be profitable for the organizations. It is important not to waste resources to use Open Data if they are not useful to add value to the customers and the procurement organization.

4.4 Benefits

The biggest challenge facing procurement organizations is how to operate in an increasingly digital world. Open Data can provide a digital support from which procurement organizations can rapidly respond and adapt to a changing marketplace, and add value to their organizations.

The ubiquitous push from governments to release more data publicly has resulted in new UK government and industry bodies being set up to address the use of Open Data for both the citizens and commercial purposes (Bates, 2012).

The benefits of Open Data are essentially five, here labeled as the 5 Vs:

- Value: Open Data are data freely available. Even taking into account the costs of getting, analyzing, and processing them, the total costs of operations are normally lower than the ones of other types of data;
- Variety: Open Data are available in different and distant sectors to help in different aspects of the procurement processes;
- Velocity: To access other data not open tends to be slower than getting information on respect to a digital analysis of existing Open Data;
- Veracity: Every Open Data normally is connected with some real life situation. So Open Data tends to be rather reliable;
- Visibility: The data can be shared publicly or selectively.

5 Experiences

Researchers (Tangi, 2015) analyzed the Italian situation through a classification model of Open Data portals in order to be able to highlight positive features and problems.

An increasing amount of public procurement data is now being ported to linked data format, in view of its exploitation by government, commercial, and nonprofit subjects (Mynarz et al., 2015). This chapter shows how to implement a portable matchmaking service that relies solely on the capability of SPARQL 1_1_. In order to show its effectiveness, the proposed service has been tested and evaluated on the RETized versions of two procurement databases: the EU's Tenders Electronic Daily and the Czech public procurement register. This author evaluated several factors influencing. matchmaking accuracy, including score aggregation, query expansion, contribution of additional features obtained from linked data, data quality, and volume.

Despite an extensive energy efficiency potential, measures are sometimes not adopted due to barriers, such as lack of information (Blomqvist, 2015). An integrated database of available energy efficiency measures is one step towards overcoming such barriers. To address this challenge, Blomqvist presented a database integrating energy efficiency data from Sweden (from the Swedish Energy Agency) and the US (from the Department of Energy's Industrial Assessment Centers). He published the data on the web, using standardized web languages and following the principles and best practices of the linked data. Additionally, he provided several demonstration interfaces to access the data in order to show the potential of the result. These are entirely new results, since this is the first database that publishes this type of data using linked data principles and standards. It integrates data from entirely different sources, making them jointly searchable and reusable. The results show that such data integration is possible and that the integrated dataset has several benefits for different categories of users, such as supporting industry and energy efficiency buyers in overcoming the information barrier for investment in energy efficiency measures, and supporting application developers to integrate easily such data into support tools for energy efficiency assessment.

6 The future

This chapter examines briefly some uses of Open Data to transform procurement. Rapidly emerging technologies for Open Data are becoming enablers to creating competitive advantages. The future looks very exciting for supporting procurement processes with new technologies that could change the ways that procurement organizations work today.

Looking to the future, there is a technology developed for a specific case, the Bitcoin virtual currency, which has the potential to change many fields including procurement. The blockchain technology is interesting in itself (see Figure 8.2). It is a clear example of how data accessible to multiple parties can change the processes and even the industry. Blockchain is based on a digital online, distributed, and encrypted public ledger. It maintains a sequential list of transactions replicated frequently among the different nodes. It is used to certify the correctness of information thanks to its presence on various network nodes. This is possible due to the fact the data is not kept in a single register center, may be private, but in its pure application it is made Open Data with copies in each node of the network. The fairness of a transaction derives from the so-called consensus method: "if everyone knows it, it must be true."

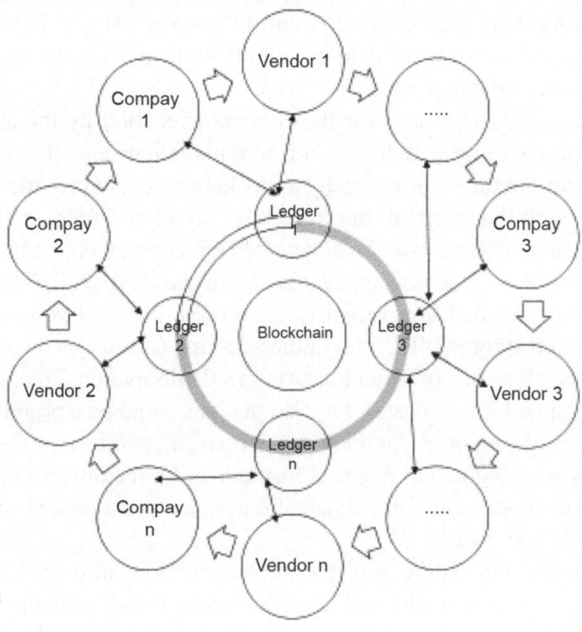

Figure 8.2 Blockchain in procurement

Blockchain can be used as an Open, or at least Shared, Data affecting the interactions between the procurement organizations and third parties: agency networks, external vendors, and customers. It can affect the portfolio management, administration, sales, and claims handling. In the more distant future, blockchain could help in setting up smart contracts with a distributed ledger solution. It could help in managing vendor identities, reference data, and assets; increasing secure visibility; and ensuring a seamless, reliable, and uninterrupted messaging service to the procurement ecosystem. It is a very cost-effective method of facilitating the availability and exchange of data between many parties interested in the procurement processes. It is a trusted utility service that boosts the effectiveness of a procurement ecosystem.

The applications of the blockchain, in all sectors of procurement, could be many. Figure 8.1 shows the typical high-level process of procurement. Blockchain could be useful along the entire cycle.

Blockchain can be applied at the time of the vendor participation to a tender or of the qualification, to verify the identity of the vendor or to limit the sourcing risks from that vendor. This is the case of Tradle. This start-up has closed the gap with where you want your company information stored with its high resilience to potential hackers and cyber-attacks (Collins et al., 2016). Allowing the partner banks to share data about their customers, the partner company of the bank can offer a very quick and streamlined process for subscribing to a product without asking for data already available in possession of the financial services institutions. Document exchange and communications could be saved and guaranteed by blockchain, which certifies these mailings. It allows the recovery of the data in full compliance with European data laws. Another example in underwriting is provided by SafeShare, a British company (Nicoletti, 2017). It uses Bitcoin's underlying blockchain technology to confirm counter-party obligations. Blockchain technology facilitates the delivery of a flexible and a responsive product to customers at a reasonable price.

Blockchain can also be used for the contract execution by the automation of the contracts for getting a reduction of administration costs for reconciliation and error. Smart contracts, powered by a blockchain, could provide procurement organizations with the means to manage claims in a transparent, responsive, and irrefutable manner. Contracts and claims could be recorded onto a blockchain and validated by the network, ensuring that only valid claims are paid (Deloitte, 2012).

The use cases detailed in a recent paper (Ølnes, 2015) show that blockchain should be of interest for public sector bodies. Storing certificates on the blockchain is a cost-effective way of storing and securing vital information. The use cases show that this is possible for certificates, but also that this could be a promising technology for all types of permanent, or relatively permanent, public or private documents (such as invoices submitted to financial institutions for factoring). Other examples could include contracts of different types (for instance, procurement contracts), certifications, and many more.

One of the most interesting potential implementations of blockchain is the so-called smart contracts, a model still in its definition in technical and legal details. The scheme turns specific contractual provisions in executable digital codes, designed for self-execution in a blockchain system.

A paper presents a brave new step in the way contracting could be performed within the US Department of Defense and how contracts could be handled (Chesebro, 2015). The contract could cease being a static document file on a computer server. The contract could manage itself. The contract could become empowered. It could take actions apart from human interactions. The potential savings could be very large. A solution exists to bring the contract to be a dynamic object. In discussions about programming, the word "object" means a component with properties and methods. Properties are what an object knows about itself and methods are what an object knows it can do. A contract, as an object, would know things about itself. It would know how much it is worth. It would know who signed the contract, who administers the contract, and when the contract is supposed to be complete. With a little additional development in the environment in which the smart contract exists, the contract could be able to interact with other objects. That would enable the contract to know how much money has been paid to the contractor and how much is left. The contract would know how to close itself out. If a problem arises, such as funds still not spent with the contractor no longer in business, the contract would know how to handle this new situation. Among its many advantages, the smart contract could eliminate the problems associated with institutionalized knowledge. The use of blockchain for smart contracts would extend their action beyond the single organization and could help the ecosystem.

An example of this type of use of blockchain is Ethereum, also a global network of computers (Marino, 2016). Examples of what this network can register and monitor are:

- Debts
- Delivery promises
- Execution of a will

Contracts may be authored in order to algorithmically specify and autonomously enforce rules of interaction. All transactions for which delivery arrangements are made can be included with unbreakable rules and agreements without an intermediary.

Further developments in advanced predictive Open Data Analytics are likely to lead to complex decision-making scenarios based on a variety of stress tests, in multiple market conditions, against several key performance indicators (KPIs). Such business simulations can support the design and redesign of procurement operations. For example, by simulating different market and competitor scenarios, Open Data can help in assessing business agility and resilience of a given vendor or risks.

7 Further research

This chapter has concentrated on the potential support from Open Data to the current procurement processes. It would be very important to extend some of the ideas mentioned in this chapter about the connection between smart contracts and blockchain.

Blockchain is a solution that could revolutionize the relationships between organizations and their vendors. The connection between smart contracts and blockchain promises substantial changes. It poses questions on the future role of the States in terms of private contracting (Atzori, 2015). Right now smart contracts are limited to the buying and selling on non-material products or services (Perugini and Dal Checco, 2015). It would be important to analyze their extension to material products.

Linked data or the Web of Data promise great advancements in the integration of processes among companies. More work is necessary in this direction.

This chapter has concentrated on the organizational aspects. There are also important considerations from an Information and Communication Technology Theory point of view that need to examine the technical consequences of some of the hypothesis in this chapter.

8 Conclusions

This chapter is a contribution to the analyses on how to use Open Data in procurement organizations. Open Data might change in several geographies and situation, but their availability will increase.

There is a wide-ranging diversity that actual practices surrounding Open Data produce. The procurement organizations should increase their ability to gather and make use of them through advances in resources, human and not, such as data scientists, software, scientific understanding, and the like. Given the current world situation, the concerns about its misuse, its errors, and the unevenness of resources to exploit will not decrease. Therefore, there will be varying degrees of openness around public data in the near future

Big Data Analytics, and in particular Open Data, undoubtedly represent a major challenge for procurement organizations, with important implications from several points of view. They are also an extremely important opportunity. In times of rapidly changing market dynamics, any opportunity is welcome (Christensen, 2013). Making use of Open Data means exploiting a treasure of data in order to provide more added value to the organizations where procurement is active and, as a consequence, to their customers. As noted by Greg Baxter, Citi's Global Head of Digital Strategy, "we are not even at the end of the beginning" of a digital disruption.[1]

Note

1 www.agefi.fr/sites/agefi.fr/files/fichiers/2016/03/citi.pdf [accessed 16 April 2016].

References

Alvarez, J. M., Labra, J. E., Cifuentes, F., Alor-Hernández, G., Sánchez, C., and Luna, J. A. G. (2012). Towards a pan-European e-procurement platform to aggregate, publish and search public procurement notices powered by linked open data: The MOLDEAS approach. *International Journal of Software Engineering and Knowledge Engineering*, 22(3), 365–383.

Atzori, M. (2015). *Tecnologia blockchain e governance decentralizzata: lo Stato è ancora necessario?* Available at SSRN.

Baškarada, S., and Koronios, A. (2014). A critical success factors framework for information quality management. *Information Systems Management*, 31(4), 1–20.

Bates, J. (2012). "This is what modern deregulation looks like": Co-optation and contestation in the shaping of the UK's Open Government Data Initiative. *The Journal of Community Informatics*, 8(2).

Benenson, I. (2016). The data revolution: Big data, open data, data infrastructures and their consequences. By Rob Kitchin, London: Sage, 2014. *Geography Research Forum*, 35, 145–146.

Bizer, C., Heath, T., Ayers, D., and Raimond, Y. (2007). *Interlinking open data on the Web.* The 4th European Semantic Web Conference.

Blomqvist, E., and Thollander, P. (2015). An integrated dataset of energy efficiency measures published as linked open data. *Energy Efficiency*, 8(6), 1125–1147.

Chesebro, R. (2015). *A Contract That Manages Itself: The Time Has Arrived.* Ft Belvoir, VA: Defense Acquisition University.

Christensen, C. (2013). *The Innovator's Dilemma: When New Technologies Cause Great Firms to Fail.* Cambridge, MA: Harvard Business Review Press.

Cole, R. J. (2012). Some observations on the practice of "Open Data" as opposed to its promise. *The Journal of Community Informatics*, 8(2).

Collins, L., Grisoni, L., Tucker, J., Seaman, C., Graham, S., Fakoussa, R., and Otten, D. (2016). *The Modern Family Business: Relationships, succession and transition.* Berlin: Springer.

da Rosa, I., and de Almeida, J. (2017). Digital transformation in the public sector: Electronic procurement in Portugal. In R. K. Shakya (eds.), *Digital Governance and e-Government Principles Applied to Public Procurement* (pp. 99–125). IGI Global, 90: 70–76.

Davenport, T. H. (2012). *Business intelligence and organizational decisions.* Organizational Applications of Business Intelligence Management: Emerging Trends: Emerging Trends, 1.

Deloitte (2012). *Open growth: Stimulating demand for open data in the UK.* A Briefing from Deloitte Analytics.

Gurstein, M. B. (2011). Open data: Empowering the empowered or effective data use for everyone? *First Monday*, 16(2).

Kimball, R., and Ross, M. (2011). *The Data Warehouse ETL Toolkit: Practical Techniques for Extracting, Cleaning, Conforming, and Delivering Data.* Hoboken, NJ: John Wiley & Sons.

Kitchin, R. (2014). *The Data Revolution: Big Data, Open Data, Data Infrastructures and Their Consequences.* Los Angeles, CA: Sage.

Kuk, G., and Davies, T. (2011). *The roles of agency and artifacts in assembling open data complementarities.* Proceedings of the Thirty Second International Conference on Information Systems, Shanghai, China.

Marino, P. P. (2016). *Optimization of Computer Networks: Modeling and Algorithms: a Hands-on Approach.* Hoboken, NJ: John Wiley & Sons.

Monino, J. L., and Sedkaoui, S. (2016). *Big Data, Open Data and Data Development*, Vol. 3. Hoboken, NJ: John Wiley & Sons.

Morabito, V. (2015). *Big Data and Analytics: Strategic and Organizational Impacts.* Cham, Switzerland: Springer.

Mynarz, J., Svátek, V., and Di Noia, T. (2015). Matchmaking public procurement linked open data. In *OTM Confederated International Conferences" On the Move to Meaningful Internet Systems*" (pp. 405–422). Cham, Switzerland: Springer International Publishing.

Nicoletti, B. (2013). *Lean Procurement*. Milano, Italy: FrancoAngeli.

Nicoletti, B. (2017). *The Future of FinTech*. Switzerland: Springer International Publishing.

Nugroho, R. P., Zuiderwijk, A., Janssen, M., and de Jong, M. (2015). A comparison of national open data policies: Lessons learned. *Transforming Government: People, Process and Policy*, 9(3), 286–308.

O'Riain, S., Curry, E., and Harth, A. (2012). XBRL and open data for global financial ecosystems: A linked data approach. *International Journal of Accounting Information Systems*, 13(2), 141–162.

Ølnes, S. (2015). Beyond Bitcoin-public sector innovation using the Bitcoin blockchain technology. *Norsk konferanse for organisasjoners bruk av IT*, 23(1), November.

Perugini, M. L., and Dal Checco, P. (2015). *Introduzione agli smart contract (Introduction to smart contract)*. Available at SSRN 2729545.

Rizzo, G., Morando, F., and De Martin, J. C. (2009). Open Data: la piattaforma di dati aperti per il linked data. *International Journal on Semantic Web and Information Systems*, 5(3), 1–22.

Soares, S. (2013). *IBM InfoSphere: A Platform for Big Data Governance and Process Data Governance*. Boise, ID: MC Press. Online, LLC.

Tangi, L. (2015). Open government data: la situazione italiana studiata attraverso un modello di classificazione dei portali di pubblicazione dei dati. Quali azioni per una Pubblica Amministrazione più trasparente e vicina ai cittadini? *Tesi Politecnico di Milano*, December, Milano, Italy.

Ubaldi, B. (2013). *Open government data: Towards empirical analysis of open government data initiatives*. OECD Working Papers on Public Governance, No. 22, OECD Publishing, Paris, France.

Ubaldi, B. (2015). *Open data e la nuova frontiera della fornitura di servizi innovativi*. Prisma Economia-Società-Lavoro.

Vafopoulos, M. N., Meimaris, M., Papantoniou, A., Anagnostopoulos, I., Alexiou, G., Avraam, I., and Loumos, V. (2012). *Public spending: Interconnecting and visualizing Greek public expenditure following linked open data directives*. Available at SSRN 2064517.

Vassiliadis, P., Simitsis, A., and Skiadopoulos, S. (2002). *Conceptual modeling for ETL processes*. Proceedings of the 5th ACM international workshop on Data Warehousing and OLAP. ACM: 14–21.

Yu, L. (2011). *Developer's Guide to the Semantic Web*. Germany: Springer Berlin Heidelberg.

Web Sites

Last accessed 8 July 2016.
cloudmate.com/about
data.gov.uk/
openparliament.ca
www.cloudmate.com
www.data.com
www.freedomdefined.org/Definition
www.leandigitize.com
www.opendefinition.org
www.skillprofiles.eu

9 Big Data for procurement – the importance of correctly acquiring and using information in public procurement

Nikola Komšić

1 Introduction

Today's society is highly dependent on information. What if there were no individuals who were curious and willing to discover facts, information, and data with the goal of improving our society in general? It is hard to imagine modern medicine, technology, law, the economy, and other aspects of our society without trailblazers and creative thinkers.

At this moment, thanks to the power of the Internet and globalization, we have access to so much information that has expanded our knowledge. However, knowledge that cannot be translated into action is of little value. This is especially important when organizing and executing public procurement.

Public procurement is the process of acquiring goods, services and works for the government. The significance of public procurement is that it represents between 15 percent and 20 percent of a state's GDP, and it fosters technological development while improving a country's social standard. All of this can be achieved through: proper planning, which includes precise financial evaluation and the allocation of funds and other available resources; the proper execution of the procurement procedure; and, the proper control and oversight of the executed procurement project. In order to achieve these goals, those who are responsible for planning, organizing and executing the procurement procedure must have the right information and, most importantly, know how to use it. This information should include everything from legal, economic, political data to environmental and technological data, especially in complex procurement projects such as public-private partnerships.

This research will focus on analyzing the following hypothesis. The success of the procurement project depends on two factors. The first is how much the information which is acquired and which is being used (such as the needs of the contracting authority, the way of fulfilling the specific need and the final outcome of that selection) is based on the reality of the situation. The second factor is the effectiveness of the audit system created by the state, combined with sanctions which the state uses to prevent possible corruption and collusion. The first factor in this research will be named the analysis and execution process, while the second factor will be named the control system.

For the purpose of this research we will analyze current best practices around the world and compare them with Serbia in order to find the best proposal to further improve public procurement in Serbia.

2 The analysis and execution process

2.1 Reasons for establishing and maintaining transparency

Every society has needs that have to be fulfilled. Some of those needs are more or less similar to the needs of other societies, such as clean water, good infrastructure, a stable power system, etc. At the same time, there are certain needs that are specific to each country. If we look at the government as a service to the public, we can say that the government is responsible for successfully satisfying the needs of the public. In order to successfully fulfil the needs of the public, the government must have a clear idea of what kind of needs the public has. The government must acquire information which must be precise, accurate and reliable.

The reasons why information needs to have these specific qualities can be explained in the following example. Because of the world financial crisis which occurred in 2008, many countries today are trying to find the best way to overcome this burden by improving the business climate and creating more opportunities for investment. One popular and commonly used method today is that the governments of two or more countries negotiate and organize events during which each country presents the benefits related to why a foreign firm should invest in that country. Such presentations and brochures have data such as which sectors are developed, the level of corporate taxes, average income, education level, etc. The state guarantees the accuracy of all the information that is provided. This information is necessary because these days it is highly unlikely for a successful company to invest in a foreign country without previously analyzing the overall current situation regarding that particular country.

Another example can be that of new medication. Large pharmaceutical companies will not sell or distribute their new product to the public unless it has been proven that there will be no negative effects on the health of the patient, which is an important public interest.

As we can see, in order for one project to be successful a specific amount of certainty has to be obtained. The way that can be achieved is to acquire information which is based on reality and not fiction.

We mentioned previously that the state must have a clear idea of what kind of needs it has, and which needs have to be fulfilled, be it on the state or local level. If the state does not know what kind of needs it has or if the state has the wrong perception of which needs have to be fulfilled, then there is a high probability that more harm will be done than good. This is the reason behind one of the main principles in public procurement – the principle of transparency.

In the Oxford dictionary transparent refers to (of a material or article) allowing light to pass through so that the object behind it can be distinctly seen (Oxford Dictionaries, 2016).

Even though this term is easy to understand, this principle requires good organization and structure in order to be achieved and maintained. There are several layers which are important to mention when talking about transparency in public procurement.

We usually presume that local authorities can easily define their needs, since their structure and obligations are not as vast or complex as on the state level. This is true in most cases. However, there are cases where local authorities lack the capacities and skills to precisely define their needs. The following is an example of such cases. If we look at small municipalities in developing countries, then we can say that the situation over there is quite different. In some African countries, small municipalities do not have the necessary administration which can handle and organize projects that can improve the standard of living in that particular municipality. Economic and legal factors combined with historical, social and cultural factors have contributed to creating an environment in which it is difficult to achieve any significant developments.

One aspect of this problem is the lack of accurate statistical data regarding the population number, industry sectors, etc. An estimated number and exact number are two different things. Without a good established state statistical data center, and without proper research, it is hard to have a clear picture of what the situation is really like. Another addition to this problem is the lack of qualified and experienced personnel who are tasked with finding relevant information and know how to use it properly. Is it justified to build a new state of the art highway in a remote part of the country where, in the case of some African countries, only a very small number of tribes live and there is no industry whatsoever? This is an example of when the principle of transparency is difficult to establish.

Another important aspect regarding the principle of transparency is accountability. Transparency is essential for determining the responsibility of state authorities. In public procurement, transparency can indicate if the state is using the taxpayer's money for public interest or not and if the system in general is functioning according to the rule of law. Transparency is an essential tool for creating and maintaining a stable democratic society. The lack of transparency creates space for corrupt practices. According to the report prepared by the European Commission, it is estimated that corruption alone costs the EU economy €120 billion per year, just slightly less than the annual budget of the EU (COM (2014) 38, final), It is more than obvious that it is in the public interest to have a procurement system that is as transparent as possible. In the following part we will analyze how developed countries have established and continued to maintain the principle of transparency.

For our first example, we will analyze how the US has established and maintained the principle of transparency.

2.2 International practice

The US has the strongest economy in the world. This status has been achieved through constant adaptation and changing the rules with the goal of creating an environment in which the public and private sector can achieve prosperity. The precondition for this was that the system had to be transparent enough so that everyone could understand how the system functions while also having easy access to relevant information.

When it comes to public procurement, the government of the US has created a very transparent system. Thanks to e-government (electronic government) projects, several websites have been created through which interested parties can find available procurement opportunities, information on how much has been spent, and federal procurement reports (Federal Business Opportunities, 2016). It is also worth mentioning that under the Federal Acquisition Regulation, all prospective contractors must be registered in the System Award Management system, also known as SAM (Federal Acquisition Regulation, 2005). This system, besides being a central register for contractors, is also a database for excluded parties: contractors that have been blacklisted (General Services Administration, 2012). Additionally, the Online Representations and Certifications Application (ORCA) database is also part of SAM. In practice, it is an application that enables prospective government contractors to electronically submit required certifications and representations for responses to government solicitations for all federal contracts, instead of using hard copies for individual awards. The representations and certifications can be considered current for up to one year (United States Government Accountability Office, 2012, p. 27) These representations and certifications include certifications of socioeconomic status, affirmative action compliance, and compliance with veterans' employment reporting requirements (United States Government Accountability Office, 2012, p. 27).

In order to further improve the principle of transparency, in May 2014 the Digital Accountability and Transparency Act of 2014 (DATA Act) (P.L. 113–101) was adopted. The purpose of this act is to:

- track federal spending more effectively;
- establish government-wide data standards in order to have reliable, consistent and searchable government-wide spending data;
- improve reporting and increase the accountability of responsible agencies for the completeness and accuracy of the data submitted.

There is one other report that is quite interesting. The Federal Government Procurement Data Quality Summary for the 2009–2014 period is specific because it states the extent to which the published information has been accurate. As stated in the report, "since January 2009, federal agencies have been required to conduct annual data verification and validation of agency procurement data captured in the Federal Procurement Data System (FPDS)" (Federal Government Procurement Data Quality Summary Fiscal Year 2014, 2014, p. 1). The report states that, when it comes to completeness/timeliness, the six-year weighted average was 97.7 percent, which means that by the required deadline, agencies had captured 97.7 percent of contract actions over this time period (2014, p. 1). Also, the report states that, when it comes to accuracy, the six-year average for agency accuracy samples was 95.2 percent. This means that, for the prescribed data elements, a random sampling of records found that the data recorded in FPDS matched the data in the contract action record 94.97 percent of the time (Federal Government Procurement Data Quality Summary Fiscal Year 2014, 2014, p. 1).

It is worth mentioning that the report additionally states that certain actions were previously executed in order to make this concept function properly. Policies and procedures were updated in order to address the quality of acquisition data contained in multiple systems as well as contractor-provided data. The next step was organizing proper training, checklists and guidebooks, since training was identified as the most common challenge to procurement data quality.

Taking into consideration that the US is a country with a vast and complex structure, and the relevance of public procurement, we have seen how their system has been improved in order to make relevant information available and to verify the accuracy of the published information. We must not forget that good infrastructure for this specific purpose is composed of a functional administration and well-established information system with the latest technological solutions.

In the next example, we will analyze the system in the EU, since Serbia is in the process of becoming a Member State of the EU. The EU represents a specific economic and political union between 28 Member States. This unique organization has a specific legal structure which is composed of primary and secondary legislation. Primary legislation includes treaties, while secondary legislation includes regulations, directives and decisions. Public procurement in the EU is regulated by directives (2014/23/EU, 2014/24/EU, 2014/25/EU, 2009/81/EC, and 2007/66/EC). It is important to mention that a directive is a legislative act which defines a goal which has to be achieved by all Member States. However, Member States have the freedom to choose which law or laws they consider appropriate to adopt in order to achieve the goal or goals defined by the directive.

Transparency is one of the main principles which is emphasized throughout the directives regulating public procurement. This principle derives from the Treaty on the Functioning of the European Union (TFEU) and it means that the procurement process, from publishing prior information notices to contract award notices, has to be transparent. In other words, as stated in the 2014/24/EU Directive on public procurement,

> the award of public contracts by or on behalf of Member States' authorities has to comply with the principles of the Treaty on the Functioning of the European Union (TFEU), and in particular the free movement of goods, freedom of establishment and the freedom to provide services, as well as the principles deriving therefrom, such as equal treatment, non-discrimination, mutual recognition, proportionality and transparency.
>
> (recital 1)

It is important to clarify one particular issue regarding directives. There must be a distinct difference between when a Member State *should* conduct and when a Member State *must* conduct a certain action. It is important to know which part of the directive is a suggestion and which is an obligation for the Member State.

It is also important to mention that the directive should apply to procurements which have a threshold equal to or above the ones defined in the directive. If the threshold for a particular procurement is below the threshold defined in the directive, then national legislation will be applied. However, national legislation has to be in harmony with the basic principles of the directives.

Regarding publication, the directive states that if the value of a certain public tender is equal or above the threshold, the contracting authority must send the contract notice to the Publication Office of the European Union, which will publish the contract notice in the Tender Electronic Daily. The Tender Electronic Daily is an online version of the Supplement to the Official Journal of the European Union, which actually represents a public procurement database. This way, all potential bidders from all member states can participate and compete. For additional help, there is e-Certis, which is an information system that helps identify the different certificates and attestations frequently requested in procurement procedures across the 28 Member States, one Candidate Country (Turkey) and the three EEA countries (Iceland, Liechtenstein and Norway) (e-Certis, 2016).

We can see that the EU has created a transparent electronic system of public procurement. It is understandable that it is not organized in the same way as within the US since the EU has a specific legal and economic background.

We should mention one project which is an additional measure for improving the public procurement system in the EU. In the EU, there is an Internal Market Information System, also known as IMI. This system was established for the purpose of sharing information between national, regional and local authorities across the Member States. The information which is being shared at the moment is regarding professional qualifications, services, posting of workers, euro-cash transportation, train driving licenses, patient rights and complaints about national authorities (SOLVIT) (Internal Market Information System, 2016). Another area of information is planned to be added to this system. There is a pilot project regarding information requests in public procurement. Precisely, the idea behind this project is intended to help contracting authorities in the EU check information and documentation provided by procurement companies from other European countries (Internal Market Information System, 2016).

In the EU, there is also a list of companies that have been blacklisted. However, only six companies have been blacklisted for fraud, corruption, involvement in criminal organizations, money laundering-definitive judgment (Blacklisting the corrupt: why the EU debarment system does not work, 2014). The EU's anti-fraud office (OLAF) has made 54 recommendations for judicial follow-up to cases it investigated in 2012 alone, indicating that quite a number of actors are known to the EU to be potentially fraudulent or corrupt (Blacklisting the corrupt: why the EU debarment system does not work, 2014).

The US and the EU have established and maintained the principle of transparency in public procurement. In the following part we analyze what kind of measures Serbia has taken in order to improve transparency in public procurement.

2.3 Serbia – development of transparency

The situation in Serbia is better than it was before, but there is still room for improvement. Because of the turbulent history in the Balkans, Serbia was unfortunately involved in the wars in the former Yugoslavia, sanctioned by the United Nations and bombed by NATO. These events devastated the economy, the entire infrastructure, and led to the loss of human life.

After these challenging circumstances subsided and the political situation was altered, the task of restoring and rebuilding the state became reasonably demanding. A part of this task was to conduct an evaluation of the situation and, based upon that, to properly organize public procurement. As the next logical step for creating an organized system of public procurement, a Law on Public Procurement was adopted in 2002. This was the first law that regulated public procurement.

Because there is no available data regarding public procurement before the law was adopted in 2002, some estimate that Serbia was losing around 200 million dollars per year (Training program for public procurement, 2005, p. 2). In relation to transparency, the law passed in 2002 stated that public funds can be used only for the purposes stated in the public procurement contract. It was also obligatory to publish a public notice in the *Official Journal of the Republic of Serbia* and in one local newspaper. Further in the provisions of the law we can find an article which stated that the public procurement procedure can commence only if it was specified in the procurement plan and if financial resources for that procurement have been provided. However, later in the same article it states that, if public procurement has investment value, the contracting authority will prepare an investment program according to both a unique methodology for its creation and the development program (Law on Public Procurement 2002–2003, article 24).

In comparison to the current Law on Public Procurement, it is evident that a huge change has been made. First, a website called Public Procurement Portal has been established as a central database where interested parties can find all available public procurements from contracting authorities in Serbia. Second, Serbia has established a registry database where all potential bidders have to be registered, which makes the process of proving that the necessary requirements have been met much more efficient. Third, contracting authorities have to publish their public procurement plan and all other documents such as public notice, award notice, etc. on the Public Procurement Portal. In 2008, the second Law on Public Procurement was adopted and that was when the Public Procurement Portal was introduced.

Serbia is following in the footsteps of the US and the EU in improving the level of transparency through the implementation of e-government. This project began operating in 2010, and there has been an ongoing, continuous effort in improving e-government. However, there is one issue that must be addressed. The current law from 2013 has been composed in order to be in harmony with the EU public procurement directives. One new element which was introduced with the new law was the debarred list. After the amendments that were made in July 2015, the debarred list was removed. Before the amendments, contracting authorities were obliged to reject a bid from an economic operator who was on the debarred list. The reason behind this change was, at least as stated in the draft proposal for the amendments, the lockdown situation. This is where only one offer was given, and that one offer, as such, was by an economic operator who was blacklisted, which then caused a certain number of public procurements to not be successfully completed. After the amendments, the contracting authority now has the possibility to choose whether or not to accept a bid from an economic operator who has a negative reference. According to the Strategy of Development of Public Procurement in Serbia from 2014 until 2018, in 2017 and after thorough analyses, amendments to the Law on Public Procurement will be made in order to fully harmonize with the *acquis communautaire*. At the time of this writing, we did not know exactly what changes would be made to further improve the level of transparency.

2.4 The relevance of proper analysis

As previously mentioned, public procurement is an activity of acquiring goods, services and works for the government. In order to ensure successful public procurement, it is important to have precisely defined needs. To gain a clear idea of what kind of needs are to be met, it is relevant that the contracting authority, be it on the state or local level, has access to an effective and thorough analysis of the situation.

Analysis, or a detailed examination of the elements or structure, is a crucial activity which determines how the procurement procedure will be organized. We will now focus on an element of analysis which is not usually mentioned.

How do we know that the data and information from the analysis that was conducted by government officials represents reality? How do we know that the methodology that was used is in accordance with international standards?

Even though the government is required to have the necessary knowledge and to update it as much as possible, in some situations it is difficult to do so. One of the reasons for this is that the financial crisis of 2008 has forced a large number of countries to reduce the number of individuals employed in the administration of state. That has led to a reduction of staff who are specialized in analyzing certain sectors such as industry, economics, etc. Even in Serbia, at this moment in small municipalities, only a small number of employees are responsible for covering more than one area relevant to that municipality. This is because the state's administrative departments have had to be reduced in order to be more financially efficient. In addition, the reduction of public funds has caused local municipalities to have more difficulty financing further education and specialized training for their employees.

Specialized training and the further expansion of knowledge are especially important when it comes to public procurement. Technology is developing so fast that not following and implementing the newest trends will cost us more than we can imagine. Constant improvements in technology have enabled the natural and social science sectors to conduct more research and gather new knowledge which is beneficial to society. This has consequently allowed the US, Japan, South Korea, the UK and other countries to have a strong developed economy and a high standard of living. We therefore have the right to question if the methodology that is being used by government officials in developing countries is up-to-date with international trends.

It is very difficult for an individual to be an expert in every possible field. That is especially true for civil servants employed within administrative departments of government in developing countries. They have to be qualified for only one or eventually two areas, and since they have to take care of matters relevant to the state, there is practically no time left to gain new knowledge.

However, developed countries have found a way to solve this issue. The government has involved both the private sector and academics when it comes to participation in projects of public interest. Cooperation with the private sector is relevant since it is the driving force of the economy, but also the initiator of innovation. It is important for government officials to foster good communication with the private sector, especially in relation to exchanging information which is relevant for further improvements. The best example of good cooperation between the government and the private sector is introducing a vocational education and training system, also known as the dual education system. This educational system is well established in Germany and Austria. Its main benefit is that it enables students to acquire theoretical knowledge and, most importantly, the necessary practical knowledge, which will improve their chances of finding employment.

The reason for creating this type of educational system was that companies noticed that students did not have the necessary experience required for gaining employment in the private sector after graduation. This situation forced companies to spend more money on additional education and they were therefore spending a lot time on finding suitable employees.

The private sector has initiated this program through various chambers of commerce and it has been a success in Germany and Austria for more than 20 years. With help from the Austrian Chamber of Commerce, Serbia is currently analyzing how to properly implement the dual education system while promoting its benefits.

On the other side, academic society is also a relevant stakeholder group. The main goal of academic society is to examine, acquire and transfer new information regarding the world we live in so that all members of society can enjoy better lives. Since they have to devote all of their time to research, and finding new methods to improve the quality information they acquire, it is suitable to state that the opinion of academic society is relevant.

Academic society has supported different forms of collaboration with government, but also with the private sector, in different fields such as military research, research for the pharmaceutical industry, etc. However, when it comes to public procurement, at the beginning there was no clear collaboration and cooperation with the private sector and academic society. For a long period of time, public procurement was considered a legal or economic activity, one which is fairly simple and does not require special preparation.

Unfortunately, this type of policy has been proven to be wrong. This view was abandoned due to the obstacles that occurred during procurement procedures. One of the most well known examples was the process of buying simple administrative equipment: pens. In every country, even in Serbia, it was discovered that the regular pen was two to three times more expensive than on the market when it was bought by different contracting authorities. In the past, this has caused the unjustified waste of public funds, and these findings were part of the reasons why centralized procurement was established.

Public procurement is an interdisciplinary activity which requires simultaneous input of knowledge from the legal, economic and technical sciences. This approach is, without exception, important for public-private partnerships, the complex form of public procurement.

The following example will demonstrate why it is important to carefully assess the situation. The M1 highway in Hungary was the first public-private partnership project in Central Europe. The main characteristic of public-private partnership is the proper division of risks between the public and private partner. The M1 highway seemed well structured and there were no indicators that there would be any problems. However, after only three years, the M1 project faced large difficulties. First, the amount of traffic was much lower than predicted by the feasibility study. This has consequently caused lower income for the private partner, which has led to the financial instability of the project. The amount of traffic was lower than expected because the private partner was allowed to independently determine the toll tariff, and the private partner was also responsible for the majority of the risks. Because of the high toll tariffs, the passengers used alternative roads instead. It seemed that the project was about to be terminated; however, because the European Bank for Reconstruction and Development was one of the stakeholders, the project was altered and luckily it continued to function properly.

There are more examples which confirm that it is important to carefully assess if the information which is available is correct and applicable in reality. If we want, for example, a wastewater treatment facility, the government has to consult both academic society and the private sector in carefully defining what type of technology must be used in order to refrain from polluting the environment. When the government plans to complete a project in different publicly relevant fields, the results of research conducted by academic society and by the private sector have to be used and carefully assessed. However, it is important to make sure that those findings are empirically proven. We have witnessed the scandal that occurred due to false claims by Volkswagen that their engines emit less CO2 than they actually do. Another example is that throughout history, it was shown that certain types of medical operations were proven to do more harm than good. It is in the public interest for findings to be verified and confirmed in order for any types of damages to be avoided.

Also, the government must deliver certain information to both academic society and to the private sector which will be beneficial in further improving research and increasing the quality of the information acquired. For these reasons, it is important that communication between parties is well established and transparent. However, in cases of national security and defence, it is justified for information that is shared between parties to be withheld from disclosure to the public for a certain period of time.

We can conclude that, in modern times, people understand that in order to successfully plan public procurement it is important to have accurate, precise, and proven information. For example, constructing a 20-km highway is not the same as constructing one that is 200 km. Procuring 200 laptops for a state institution cannot be the same as constructing a nuclear power plant. It is important that government representatives and the contracting authority have well-defined needs. In addition to that, thorough market research has to be done in order for public procurement to be properly planned. The need that has to be satisfied will determine the type of financial structure that is to be made, the type of contract to be prepared and executed and, if necessary, the type of technology to be utilized.

If the contracting authority has difficulties in defining the need, then it should cooperate with the private sector and also with academic society. In order to increase the quality of the information that is being acquired, governments must provide support to both academic society and the private sector so all can continuously improve. Practically, investment in better education and university research programs are some of the reasons why developed countries have an advantage when it comes to knowledge. Also, the provision of support to companies that are constantly making innovations is one of the reasons why developed countries have strong economies.

In Serbia cooperation and collaboration has not been on the same level as in developed countries. However, in the last couple of years the current government is trying to change this. For example, the Chamber of Commerce and Industry of Serbia, together with the Ministry of Education, Science and Technological Development, the Novi Sad Faculty of Technical Science, with support from other stakeholders, is organizing a competition for the best innovation (The best technological innovation, 2016). The winners of this competition receive a monetary prize as well as support in promoting their innovation in Serbia and abroad. It is also important to mention that there is now a program which promotes and supports collaboration between research and development organizations registered in Serbia and the private sector (The innovation fund, 2016). The goal of this program is to promote projects which are innovative but also commercially applicable. The government is now cooperating with more state institutions in completing publicly relevant projects, such as the Prokop train station, which was completed with help from the Transportation Institute.

Depending on the information that is being used by the contracting authority, and also on the type of public procurement procedure, the outcome can be either successful or harmful. Having explained why analysis is important, we will now briefly recall why it is also important to choose the right procurement procedure.

2.5 The execution of procurement procedures

In the previous part, we pointed out why it is important to precisely define the need that has to be met. The next logical steps include choosing the award criterion and what type of procurement procedure will be used.

If the need is fairly simple and precise then, in most cases, open or restricted procedure will be used. On the other hand, if the need is more complex, then it is more likely that negotiated procedure or competitive dialogue will be used.

There are two types of award criterion that are used in the procurement process: the lowest price and the most economically advantageous tender, also known as MEAT. Analyzing what type of procedure and which award criterion is commonly used gives us insight into whether the public procurement system is structured to foster improvements or not.

Using the lowest price as award criterion does not guarantee that the contracting authority will acquire the best possible goods, services and works. In practice, it is common that the contracting authority will, in the end, pay a lot more for additional costs that were not foreseen at the beginning. The lowest price as award criterion is not adequate for complex projects. In order to acquire the best possible quality, it is necessary to use the most economically advantageous tender. In other words, it is necessary to conduct a total life cycle cost analysis which will take into account other important indicators, depending on the project, such as time of delivery, type of technology, experience, whether it is environmentally friendly, etc.

In the EU, MEAT as award criterion is used in 78 percent of cases while the lowest price as award criterion is used in only 22 percent (Public Procurement Office of Serbia, 2015). In Serbia, in 2015 MEAT was used in 19 percent of cases, while the lowest price was used in 81 percent (Public Procurement Office of Serbia, 2015). It is obvious that there is a huge difference when comparing which criterion is dominant. However, we must consider that the Law on Public Procurement from 2013 was the first law in Serbia that was composed in order to achieve harmonization with EU directives regarding public procurement. It will take time to achieve the EU level, but it is important to note that progress is being steadily made.

In the Republic of Croatia, which became a Member State of the EU in 2013, a very different situation exists with regards to public procurement. According to the report for 2015, the lowest price as award criterion was used in Croatia for more than 97 percent of cases (Portal of Public Procurement Croatia, 2015).

As for the successful completion of procurement procedures, in Serbia the completion rate was 89 percent for 2015, while 11 percent were suspended. In the

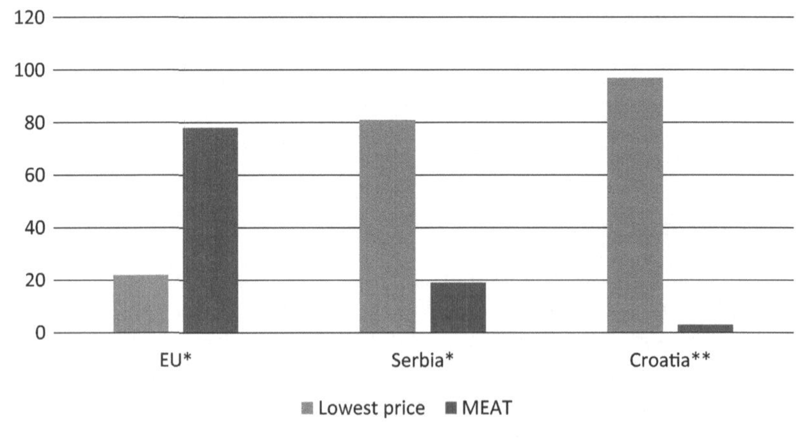

Figure 9.1 Most used award criterion

Source: *Public Procurement Office of Serbia ** Public Procurement Portal Croatia

report for the first half of 2015, it was stated that a contract is considered executed when the contracting authority has made the payment (Public Procurement Office of Serbia, 2015). Unfortunately, the only way to check if the economic operator has fulfilled contractual obligations is to review reports prepared by the state auditor for each contracting authority.

At first glance, it can be said that the majority of public procurement procedures are successfully executed and completed. However, the process cannot be complete without a proper control mechanism. In the next part we will analyze the relevance of supervision and the implementation of an audit system while trying to find new pathways to improvement.

3 The control system

3.1 The relevance of an effective control system

The funds that are allocated for public procurement represent a significant part of state and local budget. Without a proper control system, the probability of the procurement procedure being abused increases dramatically.

Corruption and collusion are the two largest problems associated with public procurement. The common element for these two activities is the intention, of an individual of a group, to achieve their personal goals or interests by avoiding the rules, and utilizing fraudulent and/or other illegal activities. The consequence of these activities in public procurement is that the government is either going to pay more than it should, or in the worst scenario the government is going to acquire goods, services or works which could be harmful to the public. One of the most well-known examples of corrupt practices was the Siemens case in Russia. The World Bank had investigated the corrupt practices of a Siemens subsidiary participating in a project in Russia. Siemens AG settled with the World Bank in 2009 and the settlement included Siemens having to pay 100 million dollars to support anti-corruption work, a four-year debarment for the Siemens Russian subsidiary and a voluntary two-year shut-out from bidding on Bank business for Siemens AG and all of its consolidated subsidiaries and affiliates (World Bank, 2009).

In some problematic cases, there is no corruption or collusion, such as when the economic operator simply did not fulfil obligations that are defined by the contract. For example, when state hospitals procure medical equipment, there have been cases where the economic operator delivered medical equipment such as medical gloves which were defective. These situations have caused more damage, especially in life or death patient situations. In Serbia, for example, a contracting authority had procured an IT system, but the economic operator did not install the IT system.

The government has an obligation to ensure that all measures have been taken to eliminate or at least reduce the possibility of failure in public procurement to the lowest possible level. In other words, it is important to establish an effective control system. In the following part, we will review different systems and compare them to the system in Serbia.

3.2 Control system comparison

One of the most important elements in the public procurement system is the control system. This system is relevant, as we've mentioned before, for the reduction of the chances of failure or abuse of the procurement procedure. Even though there are legal differences among countries, it is considered a good practice to have well-established internal controls, but more important to have an effective complaint/review policy and an audit policy. It is relevant to have a mechanism which allows both parties participating in the procurement process, and also interested parties, to question the fairness of the procurement process. For the purpose of this chapter, will only focus on the complaint and audit mechanism. For our first example, we will review the situation in the US.

In US, public procurement is audited by the Government Accountability Office, or also known as GAO. The GAO was established in 1921 as an independent auditor of government agencies and activities (Kaiser, 2008). Since then it has grown into one of the most important agencies which gives relevant support to Congress. This institution is authorized to hear bid protests that challenge government contract awards. However, it is important to mention that it is not the only office authorized to hear bid protests involving federal acquisitions. Other than the GAO, the procuring agency and the US Court of Federal Claims can also hear bid protests (Manuel and Schwartz, 2016, p. 1). In the CRS Report for Congress it is stated that the GAO hears more protests than the Court of Federal Claims, the only other forum for which data is readily available (Manuel and Schwartz, 2016, p. 1).

The bid protest procedure at the GAO can be considered efficient. The GAO is obliged to issue a final decision regarding a bid protest within 65 to 100 days. Another element which contributes to its efficiency is that interested parties can file protests on their own behalf, without legal representation, by providing that "no formal briefs or other technical forms of pleading or motion are required" (Manuel and Schwartz, 2016, p. 6). In order for GAO to consider a protest, a protester need only:

- identify the contracting agency and the solicitation or contract number;
- set forth a detailed statement of the legal and factual grounds of protest, including copies of relevant documents;
- establish that the protester is an interested party making a timely protest; and
- state the relief requested (e.g. termination or re-competition of a contract).

Also, hearings at the GAO are not usually held in person, which represents reduction in cost for parties participating in the bid protest. It is important to state that when a bid protest is filed to the GAO, the automatic stay of contract award is activated. The contracting authority cannot award the contract until the GAO has issued its decision. However, there are exceptions that allow the contracting authority to override the automatic stay. Those exceptions (Manuel and Schwartz, 2016, pp. 6–7) are:

- "urgent and compelling circumstances which significantly affect interests of the United States will not permit waiting for the decision of the Comptroller General"; or
- "performance of the contract is in the best interests of the United States."

When the GAO receives the bid protest, it will review to see if any violations occurred or not. If the GAO determines that the claims in the bid protests are justified and that there was a violation of federal law, it will issue a recommendation to the contracting authority. However, it is important to mention that the GAO recommendations are not legally binding. The reason for this is because the GAO is a legislative branch agency and cannot constitutionally compel executive branch agencies to implement its recommendations because of the separation of powers doctrine (Manuel and Schwartz, 2016, p. 16). In practice, contracting authorities in general do comply with the GAO recommendations. If the contracting authority does not comply with the GAO recommendations it has to notify the GAO, which will notify Congress. It is important to mention that Congress has the ability to exercise oversight or to take legislative action compelling agency compliance, if it decides to do so (Manuel and Schwartz, 2016, p. 18). From 2001 to 2015 there were only eight cases where the contracting authority did not comply with GAO recommendations (see Figure 9.2) (Manuel and Schwartz, 2016, p. 18).

As we can see, GAO recommendations have a strong reputation even though they are not legally binding. That can be explained by the fact that the GAO has support from Congress, and if the contracting authority does not implement GAO recommendations, there is a high probability that Congress will open an investigation regarding that contracting authority.

On the other hand, in the EU, the Member States have an obligation to establish a control/audit body regarding public procurement. However, since the EU has a specific legal and economic structure, the European Court of Auditors was established to improve EU financial management (European Court of Auditors, 2016). It is an independent external auditor which:

- audits EU revenue and expenditures;
- verifies any person or organization handling EU funds;

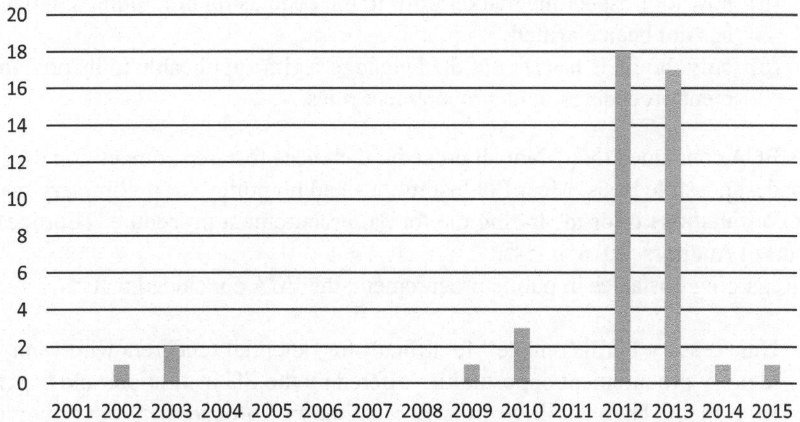

Figure 9.2 GAO bid recommendations – not fully adopted

Source: Congressional Research Service using data from GAO

- writes up findings and recommendations in audit reports for the European Commission and national governments;
- reports suspected fraud, corruption or other illegal activity to the European Anti-Fraud Office (OLAF);
- produces an annual report for the European Parliament and Council of the EU, which the Parliament examines before deciding whether to approve the Commission's handling of the EU budget; and,
- gives its expert opinion to EU policy-makers on how EU finances can be better managed and made more accountable to citizens.

The European Court of Auditors has just recently released a special report regarding public procurement by EU institutions. In this special report, it was concluded that EU institutions can do more to facilitate access to their public procurement (European Court of Auditors, 2016, p. 53). Next, it concluded that most EU institutions do not systematically measure the level of participation in their procurement procedures (European Court of Auditors, 2016, p. 20) and that: "Simply counting the number of offers received is not enough to reliably monitor the level of participation" (European Court of Auditors, 2016, p. 53).

It also concluded (European Court of Auditors, 2016, p. 54):

> When revising their procurement rules in 2015, EU institutions did not facilitate access to their public procurement by simplifying rules and clarifying grey areas to the fullest extent possible (see paragraphs 26 to 35):
>
> (a) the EU Financial Regulation and its rules of application have not been consolidated into a single document and remain an unnecessarily complex piece of legislation;
> (b) deviations from the new procurement directive are not always clearly indicated or explained;
> (c) the participation of small and medium-sized enterprises is not explicitly encouraged;
> (d) how to prospect the market prior to the conclusion of building contracts has not been clarified;
> (e) only the ECB has set out the language regime applicable to its procurement procedures in its procurement rules.

The ECA concluded that: "Not all procedural choices fostered competition on the broadest possible basis. Most EU institutions had no policy for preliminary market consultations prior to starting the formal procurement procedure" (European Court of Auditors, 2016, p. 54).

Regarding obstacles in public procurement, the ECA concluded that:

> Unnecessary hurdles make life difficult for potential tenderers who want to identify procurement opportunities offered by the EU institutions and benefit from them. The visibility of the EU institutions' procurement opportunities on the internet is poor. The information available is patchy and spread over many different websites. The search function of TED (Tenders Electronic

> Daily) did not always produce satisfactory results. Tools which allow tenders to be submitted electronically have not yet been rolled out in a comprehensive and harmonized manner.
>
> (European Court of Auditors, 2016, p. 55)

Interestingly, the ECA concluded that it is difficult for economic operators who believe that they have been unfairly treated to obtain a rapid review of their complaints and receive compensation for damages (European Court of Auditors, 2016, p. 56).

As for transparency, the ECA concluded:

> Information on the outcome of the EU institutions' procurement activities is not accessible in a way that allows effective monitoring by the discharge authority and the wider public in order to increase transparency and build up confidence. Such information is only provided piecemeal and most of the time not in a harmonized manner.
>
> (European Court of Auditors, 2016, p. 56)

The final conclusion was that:

> As the procurement activities of the EU institutions are largely decentralized, cooperation amongst them can bring improvements thanks to mutual learning and cross-fertilization. We noted considerable cooperation and exchange of experience between the different institutions and, in the case of the bigger institutions, between the different procurement units. However peer reviews, which are the most advanced tool for a structured exchange of best practices, were not used.
>
> (European Court of Auditors, 2016b, p. 57)

It is important to mention that the ECA gives expert opinion and writes annual reports, and it is up to EU policy makers to decide whether or not to accept recommendations from the ECA.

In Serbia, the control/dispute mechanism is organized in such a manner that if an economic operator considers that the procurement procedure, in which it is participating, is not being lawfully conducted, it can file a request for protection of rights to the Republic's Commission for the Protection of Rights in Public Procurement Procedures.

In the Law on Public Procurement from 2013, there was a legal gap which has created a lot of problems in practice. If a request for protection of rights was filed, automatic suspension would be activated and the procurement procedure could not continue until the Republic's Commission had reached a decision regarding the request for protection of rights. In addition to that, the definition of "interested party" who can also file a complaint was not precise, resulting in anyone being able to file a request for the protection of their rights. This consequently led to certain individuals filing requests for the protection of rights to purposely halt the procurement procedure and the Republic's Commission could not reach a decision in the lawfully defined time frame, since it had too many complaints to review (see Figure 9.3).

After amendments were made to the Law on Public Procurement in 2015, this legal gap was eliminated. Now there is a precise legal definition as to who is considered an interested party and what the conditions are for filing a request, and the automatic suspension of the procurement procedure has been removed. The contracting authority can continue with the procurement procedure even if a request for the protection of rights is filed. However, the contracting authority cannot award the contract until the Republic's Commission has reached its decision. It is important to mention that the economic operator has the right to file a complaint to the Administrative Court if it is not satisfied with the decision of the Republic's Commission.

In order to ensure that the procurement procedure has been executed according to the law, a special measure of supervision has been added to the Law on Public Procurement in 2013, and it is called a "civil supervisor". The Public Procurement Office of Serbia will appoint a civil supervisor if the estimated value of the procurement procedure is more than RSD 1 billion (€8 million). The person who is appointed as a civil supervisor will supervise the procedure with the authorization to have permanent insight into the procedure, documents and communication between contracting authority and interested parties (i.e. the bidders). The civil supervisor is obligated to file a report after the contract has been concluded or if the procurement procedure has been cancelled.

It also important to mention that, in Serbia, audits of the procurement procedure are executed by the State Audit Institution. If the State Audit Institution discovers that there were irregularities in the public procurement procedure, the responsible contracting authority has an obligation to deliver the report on eliminating irregularities to the State Audit. If the State Audit concludes that the contracting authority did not execute necessary measures to eliminate the irregularities, it will contact either the responsible institution or the National Assembly, depending on

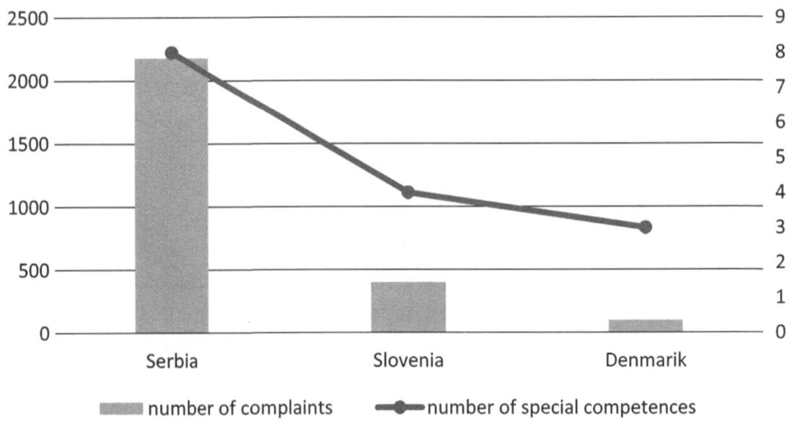

Figure 9.3 Filled complaints in 2014

Source: Republic Commission for the Protection of Rights in Public Procurement Procedures

the significance of the violation, and either suggest that the responsible individual be dismissed or that the public be informed.

One issue has to be mentioned regarding the State Audit reports on public procurement: there is no unified public procurement report in which all contracting authorities are mentioned. There are only audit reports for each contracting authority in which there is a section on public procurement.

After analyzing these several different systems we can say that there is no perfect control mechanism. As we can see, in the US, the EU and Serbia, the appointed institution will report to the highest authorities if they find that procurement procedures did not occur according to relevant laws. However, each system has its own procedure regarding the elimination or at least the maintenance of a low level of abuse throughout the procurement procedure. In order to have a fully functional control mechanism it is necessary to have the necessary financial and technical support, and also it is important to have the right amount of qualified staff. In addition, it is necessary that the relevant information is shared among the relevant institutions so that control/audit can be at its finest. Each country, according to the resources at its disposal, must devise a system which will be fully functional and efficient.

As for the situation in Serbia, a lot of improvements have been made. However, it is important to carefully choose what kind of changes will be made in order to improve the overall system of oversight. There is no reason to propose something that cannot be successfully implemented in reality. For now, it would be useful if there existed one central procurement procedure report within which all contracting authorities are to be included. Later, when considered appropriate, it would be useful to improve the communication between relevant state institutions, and to make sure that there are no delays in reviewing possible abuse that occurs throughout public procurement, or at least to make the review process reasonably faster.

4 Conclusion

Information is the most important asset in modern times. However, not all information can be applicable in every situation; similarly, not all information has the same value in every situation. It is essential to carefully asses which information will be used and when.

Public procurement is an activity which bases its success on the information which has been acquired. In order for the government to properly organize public procurement, it is necessary to have accurate, precise and up-to-date information. That is why government must function in a collaborative and cooperative manner while sharing information with both academic society and the private sector. These two parties are important partners not only when it comes to the acquisition of new information, but also throughout the process of improving the public procurement system.

Each country must continuously increase its support to both academic society and the private sector and thereby facilitate the discovery of new information and the initiation of innovations which are beneficial for everyone. In relation to that, it is important to cooperate in creating a functional system of control and oversight which will make sure that the information that is being used throughout the public procurement process is neither being abused nor is it false. It is essential to ensure that public funds and public interest are not unfairly misappropriated and taken advantage of, respectively.

It is not a problem to pass a law or any other legal act which will state and define the measures which have to be implemented in order to achieve a goal. What is more important is to create measures which can be applied in reality and lead to measurable results. That is why it is important to carefully analyze every aspect and carefully choose how to implement it in reality.

References

The best technological innovation (2016). Available at http://inovacija.org/ [accessed 10 July 2016].

DG Internal Market and Service, e-Certis (2016). Available at http://ec.europa.eu/markt/ecertis/login.do [accessed 14 June 2016].

Digital Accountability and Transparency Act of 2014 (DATA Act) (2014). (P.L. 113-101). Available at www.gpo.gov/fdsys/pkg/PLAW-113publ101/pdf/PLAW-113publ101.pdf.

Directive 2014/24/EU of the European Parliament and of the Council of 26 February 2014 on public procurement and repealing Directive 2004/18/EC, 2014 O. J. L 94/65.

EU Commission (2014). Report from the Commission to the Council and the European Parliament, EU Anti-Corruption Report, COM(2014) 38 final. Available at http://ec.europa.eu/dgs/home-affairs/e-library/documents/policies/organized-crime-and-human-trafficking/corruption/docs/acr_2014_en.pdf [accessed 10 June 2016].

The EU Single Market, Internal Market Information System (2016). Available at http://ec.europa.eu/internal_market/imi-net/about/index_en.htm [accessed 19 June 2016].

European Court of Auditors (ECA) (2016a). *Overview*. Available at http://europa.eu/about-eu/institutions-bodies/court-auditors/index_en.htm [accessed 18 June 2016]

European Court of Auditors (ECA) (2016b). *Special report – the EU institutions can do more to facilitate access to their public procurement*. Available at www.eca.europa.eu/Lists/ECADocuments/SR16_17/SR_PROCUREMENT_EN.pdf

Federal Acquisition Regulation (FAR) (2005). *4.11. System for award management, 4.1102 Policy*. Available at www.acquisition.gov/?q=browsefar

Federal business opportunities, procurement award data, federal procurement report. Available at www.fedbizopps.gov, www.usaspending.gov, www.fpds.gov [accessed 31 May 2016].

General Services Administration (2012). *Public user – identifying excluded entities system for award management*. Available at www.sam.gov/sam/transcript/Public_-_Identifying_Excluded_Entities.pdf.

The Innovation Fund (2016). *The collaborative grant scheme program*. Available at www.innovationfund.rs/program-cgs/

Kaiser, F. (2008). CRS Report for Congress, GAO: Government Accountability Office and General Accounting Office, Order Code RL30349, 4. Available at www.fas.org/sgp/crs/misc/RL30349.pdf

Law on Public Procurement (Official Gazette of RS, number. 39 from 5. VII 2002, 43 from 22. IV 2003), article 24, Belgrade.

Manuel, K., and Schwartz, M. (2016). *CRS report for congress, GAO bid protests: An overview of time frames and procedures*. Available at www.fas.org/sgp/crs/misc/R40228.pdf

Oxford Dictionaries (2016). *Transparent*. Available at www.oxforddictionaries.com/definition/english/transparent [accessed 17 May 2016].

Public Procurement Office of Serbia (2015a). *Report for 2015*. Available at www.ujn.gov.rs/ci/izvestaji/izvestaji_ujn

Public Procurement Office of Serbia (2015b). *Report for the first half of 2015*. Available at www.ujn.gov.rs/ci/izvestaji/izvestaji_ujn

Public Procurement Portal Croatia (2015). *Report for 2015*. Available at www.javnanabava.hr/userdocsimages/Statisticko_izvjesce_JN-2015.pdf.

Transparency International (2014). *Blacklisting the corrupt: Why the EU debarment system does not work*. Available at www.transparency.org/news/feature/blacklisting_the_corrupt_why_the_eu_debarment_system_does_not_work [accessed 19 June 2016]

Transparency Serbia (2005). *Training program for public procurement*. Work material. Available at www.transparentnost.org.rs/stari/javne_nabavke/materijal/Radna%20za%20konferenciju%20-%20materijal%20sa%20seminara%20srp.doc [accessed 21 May 2016]

United States Government Accountability Office (2012). *Report to congressional committees, federal contracting, effort to consolidate government wide acquisition data systems should be reassessed*. Available at www.gao.gov/assets/590/589370.pdf

USA spending, federal government procurement data quality summary fiscal year 2014 for agency data in the federal procurement data system (2014). Available at www.usaspending.gov/about/Documents/Federal%20Government%20Procurement%20Data%20Quality%20Summary%202009%20-%202014.pdf World Bank (2009). *News, Siemens to pay $100 million to fight fraud and corruption as part of World Bank group settlement*. Available at www.worldbank.org/en/news/press-release/2009/07/02/siemens-pay-million-fight-fraud-corruption-part-world-bank-group-settlement

Part 4

Renegotiation in public procurement

10 Colloquium

Francesco Decarolis and Martin Trybus

1 Francesco Decarolis – renegotiations or modifications of public (procurement) contracts: the economic view and some empirical evidence

A key tenant of the economics view about the procurement of contracts regards the key role played by the job complexity (Bajari and Tadelis, 2001). For contracts involving easily specified jobs, such as the delivery of a specific type of standardized product or the execution of a routine work (say, paving a road), it is best for the auctioneer to write a detailed contract and to auction it off as a fixed price contract through competitive procedures, such as first price auctions. In this case, renegotiations should be limited to exceptional circumstances. For contracts involving highly complex jobs instead, specifying a very complete contract would likely be very costly and could potentially still fail to anticipate all possible contingencies. In this case, it is thus best to leave some margins for ex post adaptations by awarding the contract as a cost-plus contract although with more flexible procedures, such as negotiations or scoring rule (i.e. multiple criteria) auctions. In this case, renegotiations (broadly defined as any change relative to the original contract) are a natural part of the procurement process and they should only be regulated to limit abuses (for instance, due to corruption risks).

In both situations, the economists' focus is on asymmetric information and strategic behavior. The main idea is that for simpler jobs the main information asymmetry is between the procurer, who does not know the cost of performing the contract, and the potential contractors, who are able to correctly foresee their costs. Competitive procedures in this case serve to limit the rents that contractors would earn from their private information. For more complex jobs, instead, not only the auctioneer but also firms are not fully aware of the cost of a contract when they bid. Leaving firms to bid competitively on an incomplete contract can generate perverse effects: price competition may result in greater risk of renegotiation and, possibly, even in a complete default on the contract, thus generating possibly very high transaction costs and costs to re-award the contract.

Therefore, the assessment of renegotiations depends on whether they emerge as an intrinsic element of a complex contract that had been properly specified in terms of incentives (i.e. cost-plus) and awarding methods (i.e. flexible procedures) or as a perverse outcome resulting from incorrectly chosen contract types and awarding procedures. For instance, in a seminal paper, Spulber (1990) showed that, when firms are heterogeneous in their cost of misperforming on the contract (for instance due to limited liability or to different reputation costs) and there is production cost uncertainty at the time of bidding, the enterprises with lower costs for breach of contract are at an advantage, as they can "bet" that the execution of works will not be costly. This allows them to offer particularly low prices at the time of the auction. Afterwards, if completion of the works proves to be very costly, these enterprises will prefer to withdraw and pay breach of contract costs rather than carry the project through. Therefore, renegotiations can result from the procurer trying ex post to avoid a full default by the contractor.

This is an instance of how renegotiations can emerge from the awarding procedures adopted. The only factor taken into account in first price auctions is price: this one-dimensionality prevents the mechanism from optimally selecting the enterprise with the lowest production costs while simultaneously rejecting those with the highest risk of non-completion. Instead, the incentives inherent in this format imply that the least reliable enterprises are those with the best chance of winning the award. This is a problem of adverse selection, as types that are ex ante more risky are more likely to win.[1]

A few empirical studies have confirmed the tight link between awarding procedures and the extent of contract renegotiations. Cameron (2000) compares the performance of 93 long-term power purchase contracts awarded using either first price auctions or negotiations. She finds that the use of first price auctions increases the probability of a breach of contract by 50 percent. Decarolis (2014) uses data on Italian public procurement of roadwork contracts to study the impact of the reforms prompted in Italy by 2004 EU Procurement Directives to restrict the use of automatic elimination of abnormally low tenders in favor of first price auctions. The switch to first price auctions is associated with an increase in the winning discount (about 11 percent of the reserve price) but also a worsening of performance: an increase of the delay in the completion of the work ranging between 20 and 30 percent of the contractual duration and an increase of the total price paid to the contractor ranging between 5 and 7 percent of the reserve price.[2]

Decarolis (2014) also finds that if the switch to first price auctions is accompanied by an increased discretionary screening of the bids submitted, then the increase of the winning discount is lower (about 7 percent of the reserve price), but there is no worsening of performance. This points out that having a broad view of the procurement rules and how they interact is key to understand renegotiations. Thus, renegotiations will respond not only to awarding procedures and contract types, but also to the rules on ex ante or ex post assessment by the adjudicating authority of bids' reliability. Similarly, they will also respond to the presence of third party guarantees.[3]

While the literature that looks at renegotiations from an empirical perspective is still small, a renewed interest has been spurred by the growing availability of data. Using US data on public work contracts, two recent works have analyzed both time renegotiations, Lewis and Bajari (2011), and price renegotiations, Bajari, Houghton and Tadelis (2014), confirming how both types of renegotiations can be influenced by the design of awarding procedures and contract types.

However, Decarolis and Palumbo (2015) by using a comprehensive dataset of all Italian works awarded between 2000 and 2007 have shown that time and cost renegotiations – while both systematic – are nearly uncorrelated and that many factors often suggested to explain renegotiations have opposite effects on price and time renegotiations. Further empirical research on renegotiations is thus clearly needed.

2 Martin Trybus – renegotiations or modifications of public (procurement) contracts: an EU law perspective

Contracting entities require a procurement law that allows them to achieve the objective of value for money. This normally requires a framework facilitating competition between economic operators bidding for public contracts. Competition in turn requires transparency so that contract opportunities are widely known and procurement conditions understood and sufficiently trusted to create interest. For the EU Internal Market this is connected to the opening of national procurement markets (non-discrimination on grounds of nationality) facilitating bids across borders, from other Member States.

The part of the procurement cycle regulated by EU law begins after the 'budgetary phase', when the decision on what to buy was made. It ends after the conclusion of the contract, before the 'contract management phase'. Within this procurement phase in the strict sense competition and transparency are paramount. However, this requires the foreseeability of all or most of the conditions of that contract: price, size, timeframe, context, etc., from the budget phase all through the procurement phase, and most importantly the contract management phase, which can last years or even decades.

A multitude of conditions can change during the lifetime of a contract, making the contract no longer desirable for either partner and especially the contracting authority or utility. This creates a dilemma for public procurement law and its objectives. The originally awarded contract is no longer needed to satisfy the requirements of the public authority or utility, whereas a different contract that would satisfy these requirements is needed but not in place. A possible action is to terminate the existing contract and start with the procurement of a new one. However, both the termination of the old contract and a re-tender will have disadvantages in the form of costs, time, and the continuity of the public service the contract serves. Thus, an attractive solution might be to renegotiate the originally awarded contract with the existing contract partner and thus to alter the existing arrangements to meet the changed contract requirements. This creates a problem for public procurement law since the original contract would normally have been awarded to the economically most advantageous bid on the basis of the original conditions.

Based on the new conditions, an entirely different economic operator might be successful, creating concerns about competition, transparency and non-discrimination (Arrowsmith, 2014) and ultimately value for money. EU procurement law could be undermined (Comba, 2014). Thus in EU procurement law renegotiation has to be approached from a restrictive perspective (Arrowsmith,

2014). A balance needs to be struck between the outlined competing interests and that is what lies at the heart of the EU law perspective of contract renegotiation or modification. This contribution will focus on EU procurement law as an example legal framework, looking first at the leading case on the issue, then the resulting legislation. The term 're-negotiation' is understood as a process introducing materially different amendments to an awarded contract. This is to be differentiated from 'clarifications' which are not changing the terms of the contract and are regulated by different rules and from 'modifications' which suggest contractual adjustments or revisions which do not amount to renegotiations (Sanchéz Graells, 2015).

2.1 The Pressetext judgement

The factual background of the leading case (C-454/06, *Pressetext*) of EU procurement law on 'modifications' also provides an illustrative example of the legal dilemma of renegotiations (see also cases C-337/98, *Commission* v. *France* and C-498/99P, *Succhi di Frutta*). In 1994 Austria concluded a contract for an indefinite period with APA, a news service provider, waiving its right to terminate until 1999. The contract allowed Austria to access information and press releases and use the original text service (OTS). Then in 2000 APA established a wholly owned subsidiary, APA-OTS, and to which it transferred its OTS. In 2001 when Austria joined the euro the two parties entered a supplemental agreement to the contract, rounding off some prices and substituting the price index. In 2005 there was a second supplemental agreement waiving termination rights until 2008, and reducing the price of online enquiries. Rival agency Pressetext challenged the contract on the basis that the original agreement was severed following APA's restructuring in 2000, and that the supplemental agreements were unlawful.

The European Court of Justice ruled that amendments to a public contract only constitute a new award when they are materially different from the original contract and demonstrate the intention of the parties to renegotiate the essential terms of that contract. However, in this case none of the changes were materially different. While APA-OTS had a separate legal personality to APA, it was a wholly owned subsidiary and APA continued to assume responsibility under the contract, meaning that this was an internal re-organization. Adjustment to the euro prices was minimal and objectively justified and the contract provided for updating the price index. The contract was for an indefinite period and there was no suggestion that the authority would have terminated it, so the increased waiver period did not distort competition. The price reduction could be considered to come under the terms of the contract and was to the detriment of APA, so it did not shift the economic balance in its favor.

More generally the Court ruled that an amendment may be regarded as material when: (a) it introduces conditions which, had they been part of the initial award procedure, would have allowed for the admission of tenderers other than those initially admitted, or for the acceptance of a tender other than the one initially accepted; (b) it extends the contract's scope to encompass services not initially covered, or (c) it changes the economic balance in favor of the contractor in a manner not provided for in the initial contract.

Pressetext introduces the relevant categories for the balance struck in EU procurement law regarding modifications: a new award is given when amendments are materially different and demonstrate an intention to renegotiate. A comparison with the situation of the procurement procedure with the amendments is crucial to decide if they are materially different: would they have created a different field, extended the scope of the contract, or shifted the economic balance in favor of the contractor? Thus *Pressetext* confirms the general ban on renegotiations in EU procurement law but does allow modifications.

2.2 The new public sector directive 2014/24/EU

Pressetext led to new rules regarding modifications in the 2014 Directive, although there are differences (Treumer, 2014). According to Article 72(1) Directive 2014/24/EU contracts may be modified after award without a new procurement procedure in five scenarios. First, when the modification has been set out in a review clause meeting certain requirements. Second, for additional works, services or supplies by the original contractor that have become necessary but were not included in the initial procurement. In this second scenario, a change of contractor cannot be made for economic or technical reasons and would cause significant inconvenience or substantial duplication of costs for the contracting authority. Any increase in price shall not exceed 50 per cent of the value of the original contract for this scenario and, for the third scenario, when the need for modification has been brought about by circumstances which a diligent contracting authority could not foresee when the modification does not alter the overall nature of the contract. Fourth, where a new contractor replaces the original one as a consequence of either an unequivocal review clause, universal or partial succession into the position of the initial contractor, following corporate restructuring, including takeover, merger, acquisition or insolvency, with another economic operator that fulfils the criteria for qualitative selection initially established provided that this does not entail other substantial modifications to the contract; or in the event that the contracting authority itself assumes the main contractor's obligations towards its subcontractors. Finally, where the modifications, irrespective of their value, are not substantial. Additionally, according to Article 72(2) modification is possible where the value of the modification is below certain thresholds and less than 10 per cent (15 per cent for works) of the value of the initial contract and the modification does not alter the overall nature of the contract.

Article 72(4) contains the definition of when a contract is considered substantial, which is mainly where it renders the contract materially different in character from the one initially concluded. This is the case in four scenarios. First, the modification introduces conditions which, had they been part of the initial procurement procedure, would have allowed for the admission of other candidates than those initially selected or for the acceptance of a tender other than that originally accepted or would have attracted additional participants in the procurement procedure. Second, the modification changes the economic balance of the contract in favor of the contractor in a manner which was not provided for in the initial contract. Third, the modification extends the scope of the contract considerably. Finally, where a new contractor replaces the one to which the contracting authority had initially awarded the contract in other cases than those provided in Article 72(1).

2.3 Summary

EU procurement law allows modifications to awarded contracts as long as the amendments to that contract do not constitute a new award. A new award requires a new procurement procedure. This is confirmed by Recital 107 of Directive 2014/24/EU, which provides that if the needs of the contracting authority can no longer be satisfied without introducing material changes the only option is termination and re-tender. The crucial determination of a 'new award' requires a comparison between the existing contract before and after its amendment. Decisive are the dimensions of the change and the differences in the market conditions and potential outcome of the procurement procedure. While occurring during the contract management phase, modifications are mainly a concern of the public procurement phase between the call for tender and contract conclusion, not a matter regulated by contract law. Overall, EU procurement law provides a sensible approach to modifications which strikes a balance between the interests of contracting entities in flexibility and the objectives of EU law in non-discrimination and competition. However, the rules on contractual extensions and additional awards appear rather lenient (Sanchéz Graells, 2015) and could develop into loopholes to escape the ban on renegotiations. Moreover, it can be suspected that the drafting of review clauses will develop into a prized skill of procurement lawyers.

3 Francesco Decarolis – response to paper 2

The legal perspective illustrated in the note by Trybus presents the current EU rule on renegotiations (contained in Article 72, Directive 2014/24/EU), discusses the European Court of Justice ruling that shaped this part of the new Directives (C-454/06, *Pressetext*) and offers a general perspective on the legal approach to renegotiations. Regarding the latter, the provisions in Article 72 are seen as an example of how the regulation must strike a balance between preventing costly contract termination (that would be exacerbated in an environment in which contract modifications are severely limited) and preventing distortions that could result from permitting excessive renegotiations. The latter could result from outright corruption concerns, but also from distortions of fair competition as different firms could have participated in the tendering procedure and/or won it, had the contract incorporated from the beginning what the subsequent renegotiations implied.

In the light of these considerations, my understanding is that there are a few interesting differences between the economic and legal approaches. As illustrated in my own note, the economics view on renegotiations tends to focus on the rolc of asymmetric information. The overall procurement problem is seen as a problem of information extraction: an uninformed procurer needs to extract information from better informed suppliers. For low-complexity tasks where suppliers are likely to be fully (but privately) aware of their production cost, full and open competition to award fixed-price contracts is the ideal tool to extract information. However, for more complex tasks, whose cost even suppliers might individually have a hard time to predict at the time of bidding, using negotiation-style procedures to award cost-plus contracts might be ideal to extract information. Hence, the possibility of renegotiations should be nearly eliminated for the simpler contracts, but allowed for the more complex ones.

Therefore, it appears that the legal and economic approaches to renegotiations give more prominence to different moments of the procurement process. The legal view emphasizes the point in time after the contract has already been awarded and how renegotiations serve to deal with what might come afterwards: a costly termination versus a dispute involving distortion of competition relative to that tender. The economic view tends to emphasize an earlier phase: when firms are deciding to participate in the tender and what bid to offer, they incorporate in their behavior the expectation of future renegotiations. Thus, the optimal design of renegotiation rules shall steer the behavior of contractors right from the very beginning of the process so that, for instance, no law ball bids are placed in competitively awarded fixed-price contracts, as they will not be renegotiated.

This difference is likely the result of the economists' focus on strategic behavior and equilibrium analysis. Strategic behavior refers to environments where the action of an agent influences what is the optimal action of the other agents: for instance, a strategic interaction is present if revealing the bid of a firm to its rivals can induce them to select a different bid to place. The tendering of public contracts, more than many other market arrangements, seems to fit to perfection the idea of an environment in which strategic interactions shall matter. The economist toolbox for these environments typically entails postulating "equilibrium behavior", which is a mathematical formulation used to capture a very simple and intuitive idea: we shall expect to observe agents making actions such that for each agent individually, given the actions chosen by the others, there is no deviation to an alternative action that, if taken, would strictly improve his condition.

The use of this equilibrium approach, in turn, allows the economist to make a number of useful conjectures about how the provisions of Article 72 will work. First, the fact that the Directives leave ample margins to renegotiate contracts – especially the 50 per cent bound for each successive modification – regardless of their complexity and of how they were procured, opens the door to potentially risky law ball bids. Second, the thresholds set in Comma 2 stating that, for contracts below certain thresholds, modifications of less than 10 per cent (15 per cent for works) of the initial price require even less stringent conditions will matter: winning prices will be even lower for these contracts, but renegotiations will be frequent and pooled at the 10 per cent (or 15 per cent) level. Both factors make the economist's view of Article 72 not too optimistic, but there are three elements making the picture rosier: a) the emphasis on more discretionary procedures and on the most economically advantageous offer; b) the division in lots that, while aimed at favoring SMEs, will also likely reduce the uncertainty associated to the jobs procured; c) the novel possibility of using past performance to exclude from the procedure suppliers with a poor track record. All these features reduce the benefit from opportunistic renegotiations (b and c) and give to contracting authorities the tools to select reputable bidders offering sound bids (a and c).

4 Martin Trybus – response to paper 1

Even the procurement of a standardized 'off-the-shelf' product or a routine work may require 'modification' after the public contract is awarded, concluded or made. For example, the change in the internal organization of the economic operator and Austria's adoption of a new currency in the *Pressetext* judgement were post-conclusion changes that can occur no matter what procurement procedure was used. However, it is indeed the more complex contracts where the risk of change is most present, where modifications are more likely to be required. Strictly speaking, 'renegotiation' after conclusion of the public contract should only be necessary if 'negotiation' was allowed and thus possible before conclusion. Negotiations, as such, are not allowed under the open and restricted procurement procedures (Arrowsmith, 2014) used for the procurement of standardized products or routine works. Economic operators bid on the basis of a detailed set of specifications. If such detailed specifications cannot be drawn up from the beginning, the open and restricted procedures should not be used. The same can be said about framework agreements, dynamic purchasing systems, and electronic auctions. If negotiation is not allowed before the conclusion it should not be allowed after conclusion either. The rules on modifications outlined above, which also apply to contracts awarded on the basis of the open or restricted procedures, do not contradict this ban on renegotiations.

Under EU procurement law renegotiations are ultimately not recognized as a "natural part of the procurement process only to be regulated to limit abuses", there is no recognition of an "incomplete contract". Apart from the complete ban on negotiations for open and restricted procedures, this emerges from the now extensive range of negotiated procedures in the procurement Directives and the detailed rules regulating them. Second, this emerges from the accommodating but arguably still very restrictive European Court of Justice case law on modifications and the new Article 72 Directive 2014/24/EU outlined above. Moreover, it is argued that due to the fact that EU procurement law has to strike a balance between the requirements of complex contracts on the one hand and its internal market objectives of non-discrimination, competition, equal treatment, and transparency on the other hand, renegotiation cannot be a default approach.

4.1 A wide range of negotiated procedures

The EU procurement Directives provide a wide range of procedures that accommodate negotiation. These are the negotiated procedure with prior call for tender (Article 29 Directive 2014/24/EU), the competitive dialogue (Article 30), the new innovation partnerships (Article 31), and the negotiated procedure without prior call for competition. Only the latter allows single-source negotiated procurement without competition and is restricted to a number of exceptional circumstances expressly provided in Article 32 Directive 2014/24/EU. These include extreme urgency brought about for example by natural disasters or competition being impossible due to intellectual property rights. The other negotiated procedures are designed for complex contracts, especially the competitive dialogue and innovation partnerships. Moreover, the particularly complex Public Private Partnership (PPP) contracts are now regulated in a separate new Concessions Directive 2014/23/EU providing an instrument very much based on negotiated procedures. While all negotiated procedures are limited to prescribed circumstances under the Public Sector Directive 2014/24EU, the Directives on Utilities Procurement 2014/25/EU and Defence Procurement 2009/81/EC allow the free use of the negotiated procedure with prior call for tender. Article 26 (4)(a) (iii) Directive 2014/24/EU exemplifies the approach by limiting the use of competitive negotiations and the competitive dialogue inter alia to situations in which "the contract cannot be awarded without prior negotiations because of specific circumstances related to the nature, the complexity or the legal and financial make-up or because of the risks attaching to them". However, the emphasis in all these procedures in the various EU procurement Directives is on negotiations, not renegotiations. The assumption is that flexibility, risk, complexity and long life times of contracts are extensively accommodated in these procedures; and that the factors that could lead to renegotiations to insert material modifications into the original contract after it is made can be addressed before contract conclusion. These negotiations are envisaged to produce a 'complete contract'; negotiations and not renegotiations are a natural part of complex public contracts under EU procurement law.

4.2 Again: the case law

As outlined above, EU procurement law strictly limits 'renegotiations' leading to modifications to a concluded public contract. It allows such modifications only as long as the amendments to that contract do not constitute a new award, which requires a new procurement procedure. The crucial determination of a 'new award' requires a comparison between the existing contract before and after its amendment. Decisive is the extent of the changes and the differences in the market conditions and potential outcome of the procurement procedure.

Overall, EU procurement law provides a sensible approach to modifications which strikes a balance between the interests of contracting entities in flexibility and the objectives of EU law in non-discrimination and competition. The costs and other disadvantages of having to terminate a public contract that is no longer desirable and to re-tender the contract that is needed after conditions have changed are addressed in a set of flexible negotiated procedures that allow both parties to accommodate these risks in their negotiations before the conclusion of the contract. Negotiation rather than renegotiation. Moreover, within strict limits, modifications to an already concluded contract are allowed. However, the crucial limit is that the modifications must not lead to what constitutes a materially different and thus new public contract. Each contract that falls within the scope of the Directives needs to be awarded following its rules. A materially different contract that is simply (re-)negotiated with the economic operator with who the now redundant original contract was concluded would ultimately be awarded without following the rules of the Directives, single-source, without competition and transparency. How can the contracting entity know that this is the economically most advantageous tender and that the economic operator has not been abusing the situation requiring modification, both in the original procurement procedure and when the new contract is (re-)negotiated?

5 Francesco Decarolis – conclusions

The idea that renegotiations should only be possible when "negotiations" are used to award contracts in the first place is certainly reasonable and agrees with the dominant view in the economics literature. However, this is not a principle that is explicitly stated in the Directives. Neither article 72 of Directive 23/2014, nor any other article in the procurement or concessions directives, draws links between the possibility (or extent) of renegotiations and the type of awarding procedure used. The practice tells us that contracts awarded through full and open competition are very often renegotiated and, moreover, that such renegotiations will typically undo all the benefits of open competition (Guasch, Laffont and Straub, 2008).

This problem is exacerbated by a feature of Article 72 that deserves close attention, but that this discussion has not yet addressed: the quantitative amount of potential renegotiations admissible under the Directives. For works, renegotiations up to 15 per cent of the initial value of the contract are always permitted,[4] and, moreover, in all the circumstances listed in Trybus's first document, renegotiations are also possible with the only limit that any increase in price shall not exceed 50 per cent of the value of the original contract. Where several successive modifications are made, that limitation shall apply to the value of each modification. This latter sentence is particularly ambiguous, as it does not explicitly state whether 50 per cent is an overall limit or a limit for each renegotiation. Nevertheless, in both cases, common sense says that the room for renegotiations created by this provision is substantial. This is worrying as contracting authorities are allowed to renegotiate whenever a change in contractor would cause significant inconvenience or substantial duplication of costs for the contracting authority. This implies a huge margin of discretion for contracting authorities and it adds to the other margins of discretion associated with two of the Directives' pillars: the use of negotiated procures and the preference for the most economically advantageous tender (MEAT) award criterion. Altogether, this bolsters the risk of corruption and the likelihood that firms will have strong incentives to appeal any decision that contracting authorities take which do not advantage them.

These concerns have induced some observers to stress the need to enhance transparency, competition and expertise in EU procurement.(Saussier and Tirole, 2015, p. 22) The Directives have introduced some positive innovations on all these fronts. For instance, transparency will benefit from the use of a standardized European Single Procurement Document and from the digitalization of the procurement process (by October 2018). Competition will potentially be favored by the possibility to exclude from the auction contractors with poor past performance.[5] Furthermore, Member States will also be able to limit the risk of potential abuses of renegotiations by introducing rules to further promote transparency, competition and expertise. Italy, for instance, has introduced a compulsory communication of each contract modification to its regulatory authority, ANAC.

However, what will be the overall effect of these measures and whether the increase in potential renegotiations will benefit or harm the development of an efficient and effective public procurement system is a fully open question that only a careful analysis of the data in the next years might help to answer.

6 Martin Trybus – conclusions

The basic approach of most procurement laws and EU law in particular to the renegotiation of awarded public (procurement) contracts is a restrictive one. Due to the fundamental objectives of competition, non-discrimination and transparency, there is a ban on renegotiations and 'modifications' are seen as an unavoidable evil, an unwelcome fact of life which is only grudgingly accommodated, tolerated rather than really accepted. In this context Decarolis rightly emphasized the difference between simple public contracts which can be awarded on a fixed-price basis and more complex projects which require cost-plus arrangements and ultimately some flexibility regarding renegotiation. Moreover, these complex contracts may require not only modification but negotiation (before the award). To put it in slightly colloquial terms, EU procurement law and many other procurement laws 'dislike' negotiation and thus necessarily also renegotiation. This is exemplified in the strict limitation of any negotiated procedure in the Public Sector Directive 2014/24/EU and its predecessors. These procedures are only allowed in prescribed circumstances. Allowing more flexibility, the Utilities Directive 2014/25/EU and the Defence Procurement Directive 2009/81/EC allow the free use of the negotiated procedure with prior call for tender (with competition) but also restrict other negotiated procedures and especially the variation without competition (single-source). Decarolis points to one reason for this reservation towards negotiation and renegotiation: lesser informed procurers need to extract information from better informed economic operators. The latter know more about the basic economic parameters of the contract in question and are therefore ultimately in a superior position. The inferior procurer is well aware of his or her weakness and the legislature at least initially favored rules limiting negotiation. This is at least also done to protect the procurer. Most older procurement laws favor competitive procedures (open procedures or sealed bidding for the actual award of the contract) and do not leave much room for (re)negotiation or even modification. This was the approach in the predecessors of the current Directives and largely survives in 2014/24/EU. It was the European Court of Justice which, while maintaining the ban on renegotiations, ushered in a less restrictive approach in *Pressetext*, later codified in Article 72 Directive 2014/24/EU. However, while less so, it is still restrictive. After all, limits are set to the extent of the possible modifications in question. Decarolis highlights the strategy of at least some economic operators to bid or negotiate with possible renegotiations leading to different contracts already in mind before the initial award. The public contract to be awarded is thus not taken too seriously. Economic operators bid or negotiate for the award of a contract that will actually never be fulfilled, aiming for a different contract to be renegotiated after the award, when the competition has been eliminated. This strategy is not what Article 72 Directive 2014/24/EU aims to accommodate. Procurement review boards and courts are likely to take a very restrictive approach if they detect such a strategy. Moreover, as highlighted above, some of the rules on modifications are rather lenient and the possibility of inserting modifications in review clauses may allow modifications of almost any value or relevance as long as certain requirements are met. This is likely to lead to litigation (Sanchéz Graells, 2015). What *Pressetext* and Article 72 do acknowledge is the fact that things change over time and that this requires a certain flexibility allowing for modifications within strict but not excessively strict limits. Considering a context determined by the mentioned information deficit on the side of the procurers and the possible strategies of economic operators, this might not be the best but certainly is a sensible approach. After all, value for money, tight public budgets, and the general objectives of EU procurement law are also part of that context. Adjustments might be required but, with Article 72 Directive 2014/24/EU, the legislature might well have taken a step in the right direction.

Notes

1 Isomorphic results can be obtained in at least two other situations: (i) non-equilibrium situations where, due to the complexity of the work, firms underestimate the final cost; (ii) in the presence of moral hazard behavior, so that if some unforeseen contingencies materialize, he might exploit them against the procurer.

2 An empirical confirmation of the potential good properties of negotiated procedures to limit the risk of renegotiations and defaults is presented in Bajari, McMillan and Tadelis (2009) using data on contracts awarded in the private sector building construction industry in California from 1995 to 2001. They find that projects awarded via negotiations i) are more complex and ii) are awarded to more experienced contractors.

3 For instance, like the US performance bond, which offers substantial guarantees for the execution of the contracted works. More specifically, the winning bidder takes out a policy committing a counterparty, the surer, to complete the project on schedule and at the cost promised by the winning bidder in case of the latter's breach of contract. The surety, therefore, has every interest in charging a higher price to less reliable firms. This system is typically used in the US, imposing a bond equivalent to the full value of the contract. In this way all risks deriving from failure to complete a project are shifted from the procurer to the surety, and the first price auction again becomes optimal, now of course increasing the award price by the cost of the bond. An alternative, actually adopted in Italy, is letters of credit by which one party (an insurance company or bank) guarantees that a third party will not suffer economic loss due to breach of an obligation by the contractor. In this case the intermediary does not carry out a discretional assessment of the economic risk, but only attests to the presence of the capital subject to the letter. This method is less satisfactory, since completely eliminating the risk of breach of contract would require very large guarantee sums; and this could significantly reduce an enterprise's liquidity, which would limit the field to a few large enterprises. Thus, in general, only guarantees covering a small part of the value of the contract can be required, so the risk of non-completion is not entirely passed on to the guarantor.

4 Along with modifications that are either not substantial or had been incorporated in the contract in the form of price revision clauses or clear options, regardless of their amount.

5 While this tool can reduce competition if improperly used, evidence from past experiments with reputational mechanisms in public procurement is indicative of their benefits. See, for instance, Decarolis, Pacini and Spagnolo (2016).

References

Arrowsmith, S. (2014). *The Law of Public and Utilities Procurement: Regulation in the EU and UK*, Vol. I, 3rd ed. London: Sweet & Maxwell.

Bajari, P., Houghton, S., and Tadelis, S. (2014). Bidding for incomplete contracts: An empirical analysis. *American Economic Review*, 104(94), 1288–1319.

Bajari, P., McMillan, R., and Tadelis, S. (2009). Auctions versus negotiations in procurement: An empirical analysis. *Journal of Economic Behavior and Organization*, 25(2), 372–399.

Bajari, P., and Tadelis, S. (2001). Incentives versus transaction costs: A theory of procurement contracts. *RAND Journal of Economics*, 32(3), 387–407.

C-337/98, *Commission v. France* [2000] ECR I-8377

C-454/06, *Pressetext Nachrichtenagentur v. Austria* [2008] ECR I-4401

C-498/99P, *Commission v. CAS Succhi di Frutta* [2004] ECR I-3801

Cameron, L. J. (2000). Limiting buyer discretion: Effects on performance and price in long-term contracts. *American Economic Review*, 90(1), 265–281.

Comba, M. (2014). Effects of EU law on contract management. In M. Trybus, R. Caranta, and G. Edelstam (eds.), *EU Public Contract Law: Public Procurement and Beyond*. Brussels: Bruylant.

Decarolis, F. (2014). Awarding price, contract performance and bids screening: Evidence from procurement auctions. *American Economic Journal: Applied Economics*, 6(1), 108–132.

Decarolis, F., Pacini, R., and Spagnolo, G. (2016). *Contractors past performance and procurement outcomes: A firm-level experiment*. SIEPR DP 16-036.

Decarolis, F., and Palumbo, G. (2015). Renegotiation of public contracts: An empirical analysis. *Economic Letters*, 132(2), 77–81.

Defence Procurement Directive 2009/81/EC: Directive 2009/81/EC of the European Parliament and the Council of 13 July 2009 on the coordination of procedures for the award of certain works contracts, supply contracts and service contracts by contracting authorities or entities in the fields of defence and security, and amending Directives 2004/17/EC and 2004/18/EC.

Directive 2014/23/EU: Directive 2014/23/EU of the European Parliament and of the Council of 26 February 2014 on the award concession contracts [2014] OJ L94/1

Directive 2014/24/EU: Directive 2014/24/EU of the European Parliament and of the Council of 26 February 2014 on public procurement and repealing Directive 2004/18/EC [2014] OJ L94/65

Directive 2014/25/EU: Directive 2014/25/EU of the European Parliament and of the Council of 26 February 2014 on public procurement by entities operating in the water, energy, transport and postal services sectors and repealing Directive 2004/17/EC [2014] OJ L94/243

Guasch, J. L., Laffont, J. J., and Straub, S. (2008). Renegotiation of concession contracts in Latin America: Evidence from the water and transport sectors. *International Journal of Industrial Organization*, 26(2), 421–442.

Lewis, G., and Bajari, P. (2011). Procurement contracting with time incentives: Theory and evidence. *Quarterly Journal of Economics*, 126(3), 1173–1211.

Sanchéz Graells, A. (2015). *Public Procurement and the EU Competition Rules*, 2nd ed. Oxford: Hart.

Saussier, S., and Tirole, J. (2015). *Strengthening the Efficiency of Public Procurement*. Les notes du conseil d'analyse économique.

Spulber, D. F. (1990). Auctions and contract enforcement. *Journal of Law, Economics, and Organization*, 6(2), 325–344.

Treumer, S. (2014). Contract changes and the duty to retender und the new EU public procurement directive. *Public Procurement Law Review*, 23, 148–155.

11 Procurement and renegotiation of Public Private Partnerships in infrastructure

Evidence, typology and tendencies

Josè Luis Guasch

1 Introductions

Public Private Partnerships (PPP) were introduced in emerging economies in the 1990s, with Latin American countries taking the lead. PPPs for this report include all types of private participation, whether there is or is not financial contributions by the government, the so called concessions or PPP in certain countries and Private Finance Initiatives (PFI). There is over 25 years of experience and more than 7000 projects implemented as PPP (Guasch, 2016). The findings, here presented, are based on an analysis of over 1500 concessions/PPP around the world and on the analysis of a large number of PPP programs (legal, project selection, institutions, procurement, procedures, oversight and conflict resolutions). The report shows that indeed PPP programs have been and can be quite effective to complement public works in breaching the infrastructure gap and the quality of public services. Yet, it is not automatic, and a number of things and elements have to be in place to secure the expected benefits. While PPP programs can be quite effective, they have also weaknesses that need to be addressed, the main one being their vulnerability to contract renegotiation. The incidence of contract renegotiation is staggering and can threaten the credibility of the program. A key focus of this report is to illustrate and analyze the incidence and tendencies of contract renegotiation. Plenty of mistakes have been made but most of them can be relatively easily corrected if there is the appropriate commitment, leadership, knowledge and capacity in place. PPP programs have to evolve, and many of them are doing so to reach the stage needed to secure the extensive benefits of PPP.

2 Motivation: infrastructure gap and limited fiscal space from public sector and growth/productivity impact

Growth and productivity in Latin American countries, with some exceptions for the last two decades, have been wanting, particularly for the larger countries such as Mexico, Brazil and Argentina, even with the commodity boom. It has been argued that a key factor was the level and quality of infrastructure. A large number of empirical studies show a strong linkage between infrastructure investment and economic growth and poverty impact. Investment in infrastructure is accumulated in man-made capital formation and thus contributes to GDP growth (Calderón and Servén, 2004; Fay, 2000; Fay and Yepes, 2003). A meta-analysis conducted by the World Bank (Straub, 2008) that reviews micro and macro analyses of the impact of increases or improvements in infrastructure stocks (or their variations) finds there is in general a positive link between infrastructure investments and growth. This holds for both long-run economic growth and specific factor outputs. Overall, of the 140 specifications from 64 papers considered, the majority of the empirical literature finds a positive and significant link between infrastructure and development outcomes. A small fraction of the literature (6 percent) finds a negative relationship. Analysis of developing country data led to positive results slightly more often than those exercises using data from developed economies. These results hold true for different proxies for infrastructure, including measure of public capital (i.e. investment in infrastructure, generally from public sources although not exclusively) or physical indicators. Looking mostly at the public capital stocks of the US, the macro-level literature finds very large estimates for the elasticity of infrastructure – between 0.20 and 0.40. These results survive to different proxies of changes in infrastructure's stock and output measures.

Yet infrastructure deficiencies are acutely felt throughout the region. Many people living in emerging economies remain unconnected to a reliable electrical grid, a safe water supply, sanitary sewage disposal, sound roads and transportation networks, and reliable access to health and education services. Bottlenecks are encountered in all modes of transport infrastructure services from the poor condition of roads to a lack of intraregional connectivity between the national road networks or unreliable and overall costly road transport services to an unrealized potential for rail and inland water freight transport, which has led to the excessive use of road transport to inadequate road and rail connectivity of ports with hinterlands, among others. Also, as a consequence, countries are facing high logistic costs impacting trade and access to markets by producers. In consequence all of those economies require significant infrastructure investment (roads, rails, power, telecommunications, water supply, and sanitation and social services) not only to ensure basic service delivery and enhance the quality of life of its growing population, but also to avoid a possible binding constraint on economic growth due to the substantial infrastructure gap. Without more and better investments in infrastructure, more effectively targeted project designs and better infrastructure policies, the demographic, spatial, environmental, health and safety pressures will continue to mount. This will likely foster a difficult cycle to break in which economic growth is limited by infrastructure deficiencies, which in turn further stunts infrastructure development. As a result the nexus of economic growth, shared prosperity and the infrastructure deficit, emerges as an important issue in the development prospect of emerging economies.

With all that context, the motivation for most countries to implement PPP programs has been quite straightforward. First most countries face significant gaps and deficiencies in the coverage, access and quality of public infrastructure services. Those services, as mentioned, have proven to be critical for productivity, economic growth and poverty reduction. In emerging economies, the demand for infrastructure (which broadly understood includes social services) investment is enormous but as a result of the severe fiscal constraints facing those countries, the available financial resource is limited; the capacity of the government to finance investments in infrastructure, so as to reduce the gap and improve the quality of the services, is also quite limited in most countries. They do have fiscal space problems and quite large competing needs for those limited resources. Based on information from a previous study (Fay and Yepes, 2003), Estache and Fay (2007, 2010) estimated that developing countries might need 6.5 percent of their GDP, in average, during the 2005–2015 period. Of which 2.3 percent would be needed just to maintain the existing infrastructure, whereas the remaining 3.2 percent would be required for new infrastructure projects.

A range of estimates on infrastructure financing requirements applying different assumptions and methodologies for achieving various global goals have been estimated over the years (Table 11.1). At the lower bound is Ruiz-Nunez and Wei (2014), who estimate that the region requires an annual investment in infrastructure of 3.6 percent of GDP. At the upper bound is Perroti and Sánchez (2011), who estimate an investment requirement of 5.2 percent of GDP.

The biggest gap is found in the Information, Communication and Technology (ICT) sector (41 percent of the investment requirements), followed by energy (33 percent), transport (22 percent) and water and sanitation (4 percent). In all these sectors, it is split almost equally between capital investments and operations and maintenance.

Most LAC countries suffer from an undersupply of public infrastructure, which constrains economic growth and hampers access to basic services. In the World Economic Forum Infrastructure Index, the LAC region presents a wide range in the quality and availability of infrastructure, although most countries show significant infrastructure gaps, clustering in the lower half of the 140 countries ranked. This includes the larger and more advanced economies in the region – Brazil (74th), Colombia (84th) and Peru (89th) – as well as the smaller economies – Costa Rica (71st), Honduras (93rd), Dominican Republic (100th) and Bolivia (107th). Four countries in Latin America stand relatively higher in this index – Panama (40th), Uruguay (42nd), Chile (45th) and Mexico (49th). And as shown the investments in infrastructure in Brazil are below the average for Latin American countries.

Ongoing investment in public infrastructure in the LAC region is significantly less than that required to eliminate the gap. The average annual investments, as shown in Figure 11.1, in LAC countries from 2008 to 2013 were much below the estimated requirements (assuming an average of 4.3 percent of GDP) and leading to the stated predicament of the infrastructure in most countries.

Table 11.1 Latin America and Caribbean (LAC) annual regional infrastructure requirements estimates (% of GDP)

Authors	*Estimates (% of GDP)*	*Period of prediction*
Perrotti and Sánchez, 2011	**5.2%**	**2006–2020**
Kohli and Basil, 2011	**4%**	**2011–2040**
Ruiz-Nunez and Wei, 2014	**3.6%**	**2014–2020**
Average	**4.3%**	

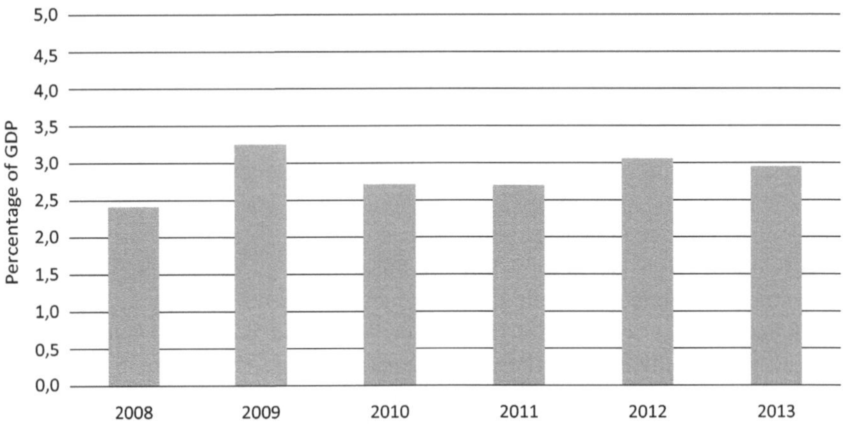

Figure 11.1 Weighted average infrastructure investments (public and private) as percentage of GDP in LAC countries, 2008–2013

Source: www.Infralatam.info. Downloaded on May 2, 2016
Note: Data points weighted by country GDP

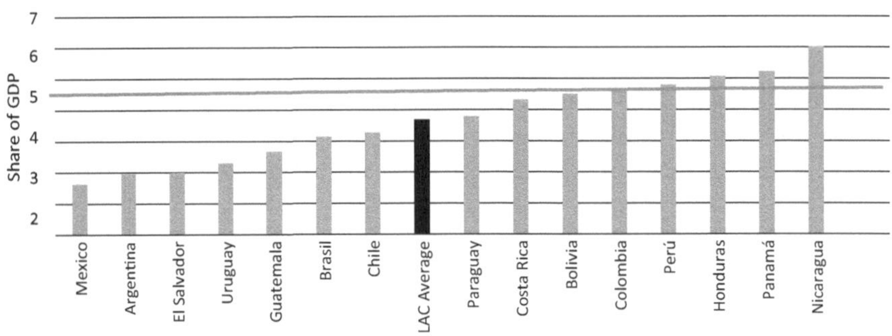

Figure 11.2 Annual average infrastructure investments (public and private) as percentage of GDP in selected LAC countries, 2008–2013

Source: www.Infralatam.info. Downloaded on May 2, 2016

There is a significant variation across countries in the region as shown in Figure 11.2. The big economies of the LAC region – Mexico, Argentina, Brazil and Chile – account for over 65 percent of the GDP of the region and they only invest between 1.6 and 3.3 percent of their GDP, affecting the overall regional investments. Small economies such as Honduras, Panama and Nicaragua invest more than 5 percent of their GDP.

3 The economics of PPP

PPP or "Public Private Partnerships" is a generic term for a contractual and long term relation between the public sector and a private operator granting to the private operator the right to provide the service and receive compensation via tariffs or government payments. PPP is a contract between the public sector and the private operator in which the public sector is expected to reap the benefits of the project and the private sector to earn its fair share of return to capital. In general, a public authority grants a private party the right to design, build (or refurbish or expand), maintain, operate and finance an infrastructure asset owned by the public sector. Often described as a concession agreement, the PPP contract is for a fixed period, say 10 to 30 years. The so called public authority may be a central/federal, regional/state or local government, or an autonomous public body such as a roads agency or a public enterprise. The term PPP describes a range of contractual agreements – such as design, construction, financing, operations, maintenance and rehabilitation, management, etc. A number of factors drive the success of that undertaking: legal, institutional, procedural, regulatory, political, financial, competitiveness/markets, risks, etc. The PPP process starts with project identification/selection/prioritization, and includes project preparation, contract design, procuring the project and ending with the oversight of project implementation.

3.1 PPP versus public works/investment projects

PPP projects are quite different from traditional procurement or public works. The main characteristics of those two modalities are the following:

- term contract: 10 to 30 years (so long term financing required);
- Usually financed by the private sector as a result of fiscal space constraints;
- Bundling of activities: construction, financing, operations, rehabilitation and maintenance, etc.;
- Ownership of assets remains with the State (few exceptions);
- Risk sharing with the private operator;
- Cost/investment recovery by private party, trough tariffs or government payments or a mixture of both;
- Private operator has the right/obligation to provide the service for the duration of the contract. His only asset oversees and regulates the implementation of the project, as well as insures compliance with the contract;
- Contract establishes all conditions, rights and obligations of both parties; and
- At the end the concession period, the service and assets revert back to the government without compensation (in general).

3.2 Public work/traditional procurement projects have the following characteristics

- A short term contract for the duration of the construction period;
- The only activity in general is the construction of the infrastructure;
- It is financed by the public sector; and
- Little or no risk transferred to the private sector. In general most if not all of the construction risks are retained by the State (turn-key projects are the exception but they are seldom used).

In summary there are three key differences between those two modalities:

- PPP transfer risks, mainly construction and demand (totally or partially), to the Concessionaire;
- PPP transfer responsibility for maintenance and rehabilitation (quality of service conditions remunerations and sanctions) to the Concessionaire; and
- PPP are financed by the Concessionaire.

3.3 Strengths and weakness of PPP

In light of the experience and track record of 25 years, PPP have shown to deliver quite systemically a number of benefits, yet also there have been a number of problems mostly driven by poorly addressing certain themes/issues that have also systemically been adversely affecting the outcomes and performance of PPP. Some of the latter are the fiscal treatment and management of liabilities, the incidence of renegotiations, the handling of land issues, misuse of the concept of financial equilibrium, burdensome procedures, information disclosure, deficient oversight, bankability issues, risk assignments, etc.

As a result, PPP have a number of strengths but also weaknesses relative to public works (see Guasch and Spiller, 1999; Guasch, Andres and Straub, 2008; Guasch, 2016a). They are outlined below.

3.4 Strengths of PPP: the following benefits are associated with and were delivered by PPP

- Increase efficiency, cost reductions, social inclusion, additionality of financing, improve welfare;
- Accelerate investment program and levels of service, coverage;
- Improve the quality of service, reliability and extent;
- Increase access to public services;
- Relieve fiscal pressure and provide fiscal space with the additionality of financing;
- Bundling effect: solves the maintenance and rehabilitation problem by internalizing it; improves quality of stock and service;
- Transfer of risks to private operators;
- Cost reductions and reduction of construction delays;
- Improved transparency of investment; and
- Focus on level of service rather than getting physical assets.

But it is not automatic, as it requires knowledge and commitment, capabilities, processes, filters, institutions, proper oversight and use of best practices to design contracts and effective regulation.

Weaknesses of PPP: They do have a number of weaknesses in relation to traditional procurement/public works. They are:

- Significantly higher costs (than public works option) of project preparation and even larger costs of project supervision/regulation for both phases – construction and operations – of project implementation;

- Lengthier project preparation time;
- Require more and better project studies and analysis than public works;
- Vulnerable to aggressive bids;
- Vulnerable to renegotiations and conflicts;
- Require long term financing – often not available in the home country;
- Unsolicited proposals often done with limited transparency and reduced competition;
- Generate contingent liabilities – with high potential fiscal costs; and
- Require effective fiscalization and regulation.

3.5 Performance of PPP versus public works/traditional procurement

The question is then what has been the relative performance of PPP versus public works? While a full coherent comparison is a complex issue, it is possible to focus on a number of indicators linked to effectiveness and/or efficiency, such as cost, time and duration of construction, and social and "political" outcomes. In a simple way, the questions we would expect to see addressed would be: (i) Has PPP been delivering better social outcomes, and meeting time and cost targets more effectively? (ii) Has the quality of the physical assets and of the service been improved under the PPP modality?

There is a fair amount of evidence that indicates that on average PPP have performed better than public works, at least relative to those indicators. With regard to their relative performance on cost overruns and delays, the differences are notable. On a sample of 500 projects of each modality, public works show an incidence of cost overruns of over 85 percent and with levels of cost overruns from 40 to 150 percent of original costs (average 85 percent). Moreover public costs show an incidence of delays of about 92 percent. Meanwhile the incidence of cost overruns on PPP was about 21 percent and cost overruns of about 18 percent of original costs and incidence of delays was about 26 percent (Guasch, 2016). And regarding the quality of the physical stock, the differences are substantial, with PPP showing much better quality than projects done under public works, mostly because under PPP the responsibility for maintenance and rehabilitation is of the Concessionaire, while under the public works is of the government and quite often the budget allocation for that task is often inappropriate (Ipsos, 2009). For example the Brazilian magazine *Veja* reported in 2013 that about half of the highway system in Brazil was not maintained for over ten years.

As a specific example of the difference in performance of PPP projects versus public investment works/traditional procurement, Table 11.2 compares the performance of those two types of modalities for implementation, with respect to three indicators: on budget, on time and user benefits. The analysis and data compilations done separately for Australia and for the UK show that PPP perform significantly better than traditional procurement regarding being on time (25 percent versus 79 percent), being on budget (34 percent versus 82 percent) and providing user benefits (27 percent versus 74 percent) (MR, 2008, Bond University).

Cost overruns are defined as the difference between the final price and the initial price at which the procurement order has been awarded. There is abundant literature reporting them (Guasch, 2016b). And cost overruns in public works do take place not only in emerging economies but also in developed countries. Landmark

Table 11.2 A survey of procurement outcomes

	On budget	*On time*	*User benefits*
Traditional [i] procurement	25%	34%	27%
ii	27%	30%	35%
iii	55%	63%	55%
Gateways Programs[iv]	69%	73%	65%
Alliance Contracting[v]	77%	78%	Refer notes
PFI (UK)[vi]	78%	76%	n.a.
PPP(Australia)[vii]	79%	82%	74%
UK Defence Contracts[viii]	17% (14%)	8% (24%)	Met requirements

Source: Guasch (2016c)

i 1999 results: NAO 2001 Modernising Construction. Delivered on or under time and price.
ii 2000–2001 results: NAO 2001 Modernising Construction. Delivered on or under time and price.
iii 2004 results: NAO 2005 Improving Services through Construction Part A.
iv 2000–2001 results: NAO 2001 Modernising Construction. Delivered on or under time and price.
v 2004 results: NAO 2005 Improving Services through Construction Part B.
vi 2004 results: NAO 2005 Improving Services through Construction Part A.
vii Fitzgerald 2005; Audit Office Reports Victoria and NSW 2004–2008; IPA 2007.
viii NAO 2004, 2006 MOD Defence Contracts.

examples of cost overruns of public works projects are the Sidney Opera House in Australia, which ended up costing 15 times the original budget, and the airport at Denver, Colorado, USA, which ended up costing more than twice the original budget and was finalized 16 months beyond the original schedule. For the Amsterdam metro line, the initial budget was set at €1.46 billion in 2002 but the costs had risen to €3.1 billion in 2009. For the Boston highway artery the ultimate price exceeded the initial price by US$1.6 billion. Substantial price increases resulted from contract renegotiation for Italian procurement contracts and for Californian procurement contracts. German procurement contracts and their cost increases are listed by Anzinger and Kostka (2015). Likewise the expansion of the Panama Canal was bid at US$3.1 billion, but ended up costing US$6.5 billion. The bid had all the traits of an aggressive bid: the second lowest bid was more than US$1 billion more than the winning bid. The low winning bid, a billion dollars less than the nearest competitor's, made a technically complex mega-project precarious from the outset. Thus, there was no surprise that there were significant cost overruns that the government had to absorb. Additionally the process has been clouded with allegations of favoritisms and corruption, and it appears to be a consensus that the expanded canal's future is cloudy at best – its safety, quality of construction and economic viability is in doubt (The New York Times, June 23, 2016). And so on. Thus the problem with cost overruns in traditional procurement is indeed endemic. Similarly on the issue of project delays, the evidence of considerable delays on traditional procurement/public works is substantial. And on both issues, projects implemented via PPP do consistently much better (Guasch, 2016c).

4 The enabling environment for PPPs

Based on the analysis of over 1500 PPP and on imputing the determinants of success, a number of salient lessons emerge. Overall, the existence of an efficient, coherent, credible and transparent enabling environment is critical so as to send the right signals, attract the private sector and indicate that there is a stable environment for private sector long-term investments. This broad concept includes a sound and coherent PPP program, policy, regulatory and legal frameworks, processes and strong institutions in place – such as PPP units – a public financial management framework and broader program governance.

More specifically, success is associated with an effective and coherent PPP program with a number of critical *building blocks or components*, based on best practices. Those building blocks are the following:

- i a PPP law and accompanying regulations;
- ii the existence of institutions responsible for managing the project and processes from identification to award and oversight;
- iii establishing clear jurisdictions for the various actions in that process including timely approvals at different stages of the process;
- iv issuing the quite critical PPP policies to be followed (such as about project selections, risk allocation, payment mechanisms, award criteria/procurement, unsolicited proposals, renegotiations, land expropriations and rights of way, government support, conflict resolution, contingent liabilities, etc. which are often embedded in the law, regulations, normatives and/or a "green book" or in the contract itself);
- v the procedures and processes to be followed in moving the project forward;
- vi the operating instruments to guide the program, mainly a reflection of the PPP policy adapted (such as Green Book risk allocation matrix, standard contract/clauses, regulatory accounting, business case for projects, financial model, impact template, TORs for required studies, etc.); and
- vii Complementary legislation such as on expropriation and right of way, on conflict resolution/arbitration, on Unsolicited Proposal (USP), on debt ceilings and management of contingent liabilities, etc.

But clearly that is the case for countries with a commitment to a relatively significant PPP program. For countries exploring the concept or with the expectations of implementing a limited PPP program, a much simpler framework suffices.

4.1 Providing the right signals

To complement the implementation of those key components, it has proven effective that to attract the private sector the government must send the right signals and frame the program in a full transparency mode in order to show their willingness and commitment to a PPP program. Some of those signals could be, for instance, a combination of enacting a specific enabling PPP law (in particular in a civil law country context), setting specialized and dedicated institutions, appointing a highly visible professional and with convening power as head of the PPP initiative, reporting to a high-level official such as president or prime minister, preparing a medium-term infrastructure plan, identifying and providing a credible and bankable portfolio of PPP project or creating an effective and well-funded

PPP unit, etc. A government can also increase its appeal to market participants, particularly international participants, by showing commitment to a significant PPP program (a portfolio of projects with an accompanying timetable) rather than just a specific project. There is indeed a cost for a foreign sponsor to enter a country, so it is unlikely that a single project would attract many foreign parties.

A PPP initiative is a major public policy initiative and global experience has shown that success is fundamentally based upon government providing compelling evidence of its ongoing commitment. A sound, transparent and predictable PPP-enabling environment (including law, policy, institutions such as a PPP unit, procedures, and governance) will communicate publicly its commitment to PPPs while attracting private sector interest and acceptability. Implementation of an overall PPP framework informs the market as to how PPP projects will be accessed, selected, funded, procured, monitored and accounted. Private sponsors and investors have choices as to where to commit their resources and will choose those markets based upon their assessment of the enabling PPP framework, the perceived bankability of projects and evidence of a credible portfolio of such projects going forward. An effective PPP framework will attract competitive bidding and private financing to affect an appropriate transfer of risk in performance-based PPP contracts, as well as lead to value-for-money for government.

When considering a PPP initiative, governments ought to (as best practice) identify a "political champion" to assist and lead the government throughout the process. A political champion is a person with influence within the government who is respected by the public and the private sectors, has convening power and is capable of articulating and aligning different interests in order to implement the PPP initiative.

4.2 Standardized procedures: a key step to generate predictability and reduce transaction costs

A key success factor in implementing a PPP program is that the various public authorities within a government utilize common policies and procedures (HM Treasury, 2007). As noted previously, polling results for the LAC region indicate that the private sector perceives government processes to be overly cumbersome, bureaucratic and complex, and having a slowing impact on project development and delivery. However, in recent years, most LAC countries have enacted and/or revised their PPP legal framework and are converging towards the standardization of the elements of the PPP program, adopting official policies and procedures for PPPs and some countries, such as Peru, have gone so far as to issue model contracts and a comprehensive "Green Book" which sets guidelines for project selection and structuring, risk allocation, procurement, dispute resolution, etc. Such initiatives will increase transparency and predictability while reducing delays. In addition, the many new PPP units will improve coordination across government and standardization of procedures.

4.3 Proper and timely approvals

It is also important that the government approval process not unduly impact the procurement process. Ideally, the approving agency (usually a cabinet committee or the Ministry of Finance, but never the Granteur) should require approval of the project priority in the early stages and to approve affordability and the use of the PPP model at the commencement of the public competitive selection process, and also at the end of the process just before launching the project for bids. An approval requirement only at the end of the selection process is typically too late to be effective and, if approval is not given, the sponsors or participants will lose confidence in the government's commitment to the market.

4.4 Moving forward

Governments in the LAC region have been using PPP as a procurement method since the late 1980s and have created relatively sophisticated PPP frameworks/markets: 19 LAC countries have implemented PPP legislation (including 17 with some form of PPP unit) and many frameworks/markets have consistently been revised and improved. Nevertheless, challenges remain: in many countries projects tend to be rushed into the procurement phase without adequate preparation, which leads to counterproductive and costly delays in reaching financial closing. Public authorities strive to identify and structure bankable PPP projects that attract sufficient interest among sponsors and lenders to generate aggressive competition. These challenges appear to result from a lack of systematic and coherent investment planning and long-term government policy and credible government commitments, a lack of internal capacity and budgets, and insufficient private sector market participants (sponsors, investors, lenders). As observed in developed markets, comprehensive project preparation and a correctly managed tender process can reduce the time between PPP contract signing and financial close, increase participation and competition, and deliver better value-for-money to the public authority.

A common response in LAC countries to a lack of bankability is for governments to provide additional support to the transaction by offering viability gap funding and financial guarantees, thereby assuming increased commercial risk, offering generous and inefficient payment mechanisms, and/or accepting less favorable contractual terms. Value for money is maximized when public authorities find the appropriate balance between attracting private finance and transferring commercial risks to the private partners. Despite the availability of development bank financing and corporate lending in the LAC region (Mexico and Brazil are excellent examples), which has enabled many PPP projects to move forward, there remains a critical lack of effective project financing, and this is fundamental to the ability of governments to achieve the best deals possible. This section describes the enabling PPP frameworks in LAC countries with international best practices in more mature and developed PPP markets (and in some aspects also in some LAC countries such as Chile and Peru).

Specific PPP legislation will greatly simplify the PPP framework for market participants, and further increase the appeal of the market, even in those jurisdictions that do not necessarily require such legislation in order to implement a PPP project. The enabling PPP legislation should be coherent, unambiguous, predictable and stable. It can provide new powers and jurisdictions, or simplify and clarify existing powers or jurisdictions.

An effective framework also requires government to have made policy decisions (some embedded in the PPP Law and regulations) regarding risk allocation and payment mechanisms in PPP contracts; and procurement processes including evaluation criteria, unsolicited proposals, renegotiations, land expropriations and rights of way, government support, oversight, conflict resolution, and treatment and management of contingent liabilities.

The effectiveness of a PPP framework will be greatly assisted if there is a dedicated institution (in some form of a PPP unit) responsible for managing the project and processes, from project selection, through procurement and award, and to construction oversight. These institutions must have clearly defined jurisdictions and mandates, with sufficient capacity to execute the mandate. Typically, in developed countries there is a PPP unit with expertise and mandate to provide an interface between government and the private sector, to assist or undertake project structuring and contract design, to provide a memory of previous transactions and ultimately to increase value for money in project delivery.

A well-designed PPP project selection process can save government resources by pre-screening projects to ensure, first, that projects meet political, economic, fiscal and environmental priorities; second, are technically and legally feasible; and, third, are worthy of further comprehensive assessment as PPP projects. After pre-screening, a more detailed business plan for selected projects ensures final affordability, viability as a PPP in terms of bankability, and whether the PPP model generates value for money in comparison to traditional procurement. To assess government affordability, the business plan will comment on both project funding and also any contingent liabilities of government, whether or not such commitments required are consolidated into the financial statements of the government.

Finally, it has been found in developed markets that investment plans and business case planning can be used to determine the optimum combination of the use of public funds with private financing. The optimum combination can reduce overall project costs and also ensure that there is no "viability gap" that blocks the bankability of private financing. The "optimal" amount of private financing is that minimum amount required to secure bankability of the project under the appropriate risk allocation and transfer the risks in the project agreement to the private partner, but retain sufficient welfare effects and value for money to make the project desirable for the country. Credit enhancements might or might not be needed, depending on the context, and on the extent and availability of direct government credit or grants that can be raised using very high credit ratings.

While LAC countries have been implementing PPP programs since the 1990s, there is a fair amount of heterogeneity and most have missing key components of those building blocks frameworks. Also there is the issue of enforcement: that is, a number of countries might have an adequate, on paper, enabling environment, but it might not be enforced or acted upon. For example Brazil and Mexico are examples of having an adequate legal framework to handle register and manage contingent liabilities, yet they do not have a structure to do so. In addition, there is the critical issue of coordination and collaboration among all the relevant government institutions that have some type of jurisdiction on the process of advancing PPP toward the market. What has also been a bottleneck and a source of problems in many countries is the absence of a coordination framework or working protocols across those government institutions. Yet, as we describe in the new practices and innovation section, countries are improving in implementing working protocols and virtual project teams, as well as bounding the process and evaluation times so as to make the process more agile while doing due process. Some countries have even gone further by creating Solutions Units and/or high profile Ombudsman-type roles to handle impasses.

Overall and perhaps not surprisingly, the results, although generally positive, have shown weakness. The country in LAC closer to the best and more coherent program is Peru, as reformed in 2016. Colombia and Chile are improving, and Mexico and Brazil are a few steps back. Relatively new entrants in LAC such as Uruguay and Paraguay have incorporated some of those components in their PPP program, but are missing others. Central American countries have had a stop-and-go practice since the early 2000s, yet despite those efforts and experience (or because of it) they are still struggling in defining and seriously committing to a PPP program.

5 Main typology of PPP projects

All contracts as defined above are and should be denominated PPP contracts regardless of their characteristics and mode of cost recovery and so on. Yet some countries and some literature make an (artificial) distinction between contracts for which investment is recovered solely via user tariffs and contracts for which investment is recovered via government payments – often called availability payments. They call the former PPP projects and the latter PFI (Private Finance Initiative) projects. The name of the latter is adopted from the lexicon of the UK, which portfolio of projects was practically financed via government payments or availability payments. To us, PFI is just a type of PPP, but nevertheless a PPP.

5.1 PPP or user-fee based

Under this mainstream modality, as mentioned, the private party recoups its investment, operating, and financing costs and its profit by charging members of the public a user fee (for example, a road toll). Thus a key feature is that the private party is usually allocated the risk of demand for use of the asset, in addition to the risks of design, finance, construction, and operation. That is the user-fee project in its purest form. However, there are slight variations where, while the government does not make a firm annual payment to the Concessionaire, it might offer some credit enhancement or guarantee that generates contingent liabilities. Typically this is in regard to the allocation of demand risk that may be allocated in various ways: for example, the public authority may share the risk by underwriting a minimum level of usage, and, therefore, the public sector may also be involved in making payments to the private sector under certain circumstances. It may also do so in the form of a subsidy for the capital costs. In other cases, it may extend the concession contract period to enable the private party to collect user fees over a longer period. The level of user charges may be prescribed in the PPP concession agreement itself, by a regulator (implementing a tariff adjustment mechanism set out in the legislation or in the concession agreement), or even by the Concessionaire. Typical examples of these types of PPP include toll roads, railways, urban transport schemes, ports, airports, and even the provision of power, water, gas distribution, and telecommunications. The competence and autonomy of a regulator or of a monitoring entity, where it is required, are crucial features of these types of PPP.

5.2 PFI or availability-based PPP[15]

These projects or contracts as mentioned are very much like the mainstream PPP or user-fee PPPs, in that they also involve a private party designing, financing, building or rebuilding, and subsequently operating and maintaining the necessary infrastructure. However, in this case,[2] the public authority – not the end users – make payments (usually annual) to the private party. These payments are usually made as, when and to the extent that a service (not an asset) is made available. Hence the main difference is the demand risk. And payment is made only on the basis of availability of the service. Whether the service is used or how much demand there is for it is irrelevant and does not affect the payment to the Concessionaire. Under the PFI type, the demand or usage risk usually remains with the public authority. This form of PPP has important implications for the detail required to define, monitor and pay for the service by the public sector; the implications for affordability for the public sector; and the procurement methodology used (under PFI the most common procurement modality is to award the project to the bidder requesting the minimum government payments, where under the standard user-fee PPP, the most common procurement modalities are minimum tariffs or maximum payment of the Concessionaire to the government for the right to provide the service). A hybrid of the user-fee (demand risk) and availability-based PPP is the use of "shadow tolls" in PPP road projects, where the payment is made by the public sector, based on usage by drivers. And of course there is also a more typical hybrid where cost recovery is done via a mix or combination of users' fees and government payments.

The PFI or availability payment modality is very commonly used in projects for which is quite difficult to levy fees on the users (or is politically undesirable), such as in social infrastructure projects (e.g. schools, hospitals, prisons, or government buildings, cultural centres, museums, etc.), as well as in other projects that are not "self-funding" (e.g. rural roads). Such modality is used where accommodation is provided or where equipment or a system is made available. In all these cases, payments are again generally based on the availability of the accommodation facility, equipment or system to a defined standard and not on the volume of usage. The mechanism that determines the level of payment for the service is usually set out in considerable detail in the project agreement itself and, accordingly, the role of a regulator may be much less extensive or even nonexistent beyond the fiscalization of and for the duration of the construction period. Where the requirement can be well defined and is unlikely to vary significantly over the life of the agreement, governments have found these types of PPPs to be very effective in ensuring that public facilities are delivered on time and on budget, are properly maintained and are able to deliver public services in the context of constrained resources. As mentioned, the UK pioneered the use of this form of PPP for the provision of social infrastructure (known as the Private Finance Initiative [PFI] Program), and many other countries – such as Australia, Brazil, Canada, Japan, Brazil, Peru, Chile, the Republic of Korea, Mexico and South Africa – are using this approach. In general private sector is quite keen and favors PFI mainly on the grounds that it does not have to worry about or manage demand risks, and also that makes the project easier to finance.

Whether to pursue a user-fee or an availability-based PPP is both a policy decision and a reflection of who is best placed to pay for the service. The affordability of availability-based PPPs is likely to be an issue in some developing countries, because such projects require public resources and do not themselves raise revenue through user-payment mechanisms. Availability-based PPPs also require that the long-term payment obligations of the government are acceptable to investors, especially since such payments may rely on multiannual budget approvals. However, user-fee PPPs also present their own challenges with regard to demand risk and user affordability (see Harris and Patrap, 2008 on how these risks may be higher in some sectors and play a role in the cancellation of projects). Faced with these challenges, the solution in a particular situation may involve blending user fees and public service charges and, in some cases, tailoring overseas development assistance into longer term, performance-based contracting support. These mechanisms can often create much more stable projects, as demand risk – a common cause of project failure – is shared. On the funding side, the solution may also involve mixing different forms of finance and funding support (as is happening even in mature PPP markets in the current climate). In many markets, particularly those with availability-based schemes, PPPs are now seen as a method of procuring public services, not just as a means of financing infrastructure. Looked at in this light, other forms of partnership are also developing to provide greater flexibility (although they often are more complex). These may involve partnerships to manage whole programs of investment and service delivery (rather than individual projects), particularly in cases where the timing or nature of future requirements may vary, but where there are still significant benefits to sharing risk and taking a strategic approach with a private sector partner. The UK adopted this approach for some of its primary health care and school infrastructure under which the private and public sectors become partners to deliver a whole program of infrastructure investment within a region over a defined period, with the identification and timing of delivery of many of the individual facilities taking place over the life of the program.

6 Good practices in contract renegotiation

While the ex-post contract award management of PPP projects is indeed critical for securing the expected benefits of PPP projects, it has in general not been an important priority for governments or has been treated lightly or as a sort of residual to be taken care somehow. That is a source of concern because most PPP contracts have durations of 15–30 years. And for PPP in social sector, which can involve more complexity (i.e. the health sector), these being set up based on the level of service and its monitoring is a big challenge. Issues do and will come up, and are often not well specified or detailed in the contract, in particular in dynamic markets in which cost structure is changing in ways aligned to the main drivers (high prices of commodities) or the demand has increased over the expectations. All that creates opportunities for abuse and opportunism, as well as raises the likelihood of conflicts among the two parties quite significantly. The conflicts appear at all levels: i) contract based, and ii) beyond the contract through renegotiation.

To some extent, disputes and differences in interpreting the contract are to be expected and are part of the business as usual – but only those contracts based not on renegotiation (contract/risk modifications). Yet the incidence of both has been and is a concern, particularly that of renegotiations. A big legacy of PPP contracts in Latin America (LCR) along the last 25 years is a large number of renegotiations. Renegotiations have been by and large the most critical and impacting problem facing PPP. Given its implications on value for money and the legitimation of PPP over traditional procurement, there is a need to be prepared and to diffuse, pre-empt and address the issue.

The PPP contract, processes and institutionality are the key determinants, along with the contractual integrity, that impinge on the likelihood of securing those benefits and avoiding conflicts. If the key contractual clauses are not well written (or risks are not well allocated), the benefits will be reduced and the incidence of conflicts significantly increased. If the oversight/fiscalization and regulation is not properly set up, again the benefits will be reduced and the conflicts increased. If the conflict resolution mechanisms are not predicable and transparent enough, interest and benefits will likely decline. Thus it is indeed critical to understand the issue, its causes and how best to address it so PPP programs can generate their expected benefits.

"Renegotiation" refers to modification of the PPP contract. The contract is awarded to the winner of the auction (or to the selected sponsor in the case on a non-competitive adjudication, but that is the exception in LAC) at the so-called commercial closing. After that there is a period between six to 12 months until the financial closing. Renegotiation refers to the modification of the contract either during the period between commercial and financial closing and also modification after the financial closing.

In particular a renegotiation is an unforeseen modification of the contract. In particular the modifications are via:

i A change in the risk assignment matrix or of its extent;
ii A change in the scope of the project, the so-called complementary contracts, additionality of investment/works, etc. (but even then it depends on whether it was foreseen and guided in the contract);

iii Other changes (derived) on the contract conditions (such as duration/term, schedule and timing of investment, investment levels, tariff structure, service levels, performance indicators, etc.); and
iv Clarification or corrective changes in the contract – often of reduced impact.[3]

That context suggests poor project preparation and limited or poor studies critical to assess the real dimension/scope of the infrastructure projects (for example the ones behind the need for additional investments in infrastructure that were not included in the original PPP contract). Overall the changes come with requests, which are often granted, of additional payment commitments increasing the fiscal impact and affecting the value for money of the PPP project.[4]

In this context, a deficient effort in project preparation studies by the government (risk allocation, minimum requirements, selection criteria and PPP procurement procedures) and lack of effective contract monitoring can lead to potential contract renegotiation from both parties – public and private. Additionally, political reasons to accelerate the implementation of PPP projects with limited project preparation, or lack of such, and proper filters (for example, feasibility studies and proper evaluations by experts) can motivate consecutive renegotiations to accommodate the continuity of the PPP contract and the implementation of the contract commitments.[5]

Renegotiations of PPP contracts are perhaps the most serious problem affecting PPP projects and indeed the weakest link of PPP programs. The concern about renegotiations arise from its consequences:

- *Eliminate the competitive* effect of the auction, and distorts the public tender, in that the most likely winner is not the most efficient operator but the most expert/qualified in renegotiations, thereby questioning the credibility of the model/program;
- *The outcomes of the renegotiation show that on average decreases the benefits*/advantages of PPP and the welfare of users; usually it has a fiscal impact by increasing liabilities to the government; on average, terms of contract improve for private operator/investors, efficiency and value for money generally decrease and users are generally adversely affected;
- *Lack of transparency in the process* since it is done in a bilateral mode between the Granteur and the Concessionaire behind closed doors; and
- *Overall the high incidence of renegotiations questions the credibility of the program* and facilitates backlash from the users against the PPP program.

The relevance of the issue is ratified by the significantly high incidence of renegotiation of PPP contracts in Latin America – and also elsewhere. The evidence is substantial such as in Guasch (2004, 2016a), Guasch, Laffont and Straub (2003, 2006a, b), Guasch and Straub (2007), Guasch et al. (2016), Bitran, Nieto-Parra and Robledo (2012). Because of the nature of the contract (long-term and informational issues), some renegotiations are to be expected. Yet its high incidence is beyond the standard conceptual analysis of the issue. A very significant number of PPP have been renegotiated shortly after the contracts have been signed. These renegotiations occur frequently in a short period of time after financial close (or even before). And often the same contract is renegotiated several times (as we show below). The problem is especially acute in some sectors, notably transport and water and sanitation and beginning to appear in social sectors. Most of renegotiations are initiated by private sector operators and to a lesser extent by the government. Table 11.3 shows the data for LAC countries for three periods from 1990 to 2015. And, as shown, it does not appear to go away. After more than 25 years and of over 7000 PPP awarded, the incidence of renegotiation remains astonishingly high, in the 50 percent to 80 percent range. As an example of a single country, the incidence of renegotiations in Peru from 1998 to 2012 was 69 percent for all sectors and 84 percent for the transport sector; and the average number of renegotiations per Concession/PPP was 2.3 times.

But renegotiations are not a problem exclusive of emerging economies. As Table 11.4 shows, renegotiations are also quite prevalent in developed economies.

While some renegotiations can be efficient, many of them are opportunistic and ought to be dissuaded and/or rejected. Yet governments have proven unable to commit to a credible commitment to reject opportunistic or inappropriate petitions policy. In general the governments opt to accommodate the petitions so as not to risk discontinuity of service and transaction costs. That is confirmed by the data in Table 11.5, which shows than less than 3 percent of the PPP projects have

Table 11.3 Incidence of renegotiations of PPP contracts by Sector Y period

	Period 1990–2004	*Period 2004–2010*	*Period 2010–2015*
All sectors	42%	68%	58%
Electricity	10%	41%	30%
Transport	55%	81%	60%
Water and sanitation	75%	76%	66%
Other sectors: social et al.		42%	40%

Source: Guasch (2016a)

Table 11.4 Incidence of renegotiations around the world

Region/country	*Sector*	*% of renegotiated contracts*
Latin America and Caribbean	Total	68%
	Electricity	41%
	Transport	78%
	Water	92%
US	Highways	40%
France	Highways	50%
UK	All sectors	55%

Note: Percentage of renegotiated contracts by region and sector.

Source: Estache and Saussier (2014, pp. 8–13)

Table 11.5 Incidence of PPP projects cancelled

Period	*Total PPP projects in infrastructure*	*Cancelled*	*Percentage*
1990–2001	**2,485**	48	2.1%
		Composition	***Per sector***
		19 Toll roads	5.8%
		9 Energy	1.9%
		7 Water and sanitation	3.5%
		8 Telecom	0.3%
		48	
2001–2013	4.185	145	3.5%
		Composition	***Per sector***
		Toll roads	
		Energy	
		Water and sanitation	
		Telecom	

Source: Guasch (2016a) and Harris and Patrap (2008)

been cancelled. Then that in turn confirms the rational expectations of sponsors/Concessionaires who expect tolerance when requesting renegotiations under a variety of arguments.

To illustrate the effects of renegotiations, Table 11.6 illustrates the case of contract renegotiations for PPP transport projects in three LAC countries: Chile, Peru and Colombia. The table shows not only the high incidence of renegotiations, but also the number of times the same contract had been renegotiated in that ten-year period: 3.3 for Chile, 20 for Colombia and almost five for Peru. It also shows the speed of the renegotiations a few months after signing the contract. And perhaps more damaging, it shows the mean fiscal costs to the government per renegotiation: US$47 million for Chile, US$266 million for Colombia and US$28 million for Peru.

The most common triggers of renegotiation request are: i) additions or changes in the scope of the project, usually originated (but not always) by the government; ii) shortfalls in demand/revenues; iii) delays in expropriations and liberations of rights of way; iv) payment structure (bankability); v) rent-seeking opportunities; vi) political opportunities; and vii) aggressive bids or mistakes in the bids (an aggressive bid is defined as a bid in which expected net profits do not cover return to capital from day one and is intended to win the project, but with the objective of subsequently renegotiating better terms and positive returns).

Also the common use of contract clauses, such as the "economic and financial equilibrium of the contract," when they are vague, favors the sponsor and opens the door for claims and requests to renegotiate. This can also blur the definition of roles and risk allocations within the private partnership. In addition such clauses can also discourage the availability of project finance, as investors and lenders face increased uncertainties as to project returns and creditworthiness. That has been common in Brazil, particularly in the earlier stages of its PPP program.

Table 11.6 Renegotiation of PPP transport contracts in Chile, Colombia and Peru, 2000–2010

	Chile	*Colombia*	*Peru*
Total road concessions	21	25	15
Mean initial value of contract Constant US$ Dec. 2009, million	246	263	166
Mean initial term Years	25.2	16.7	22.1
Mean concession length Km	114	195	383
Mean concession years elapsed	12.5	9.0	4.6
Renegotiated road concessions	18	21	11
Total number of renegotiations	60	430	53
Mean number of renegotiations per concession	3.3	20.5	48
Mean time of first renegotiation Years	2.7	1.0	1.4
Mean fiscal cost of renegotiations Constant US$ Dec. 2009, million	47.2	266.8	289
Mean fiscal costs/initial value Percentage	17.4	282.8	13.4
Mean added term Years	0.9	6.3	08
Mean added length Km	0	54.6	0
Number of renegotiations/ concession years elapsed	0.2	1.9	0.9

Source: Bitran, Nieto-Parra and Robledo (2012)

Most countries are beginning to address this serious issue establishing a platform for renegotiations (for further details on the platform see Guasch (2016a). The principles behind that platform are:

- Preserve the value for money of the PPP project/contract.
- Inviolability of the Contractual/Bid Offer. When confronted with requests for renegotiation, the sacred character of the original contract/bid including the contractually agreed risk allocation must be respected. And the operator should be held responsible for its offer.
- The financial equation of the winning offer should always be the reference point, and if the contract would be modified in the case of the renegotiation or adjustment, the outcome should be an impact of zero net present value of the benefits and risks, and without changing the allocation matrix. Compensations to the other party have to be considered to insure any extraordinary benefit.
- Renegotiation must not be used to correct errors in the basis for tender or excessively risky or aggressive bids.

Yet, even under a context of renegotiation, the PPP programs have proven quite effective on average to bring about the desired benefits and reduce the infrastructure gap that most countries face. While the benefits have been quite significant, they could have been even higher had the program and project been better designed and implemented. There have been issues and problems most related to the post contract award management of projects and countries are beginning to address them. Important lessons learned in PPP renegotiations in Latin American countries have been accumulated and motivated Latin American countries to introduce key changes in the PPP legislation in countries with PPP experience (Peru, 2008, and Chile, 2010) and recently Colombia (2011) and Mexico (2012) through a renegotiation platform. A number of elements of that platform are:

i Establishing a matrix of risks with detailed risks identification and allocation, establishing that modifications of the contract must not alter the risk allocation (via a statement in the law or regulations);
ii Requesting that the financial model of the winner at the time of the bid be turned over to the Granter and be the basis for the analysis of petitions;
iii Establishing in the contract the right to evaluate and reject aggressive and reckless bids, defining the criteria and standards, including submission of financial model for those bids or additional guarantees (financial bonds);
iv Establishing that the performance bond will be adjusted upwards if the bid offer appears to be aggressive (as measured by the difference between the highest bid and the second highest and the average bid);
v Establishing a transparent framework of conflict resolution (panel of experts and arbitration);
vi Using proper panels of experts (which composition is based on the technical profile and selected at random from a pool of experts) to address issues such as aggressive bidding, renegotiation requests, arbitration, regulation-resetting tariff structure; and
vii Establishing a freeze period for considering renegotiation requests.

7 Issue about financial/economic equilibrium clauses

A critical and misunderstood factor that has facilitated renegotiation of contracts has been the ill-applied clauses of financial equilibrium in PPP contracts. In the early period of PPP programs, around the 1990s, it was common in most contracts to have a clause that, in the event that the original financial equilibrium would be reduced, it would grant the right to the Concessionaire to restore its financial equilibrium through interventions of the Granter and/or modifications of the contract. The clauses ranged from absolute to guided by specific events. Brazil was a foremost example of that use, but contracts in many other countries did have various versions of that clause. The re-equilibrium tool is a mechanism foreseen in Brazilian law to guarantee the rebalance of the contract's financial conditions in the event of risk occurrence that changes the contract's initial financial equilibrium. That practice has proven to be not only inappropriate and unnecessary but highly impacting (adversely) to the users and to the overall expected and/or potential benefits to the country. It led to a continuing request for contract modifications/renegotiations in light of adverse outcomes for the Concessionaire, even if the risk of the event was assigned to the Concessionaire (examples would be a decline or unrealized increases in demand, when the demand risk was assigned to the Concessionaire). It led to a cascade and flurry of unwarranted and not appropriate renegotiation demands (see Guasch et al., 2010). As a result most countries are eliminating that type of clause. In replacement, and following best practices, the contract has only to state that in the event of an action that affects the cash flow of the Concessionaire (as stated in the contract, where the responsibility and risk is assigned to the government), he is entitled to a compensation for the damage done by the action or event (or in the event of a positive effect, the government is entitled to receive the compensation from the Concessionaire). That is sufficient and voids the need to refer to restoring the financial/economic equilibrium.

The mentioning of restoring the financial/economic equilibrium has led to abuses and tergiversations of its objective. For instance, it can be the case that as a result of normal operations and poor luck, say on the level of demand, the financial equilibrium is already broken. Then if that event or action (which risk is assigned to the government) takes place that affects the cash flow, the Concessionaire has often argued and requested that the government restores the financial equilibrium, which now is broken as a result of two different causes, one where the Concessionaire is entitled to compensation, but not for the other. So it should not be correct to restore the financial/economic equilibrium. That is an example of why such language should not be used in the contract.

8 Conclusion

Overall the experience of PPP around the world has proven to be positive, delivering in general and on average value for money. Yet the process has not been a smooth one. It has been riddled with conflicts and with a high incidence of contract renegotiations that have reduced the expected benefits of the projects. Part of the problem has been that the PPP programs implemented were not fully coherent and that they were missing key components. That led to poor project selection, questionable prioritization, poor project structuring, risk allocation, weak contracts and careless oversight. Yet after more than 25 years of experience, countries have begun to tackle those issues, revisiting their PPP programs, via changes in the legal context, on institutionality, procedures and associated policies; as well as implementing renegotiating platforms and adding significant transparency in the process. That has led to improvements in the outcomes and has increased buy-in from the different stakeholders.

Notes

1 This section is adapted from Farquhason, Clemencia Torres and Yescombe, 2011.
2 The availability-based PPP had its genesis in the power purchase agreements used in independent power producer projects (IPPs), where the power off-taker was a public authority. In such projects, private investors typically build a power generation plant and contract to sell the electricity generated to a publicly owned power utility (or to a private

distribution company). The public authority assumes part or all of the demand risk and makes a minimum payment for a service, in this case the availability (or capacity) of the power plant, whether or not part or all of its output (energy) is actually required – in effect a form of "take-or-pay contract."

3 Clarification: Compensations to sponsor for the occurrence of specific events are not renegotiations, when it is specified in the contract. They do add to the costs of the contract, and do have adverse fiscal consequences. And they do generate conflicts on two accounts: on assessing the causality of the event – who is responsible – and on determining the proper level of compensation.

4 That is the case of Chile, where most of their renegotiations were driven by request for additionality of investment.

5 For example, in 2005 three PPP roads (Interoceanic 2, 3 and 4) were awarded in Peru without cost-benefit analysis. The government's approved plans avoid this important step. In 2006, a third amendment was signed to allow the financial close of the projects. In 2009 and 2010, based on the global financial crisis, the government decided to avoid or relax the cost-benefit analysis, reduce the filters (value for money analysis was postponed during these years) and relax the deadlines during PPP project preparation for a selected group of candidate projects.

References

Anzinger, N., and Kostka, G. (2015). *Large infrastructure projects in Germany*. Available at https://www.hertie-school.org/fileadmin/2_Research/2_Research_directory/Research_projects/Large_infrastructure_projects_in_Germany_Between_ambition_and_realities/4_WP_Offshore_Wind_Energy.pdf

Bitran, E., Nieto-Parra, S., and Robledo, J. (2012). *Opening the black box of contract renegotiations: An analysis of road concessions in Chile, Colombia and Peru*. Available at www.oecd.org/officialdocuments/publicdisplaydocumentpdf/?cote=DEV/DOC(2013)2&docLanguage=En

Calderón, C., and Servén, L. (2004). *The effects of infrastructure development on growth and income distribution*. Policy Research Working Paper No. 3400, World Bank, Washington, DC.

Estache, A., and Fay, M. (2010). *Current debates on infrastructure policy*. Policy Research Working Paper No. 57748, November, The World Bank, Washington, DC.

Estache, A., and Saussier, S. (2014). *Public-private partnerships and efficiency: A short assesment*. CESinfo DCE Report.

Farquhason, E., Torres, C., and Yescombe, E. R. (2011). *How to engage the private sector in public-private – partnerships in emerging markets*. PIAFF, The World Bank.

Fay, M. (2000). *Financing the future: Infrastructure needs in Latin America, 2000–05*. World Bank Working Paper No. 2545. The World Bank, Washington DC.

Fay, M., and Morroson, M. (2007). *Infrastructure needs in Latin America and Caribbean, directions in development*. The World Bank.

Fay, M., and Yepes, T. (2003). *Investing in infrastructure: What is needed from 2000–2010*. World Bank Policy Research Working Paper, 3102.

Guasch, J. L. (2003). Infrastructure concessions in Latin America and the Caribbean: The renegotiation issue and its determinants. *Infrastructure and Financial Markets: Review*, 9(2), 1–6.

Guasch, J. L. (2004). *Granting and Renegotiating Infrastructure Concessions: Doing It Right*. Development Studies. Washington, DC: World Bank Institute.

Guasch, J. L. (2009a). Past and future of the private participation in infrastructure. In ICEX (ed.), *Claves de la Economia Mundial*. Madrid, Espana: Instituto de Comercio Exterior (ICEX).

Guasch, J. L. (2009b). Regulatory governance and sector performance: Methodology and evaluation for electricity distribution in Latin America. In M. Ghertman and C. Menard (eds.), *Regulation, De-Regulation, and Re-Regulation*. London: Edward Elgar Publishing Press.

Guasch, J. L. (2016a). *Granting and Renegotiating Infrastructure Concessions II: Doing It Right*. The World Bank.

Guasch, J. L. (2016b). The evolution and performance of PPP programs and new trends. *Mimeo*.

Guasch, J. L. (2016c). *Private and public investments in infrastructure-PPP/concessions: International experiences and identification of new practices and conditions for success*. IPEA Research Paper 568, Rio de Janeiro Brazil.

Guasch, J. L., and Andres, L. (2008). Negotiating and renegotiating PPPs and concessions. In G. Schwartz (ed.), *Public Investment and Public-Private Partnerships*. London: Palgrave Macmillan Press.

Guasch, J. L., Andres, L., and Correa, P. (2005). Infrastructure reforms and the performance of privatized utilities in Latin America: The way ahead. June, *Revista do Tribunal de Contas da União*, 36(104), 41–52.

Guasch, J. L., Andres, L., Haven, T., and Foster, V. (2008). *The Impact of Private Sector Participation in Infrastructure in Latin America: Lights and Shadows and the Road Ahead*. The World Bank.

Guasch, J. L., Andres, L., and Schwartz, J. (2013). *Uncovering the Drivers of Utility Performance*. Washington, DC: World Bank Press.

Guasch, J. L., Andres, L., and Straub, S. (2008). *Does Regulation and Institutional Design Matter for Infrastructure Sector Performance. Part II?* IEA World Congress Volume. Palgrave-MacMillan Press.

Guasch, J. L., Benitez, D., Portables, I., and Flor, L. (2016). *The Renegotiation of Public Private Partnerships Contracts (PPP): An Overview of Its Recent Evolution in Latin America*. Revista Chilena de Economia y Sociedad.

Guasch, J. L., Estache, A., Izimi, A., and Trujillo, L. (2009). Multidimensionality and renegotiation: Evidence from transport-sector public-private-partnership transactions in Latin America. *Review of Industrial Organization*, 35, 41–71.

Guasch, J. L., Gonzalez, J., and Serebrisky, T. (2010). The infrastructure challenge: Cost and benefits. In B. Lomborg (ed.), *Latin America Development Priorities: Costs and Benefits*. Cambridge: Cambridge University Press.

Guasch, J. L., and Haven, T. (2008). Lessons from Latin America: Evaluation of PPPs and efficiency gains. In J.-H. Kim (ed.), *Performance Evaluation and Best-Practice of Public-Private Partnerships*. Seoul, Korea: Korean Development Institute Press.

Guasch, J. L., Laffont, J. J., and Straub, S. (2003). *Renegotiation of concession contracts in Latin America*. Policy Research Working Paper 3011, April Rand Journal of Economics.

Guasch, J. L., Laffont, J. J., and Straub, S. (2006a). Renegotiation of concession contracts: A theoretical approach. *Review of Industrial Organization*, 29(1–2), 55–73.

Guasch, J. L., Laffont, J. J., and Straub, S. (2006b). Concessions of infrastructure in Latin America: Government – led renegotiations. *Journal of Applied Econometrics*, 22(7), 1267–1294.

Guasch, J. L., and Spiller, P. (1999). *Managing the Regulatory Process: Design, Concepts, Issues, and the Latin America and Caribbean Story, Directions in Development*. Washington, DC: The World Bank, Press.

Guasch, J. L., and Straub, S. (2007). Renegotiations of infrastructure concessions: An overview. *Annals of Public and Cooperative Economics*, 77(4), 479–493.

Harris, C., and Patrap, K. (2008). *What drives private sector exit from infrastructure?* Gridlines Note 46, PPIAF, Washington, DC.

HM Treasury (2007). *Standardisation of PFI contracts – version 4*. Available at www.gov.uk/government/uploads/system/uploads/attachment_data/file/221556/infrastructure_standardisation_of_contracts_051212.pdf

Ipsos Mori Social Research Institute (2009). *Investigating the Performance of Operational Contracts*. London: Ipsos Mori, March.

Kohli, H. A., and Basil, P. (2011). Requirements for infrastructure investment in Latin America under alternate growth scenarios: 2011–2040. *Global Journal of Emerging Market Economies*, 3(1), 59–110.

Mandri-Perrott, C. (2014). *Financing PPP in LAC and Brazil: Lessons*. World Bank PPP.

MR (2008). Survey of procurement outcomes. Bond University, Australia.

New York Times (2016). The expansion of the Panama Canal. June 23.

Perrotti, D., and Sánchez, R. (2011). *La brecha de infraestructura en América Latina y el Caribe. Santiago*. CEPAL, Chile.

Private Participation in Infrastructure (PPI) Database website (2016). Available at http://ppi.worldbank.org/

Ruiz-Nunez, F., and Wei, Z. (2014). *Infrastructure investment demand in emerging markets and development economies*. Policy Research Working Paper 7414, The World Bank, Washington, DC.

Straub, S. (2008). *A meta-analysis of the impact of infrastructure investments on growth*. World Bank Report 2367.

Vassallo Magro, J. M. (2015). *Asociación Público Privada en América Latina. Aprendiendo de la experiencia. Bogotá: CAF*. Available at http://scioteca.caf.com/handle/123456789/758

World Bank (2014). *Public-Private Partnerships: Reference Guide Version 2.0*. Washington, DC: World Bank Group. Available at http://documents.worldbank.org/curated/en/600511468336720455/Public-private-partnerships-reference-guide-version-2-0

World Bank (2015). *Prioritizing infrastructure investment in South Asia: A methodological framework*. WB Report 12245.

World Bank (2016a). *Asistencia Técnica al Ministerio de Economía y Finanzas del Gobierno de Perú | Mejora del Mercado de Asociaciones Público-Privadas: Guía de Apoyo para el Desarrollo de Estudios Técnicos de Pre-Inversión*.

World Bank (2016b). *Benchmarking PPP procurement 2016 – assessing public procurement systems in 77 economies*. Available at http://bpp.worldbank.org/~/media/WBG/BPP/Documents/Reports/Benchmarking-Public-Procurement-2016.pdf

World Bank Institute (2012a). *Best practices in PPP financing in Latin America: The role of subsidy mechanisms*. Available at https://ppiaf.org/sites/ppiaf.org/files/publication/BestPracticesroleofsubsidiesmechanisms.pdf

World Bank Institute (2012b). *Best practices in PPP financing in Latin America: The role of innovative approaches*. Available at https://ppiaf.org/sites/ppiaf.org/files/publication/BestPracticesroleofinnovativeapproaches.pdf

World Bank Institute (2012c). *Best practices in PPP financing in Latin America: The role of guarantees*. Available at https://ppiaf.org/sites/ppiaf.org/files/publication/BestPracticesroleofguarantees.pdf

World Bank, MEF Peru (2016). *Greenbook – Perú APP: Asistencia Técnica al Ministerio de Economía y Finanzas (MEF) para la mejora del mercado de APPs*.

12 Renegotiation and anti-corruption measures in public procurement

Biancamaria Raganelli and Ilenia Mauro

1 Introductions

How to ensure integrity, accountability and transparency of public authorities and economic operators across countries?

Non-transparent economic interests may influence legislation, its implementation, competition in the market and finally economic growth and competitiveness. It may underpin corrupt behaviours and result in the creation of a kind of barrier in the market: new borders and constraints within the economy. This effect is particularly evident in public procurement and the renegotiation of the contract.

A community of values is growing in the wider context of transnational and international bodies such as OECD, UN, and single Member States to promote a joint system against corruption, but still needs a clear means of action.

2 Corruption, human rights and economic implications

How to ensure integrity, accountability, and transparency of public authorities and economic operators across countries?

A community of values is growing in the wider context of transnational and international bodies such as the OECD, the UN, and in single Member States to promote a joint system against corruption, but it still needs a clear means of actions.

The lack of integrity and corruption affects human rights and the market, and are an issue in public procurement. Non-transparent economic interests supported by lobbies and conflicts of interest may influence the legislation, its implementation, competition and, ultimately, the economic growth and competitiveness of the market itself.

As is well known, corruption is not considered a criminal offence in most criminal codes around the world, and it also does not have a legal definition in most international treaties. However, international scholars have highlighted the effects of corruption on economic performance and consider them to be strong constraints on growth and development. Some scholars consider corruption a 'grease the wheels' instrument. In this perspective, it helps to overcome cumbersome bureaucratic constraints, inefficient provision of public services and rigid laws (Huntington, 1968; Lui, 1985), especially when countries' institutions are weak and function poorly (Acemoglu and Verdier, 2000; Méon and Weill, 2010). Others argue that corruption only reduces economic performance. This is due to rent seeking, an increase of transaction costs and uncertainty, inefficient investments, and misallocation of production factors (Murphy et al., 1991; Shleifer and Vishny, 1993; Rose-Ackerman, 1997) that come with corruption. A third stream finds ambiguous effects of corruption can be illustrated with respect to public finances in new EU Member States. Hanousek and Kocenda (2011) show that reductions in corruption either increase or decrease public investment, depending on the country and its institutions. Data shows that bribery behaviours are widespread in Europe, and more significantly in southern countries. According to Transparency International's Global Corruption Barometer, perceptions of corruption and faith in governmental institutions are on the rise in the region, in particular in Greece, Italy and Spain. However, according to part of the literature, there is no linear relationship between corruption and economic growth in regimes rated as "free" by Freedom House. (Mendez and Sepulveda, 2006). The growth-maximizing level of corruption – in the so-called free countries – is significantly greater than zero, with corruption being beneficial to economic growth at low levels of incidence, while abnormally high levels of corruption are detrimental, regardless of the government type.

Last but not least, the quality of the institutions in a given country is a major determinant of the effects of corruption (Aidt and Dutta, 2007). In countries with deficient institutions, corruption has little to no effect on economic growth, because voters cannot punish corrupt politicians, while researchers concluded that in countries with relatively strong democratic institutions, corruption does damage growth, but economic growth itself is a strong guarantor of reducing corruption, because it means that the resource base from which leaders extract rents expands over time. This makes them more eager to hold on to political power and creates a positive feedback loop between economic growth and corruption: high growth reduces corruption, which increases growth.

The phenomena of corruption in its different forms and implications – such as lobbying and conflicts of interest, for example – could potentially build new kinds of borders and boundaries in the economy and in the market. Those include real barriers, new walls aiming at keeping economic interests and groups within the market and society separate. They are negative borders and boundaries, affecting human rights and the market, with dangerous implications on growth, development and employment.

On the other hand, there are traditional borders and boundaries among countries that need to be crossed if we want to prevent and fight corruption successfully. An increasingly popular way for some States to prevent bribery committed overseas is adopting measures with extraterritorial implications, or asserting direct extraterritorial jurisdiction in specific instances. Such measures may affect companies on the international market and clearly show a difference in the strategies of the so-called zero-tolerance countries compared to the so-called more tolerant ones.

The first part of the chapter investigates two different profiles linked to the same phenomena, with a comparative approach. The legal boundaries of lobbying combined with conflicts of interest and corruption, on the one hand; the effects of some extraterritorial legislation, such as the US and the UK anti-bribery models, on the other hand. It analyzes the role of private and public preventive anti-corruption measures as a means of action in the international market. The aim is to contribute to the current debate in the literature, aiming at developing a model supporting integrity in public procurement, in order to prevent corruption and its implications (as well as conflict of interests and lobbying) and their negative externalities; and to mitigate the negative externalities linked to the measures adopted by the zero-tolerance countries.

The second part of the chapter will deal with the renegotiation issue linked to the risk of corruption. It investigates the tendering process, with special focus being placed on the selection stage and the risk of corruption related to the submission of overly aggressive offers designed solely to ensure selection, with the hidden purpose of renegotiating the contract at a later stage.

3 International anti-corruption instruments

The most common definition of corruption is the one used by the Transparency International NGO, according to which corruption is the "abuse of entrusted power for private gain." The World Bank – by referring to the definition adopted by the United Nation's Global Program against Corruption – specified that corruption involves such acts as bribery to circumvent public policies, through patronage and nepotism, the theft of public resources, or through the diversion of state resources (Racca– and Perin, 2014).

Such definition mainly covers bureaucratic/public sector corruption, and particularly emphasizes phenomena such as administrative bribes and kickbacks (PwC and Ecorys, June 2013, p. 56).

Corruption follows the unofficial laws of the market, thereby circumventing the rule of law that is a necessary condition for the respect of human rights. The fight against bribery has become a universal issue in several countries. Moreover, considering the importance of international trade for global economic growth, the costs generated by non-tariff barriers – such as those related to the lack of integrity in border control and customs administrations – can be quite significant for the public and private sectors, and for citizens and society as a whole. Indeed, corruption is considered one of the most serious crimes with a cross-border dimension (Racca and Perin, 2014).

Corruption impacts societies in a multitude of ways and has an important human rights dimension. The UNCAC not only underlines the economic consequences of corruption but also the developmental and political impacts. It refers to the impact on ethical values and justice, but there is no explicit reference to the impact of corruption on human rights. (Wouters, Ryngaert and Cloots, 2012).

Only recently has a human rights perspective been introduced in the anti-corruption narrative. Its costs impact on different aspects, including political, economic, social and environmental ones. It may occur in several different fields, thus affecting both the public and private sectors, including the health system, climate change, education, humanitarian assistance, public procurement, the legal system, or politics and government. Moreover, corruption crucially affects the development of Third World countries. Actually, briberies as well as different indirect forms of corruption are barriers to the development process of those countries, which are difficult to fight. Worldwide, over the last decade, corruption has received special focus in the development and political economy debate. It has been seen as a primary impediment to growth, with dramatic consequences in the developing world (OECD, 2016).

Over the last decade, some efforts have been made to reduce corruption at an international level. In the EU, corruption remains one of the biggest challenges for all societies (Racca and Perin, 2014). Corruption allows the creation of a kind of barrier that builds new borders and constraints within the single market. In this perspective, it restricts the four fundamental freedoms established in the year 2000 Charter of Fundamental Rights of the European Union. The Treaty on the Functioning of the European Union recognizes that corruption is a serious crime with a cross-border dimension, and art. 83(1) includes it among those crimes for which directives providing minimum rules on definition of criminal offences and sanctions may be established. Article 83(1) of the Treaty on the Functioning of the EU reads: “the European Union has a general right to act in the field of anti-corruption policies”, in particular, the EU should ensure a high level of security, including by preventing and combating serious crimes, which are often linked to corruption and cannot be addressed by the EU Member States alone. In this perspective, the recent EU Anti-Corruption Report confirms that this objective “cannot be sufficiently achieved by the Member States” and will require an intervention at the Union level.

The European anti-corruption framework is based on the accession (OECD, 1999) of the EU to the United Nations Convention against Corruption (UNCAC), on the role played by Transparency International, and on the joining of the OECD Convention on Combating Bribery of Foreign Public Officials in International Business Transactions. The setting up of Transparency International in 1993 was the first crucial milestone in terms of the work of civil society organizations and networks, both national and international, dedicated to controlling corruption (OECD, 1999).

The implementation of the anti-corruption legal framework remains uneven in the various EU Member States and, overall, unsatisfactory. The EU anti-corruption legislation has not been implemented in all Member States. Prior to the entry into force of the TFEU, the Commission had no power to take legal action against those Member States that did not implement measures adopted under the Third Pillar of the Treaty. Since 1 December 2014, instead, it is possible for the Commission to take such legal actions pursuant to Art. 10 of Protocol No. 36 on Transitional Provisions of the Treaty of Lisbon.

From a national point of view, some countries have still not ratified the most important international anti-corruption instruments and, even where anti-corruption institutions and legislations are in place, there are strong weaknesses on the enforcement side. It is now clear that finding appropriate tools and solutions to tackle corrupt practices in trade is not a simple “endeavour” and there is no single-fix solution. The need has been underlined to establish and enforce clear provisions against bribery and corruption for both public and private sectors in order to promote integrity, facilitate trade, ensure a more effective distribution of benefits, and contribute to sustainable, fair and inclusive economic growth (OECD, 2016).

As stated in a 1999 OECD survey, public procurement is the most affected sector by corruption and collusion. The allocation of public resources in the public interest through public contracts and procurement functions provides a large number of opportunities for corruption. Hence, public procurement has been targeted by various national, international and multilateral anti-corruption initiatives as an area in need of reform (Arrowsmith, 2010).

In public procurement, corruption can add as much as 50 percent to a project's cost, while reducing the quality of works or services. However, until 2014, the EU legal framework on public procurement did not include any specific provisions on the prevention and sanctioning of conflicts of interest, as it only included few specific provisions on sanctioning favouritism and corruption. The 2014 Directives on public contracts and concessions tried to bridge the gap, but there is still a long way to go.

At an international level, the OECD Convention on Combating Bribery of Foreign Public Officials (OECD Convention) entered into force in 1999, and only covers corruption to the extent it is related to business transactions. Moreover, it only covers "active" corruption. Only in 2003 did the UN Convention against Corruption target the passive side of the phenomenon. Moreover, while the OECD Convention only referred to corrupt practices in transnational business transactions, the UN Convention against Corruption (UNCAC) also covers corruption beyond transnational business transactions. In this perspective, the Preamble to the UN Convention against Corruption refers to the detrimental effects of corruption on political stability, on the rule of law, on ethical values and democracy, while the OECD Convention mainly focused on the market-distorting effects of corruption. Such idea on the detrimental impact of corruption beyond the traditional economic notions may be also found in the Inter-American Convention against Corruption (OAS Convention), which focuses more on democratic institutions (OAS Convention, Preamble, 1996).

The United Nations Convention against Corruption (UNCAC) was the first truly global anti-corruption Treaty. Broad international consensus on the Convention was not only shared by the relevant States, but also by international private sector actors and civil society. As a consequence, on 1 July 2012, 160 States – including important global players such as the US, China and India – became parties to the UNCAC (Wouters, Ryngaert and Cloots, 2012). The UNCAC is also open for signature by regional economic integration organizations, provided that at least one Member State of such organizations has signed the Convention. The EU signed the Convention on 15 September 2005 and ratified it on 12 November 2008. Currently, it is the only regional economic integration organization that is party to the Convention. Despite its innovative approach, the UNCAC monitoring was not ground-breaking. It merely established a Conference of State Parties with the aim of "regularly" monitoring the implementation of the Convention. It requires the State Parties to set up domestic corruption-preventing and corruption-combating bodies. In order to be effective, such bodies should meet the requirements laid down by the Convention as, inter alia, independence, adequate resources, training and specialization.

According to an OECD study, those anti-corruption bodies should focus at least on four areas of anti-corruption efforts. Some States have adopted multi-agency models, which focus on strengthening anti-corruption measures in existing governmental agencies, while other countries opted for the single-agency model, which gives one anti-corruption agency the primary responsibility of implementing an anti-corruption program. There are also countries where the strength of internal monitoring by governmental agencies is mixed.

In fighting corruption offences worldwide, huge efforts have also been made by private initiatives. Established by a former World Bank director in 1993, the Transparency International NGO has been the driving force behind the global anti-corruption movement. Its most influential corruption tool is the Corruption Perception Index. In addition to the CPI, TI publishes a Bribe Payers Index (BPI) and a Global Corruption Barometer (GCB). Moreover, already in 1977, the International Chamber of Commerce (ICG) adopted its first set of flagship rules against corruption.

In the last decades, the EU has also been broadening its focus on anti-corruption policies, but despite the effort, data shows a low level of trust of EU citizens in the EU's ability to fight corruption. Major efforts are expected in this direction, while adequate EU legislation, mechanisms and standards against corruption are needed to tackle the issue at its roots. As it has already been pointed out, civil society has a key role to play in preventing and combating corruption offences, which ranges from monitoring public procurement and services to denouncing bribery and raising awareness of the risks of wasting public money (Racca and Perin, 2014). The international anti-corruption legal framework has been substantially strengthened in the past two decades, with impressive progress being made at both global and regional levels. Nevertheless, the work is far from over.

Since the various anti-corruption instruments were rather fragmented and the idea that streamlining a coherent anti-corruption policy in all its activities would enhance success on this issue, the EU has developed a comprehensive anti-corruption framework, focused on the enforcement of existing instruments. The communication set up a new EU Anti-Corruption Report mechanism, with the aim being to work closely together with GRECO, the anti-corruption enforcement mechanism of the Council of Europe, and avoiding overlapping reporting mechanisms (EU Commission, 2011).

4 French and Italian models compared

Under the French law, corruption and conflicts of interest have many legal qualifications: active and passive corruption (Criminal code, art. 432–11 and 433–1), influence peddling (Criminal Code, art. 432–11, 433–1, 433–2) and conflicts of interest. It is not possible to assimilate corruption, lobbying and conflicts of interest. The object of the three practices can be the same, but their aims are different. Lobbying has been defined as an influential action, motivated by particular, category-specific and divisive interests, which is brought to the attention of a particular public officer or a producing branch of imperative legal rules without any counterpart (Houillon, 2014). In other words, lobbyists solicit administrative or legal protection for their particular interests.

At an international level, conflicts of interest are defined as conflicts between the public duty and private interests of a public official, in which the public official has private-capacity interests which could improperly influence the performance of his/her official duties and responsibilities (OECD, 2003). Within the procurement procedure, conflicts of interest may occur at any stage of the process, regardless of whether the procedure is open, restricted or negotiated. They arise at the time of defining the specifications of a project and the awarding criteria, or at the verification and selection stage or, lastly, at the awarding stage (White, 2014).

The necessity to establish legal boundaries between the three above-mentioned practices stems from the fact that corruption and conflicts of interest are regulated by *law*, whereas lobbying still remains in the domain of *facts*. Hence, it is necessary to define the cases in which defending a particular interest with public authorities, which is allowed by law, exceeds permissible limits and becomes an unlawful behaviour.

As a matter of urgency, the French policy-maker has adopted two laws: the *Loi organique* n° 2013–906 and n° 2013–907 of 11 October 2013 on Transparency in Public Life. Awareness is raised on the need for a preventive approach in the fight against conflicts of interest, as opposed to the repressive method that has been used so far (French Criminal Code, art. 432–12).

Article 2 of Law of 11 October 2013 defines conflicts of interest as interferences between a public and a private interest, able to compromise the independent, impartial and objective exercise of a public function. It also covers the hypotheses that appear to influence said independent, impartial and objective exercise of a public function.

The first requirement is the obligation of restraint imposed on the members of the government or of the Committee of Independent Authorities, either private or public, or on local office-holders with executive functions and on public service agencies. On the other hand, there are the disclosure requirements on property and income, in the frame of the fight against corruption and the so-called disclosure of any conflicts of interest (articles 1 and 26). Nevertheless, the French Constitutional Court has modified the impact of the law under consideration, in response to privacy concerns, and defined the boundaries between the principle of publicity and the opposite principle of confidentiality.

At the EU level, the debate on lobbying focuses mainly on direct representations by pressure groups in the legislation-making process. A more comprehensive approach includes different forms of communication and research activities that underpin, inform and support the preparation of policy proposals before lobbyists send them to the legislators and decision-makers (Inter-Institutional Agreement, the European Parliament and the Commission OJ L (2011) 191/29).

As noted before, the issue concerning lobbying in the French legal system is related to the absence of a legal definition of the phenomenon. However, despite the absence of a legal definition, lobbying exists in fact, and doctrine tries to elaborate a definition in order to recognize when it is implemented in practice.

Lobbying is considered as a spontaneous action taken with the aim to consider a specific interest while exercising decision-making powers. No compensation is involved in the process leading to the adoption of a legal act specifically adopted or modified in order to satisfy that particular interest (Houillon, 2012). As a consequence, in France, lobbying does not have proper "juridical evidence", but it could be the base for further legal action. Actually, it does not cause any direct modification of the legal system, but it may produce effects on the current legal order.

As some scholars maintain, lobbying is a freedom. The first concern for the French policy-maker is to understand when exercising said freedom goes beyond what is legally feasible, and how to prevent this and punish illegal actions. In fact, any reprehensible behaviour can be indicated in the activity carried out by groups of interest that try to raise the awareness of the decision-making authorities on a specific issue in order to adopt a better designed policy. It is important to clarify when such freedom becomes relevant and could be pursued vigorously as a criminal behaviour. The boundary between the legitimate exercise of lobbying and corruption is the core of the issue, and it is linked to the concept of "absence of compensation". The interest can come into consideration of the decision-making agent without any direct or indirect compensation. Any offer, as well as any request of compensation, can be considered a means of corruption. On the contrary, when the action of the decision-making agent is not driven by any compensation, but it is only based on simple recommendations or suggestions made by the groups of interest, it can be considered lobbying.

Consequently, transparency in lobbying becomes essential in order to avoid the lack of legality that badly influences public confidence in public institutions. Both particular and public interest should be taken into account. In this perspective, in 2009, the internal rules of the French Parliament have been amended in order to introduce a Register of lobbyists. Registration in the Register is voluntary and aims at regulating access to the House and Senate (Art. 26 III, B de l'Instruction générale du Bureau de l'Assemblée nationale and Chapitre XXII*bis* de l'Instruction générale du Bureau du Sénat). Penalties are not imposed in the event of breach of procedural and conduct rules. The only possible consequence is removal from the Register, which is decided by the *Direction de l'Accueil et de la Sécurité* (TI France, 2013). That was the first reform that represents a step in the right direction, but it is still not enough to regulate a wide-spread and potentially highly dangerous phenomenon.

Moving towards the second civil law model, Italy made some effort in the strategy against corruption.

The so-called Anti-Corruption Law of 6 November 2012, no. 190, made the sanctions harsher for offences such as corruption in the performance of act in breach of official duties. Together with a more dissuasive effect, there is also the extension of the limitation period for each of the officers. Furthermore, a special Ministerial Study Commission – the so-called Commissione Fiorella – was set up in 2013 to study the possibility of a more systematic reform in the field of time limitation (article 1, paragraphs 15, 16, 32 and 33).

In public procurement, Law no. 190/2012 provides for rules fostering transparency in order to prevent corruption in public procurement.

> The contracting authorities shall publish on their web sites information on the ongoing tendering procedures and send such information in digital format to the Authority for the Supervision of Public Contracts, which was replaced by the Anti-Corruption Authority in 2014. The supervisory Authority shall publish it on its web site, in a section that is freely accessible to all citizens, listed by type of contracting authority and Region. As additional information requirements, public administrations shall publish on their websites information on budgets and final accounts, as well as on unit costs for construction works and the production costs for the services provided to citizens.
>
> (Law No. 114 of June 24th 2014)

Among the most innovative aspects, the abovementioned law introduced, for the first time in Italy, a provision specifically related to the whistle-blowing regulation in the public sector. The whistle-blower cannot be punished, dismissed or discriminated on grounds that are directly or indirectly connected to him/her blowing the whistle. During any disciplinary proceedings, the identity of the whistle-blower cannot be disclosed without his/her consent, unless this is a *sine qua non* condition for the defence of the accused person. Any discriminatory measure must be reported to the Department for Public Administration by the whistle-blower or by the trade unions representing the administration involved (Chapter 3.1.11 of National Anticorruption Plan).

In general terms, it is important to underline that Law no. 190/2012 places emphasis on the relevance of training for public employees in the prevention of and fight against corruption. Such training activities are coordinated by the National School of Administration – SNA (paragraph 3.1.12 of National Anticorruption Plan).

It is also important to remind the action taken through the adoption of Law Decree no. 62/2013, the Code of Conduct for Public Employees. The Code includes rules and provisions that contribute to counter the bribery phenomenon. Each administration is required to adopt its own Code of Conduct.

5 US and UK models: the common law approach

One increasingly popular way for States to prevent bribery committed overseas is by adopting measures with extraterritorial implications, or by asserting direct extraterritorial jurisdiction in specific instances. Such measures may have implications for companies operating in different countries.

The international fight against corruption, and the fight against transnational bribery in particular, received a strong impulse from the effort of the US legislation against bribery offences of foreign public officials. Reference is to the adoption of the Foreign Corrupt Practices Act (FCPA), in 1977, which was thoroughly reformed in 1988 when President Ronald Reagan signed the House Report 4848, the Omnibus Trade and Competitiveness Act. Some issues arise because firms face different kinds of illegal behaviour. As argued above, in many countries, engaging a local agent or having a local sponsor is a requirement for doing business in that country (Koelher, 2012).

The FCPA prohibits the payment of money or anything of value to a foreign official in order to assist the payer in obtaining or retaining business (15 United States Code (USC), par. 78dd-1). It also provides for the right to prosecute any foreign enterprises and their officials, agents, shareholders or employees involved in such illicit behaviour whenever there is a link (even a weak one) between the foreign enterprise and the American territory. This is under the jurisdiction of the Department of Justice (DoJ) and of the Securities Exchange Commission (SEC). The sanctions legal framework envisages tough penalties for both the enterprise and individuals (USC, par. 77dd-2). In order to benefit from the suspension of the jurisdictional prosecution, some French enterprises involved in foreign corruption practices and prosecuted by the DoJ and by SEC signed transnational agreements with the American authorities for an amount of US$1,645 million (2014 Report issued by the *Service Central de Prévention de la Corruption*). This is why the fight against corruption in international business transactions becomes a relevant issue in the French debate and, for the same reasons, it is a global problem for governments and companies doing business internationally.

In recent times, new legislation with extraterritorial effect has been developed, which is a reality in the framework of international law. As it has been pointed out by some scholars, the debate on extraterritorial effect is closely linked to the framework of globalization of economic and financial flows, which leads to a fragmentation of national sovereignty and of the national legal systems. Under international law, based on the principle of territoriality, States may regulate acts committed in their territory and can exercise territorial jurisdiction over individuals and companies within their territory. This means that territorial jurisdiction may be exercised over natural or legal persons even when the conduct under consideration takes place abroad (Scott, 2014). Extraterritoriality formally occurs when a national legislation is applied to a foreign person/enterprise that is subject to the jurisdiction of the regulating State, due to acts committed, at least partially, outside the territory of that State. The issue concerns the demonstration of the existence of a link between the individuals or the acts committed on the one hand, and the territory of the regulating State on the other hand.

As outlined before, the 1977 US Foreign Corrupt Practices Act, which prohibits bribery of foreign public officials, is extraterritorial by nature. Anyway, it does not infringe upon the sovereignty of other States, because the ability of a State to punish acts of foreign individuals or legal entities that operate on its territory does not contravene the principle of territoriality, when the relevant nexus exists between those persons or the acts committed and the territory of the regulating State (Cohen-Tanugi, 2015).

The UK has also recently adopted a zero-tolerance approach through a special regulation prohibiting bribery of foreign officials for business purposes. The UK Bribery Act (UKBA), which entered into force on 1 July 2011 (Bribery Act 2010, Chapter 23), prohibits improper payments to both domestic and foreign public officials, as well as bribes and kickbacks in purely commercial contexts (The UK Anti-corruption Plan, 2014). It also provides for an autonomous title of company's liability when there is a lack of effective arrangements to prevent corruption within the enterprise (Section 1, 2.6 and 7 of UKBA).

In the circumstances referred to in Section 7 of the UKBA, relating to the failure of commercial organizations to prevent bribery, the *respondeat superior* principles apply if an isolated incident of bribery occurs within a commercial organization. However, in the Bribery Act Guidance, the Ministry of Justice pointed out that the organization concerned would have a full defence if it can prove that, despite a particular case of bribery, it nevertheless had adequate procedures in place to prevent persons associated with it in from bribing (Ministry of Justice, The Bribery Act 2010, Guidance15).

Going back to the issue of extraterritorial legislation, it may be stated that even the UKBA regulation is not a piece of extra-territorial legislation. It provides the company's liability for the act committed by a person associated with it, regardless of where the act was committed. Section 7 also requires that the commercial organization carries out business or part of its business in the UK, wherever in the world it may be incorporated or formed. Thus, the requirement of a link with the territory of the regulating State always needs to be met.

As a result, it is possible to talk about the extraterritoriality of law in relative terms. Looking at the application of specific legislation that spreads its effects over a foreign legal or natural person, is not possible to give a trenchant answer – yes or no. One could, on the contrary, imagine different degrees of extra-territorial application of law. Hence, pure territoriality does not exist. Even with the so-called universal jurisdiction – whose best example is the legislation countering crimes against humanity – a link with the territory of the regulating country is always required for the jurisdiction of the regulating country over a foreign person to be recognized. It might even be a very tenuous link – such as the presence of the guilty person in the territory of the country, or the fact that he/she is captured in that country – but it has to be there.

All the above leads to further considerations. Besides the financial risk for enterprises, which arises in the framework of foreign legislation against corruption in international trade, there are several consequences of the application of a foreign legislation with extra-territorial effects, and more specifically the FCPA and UKBA, which are analyzed in this chapter.

Bribery causes reputational risks and dents the worldwide image of companies. Suffice it to think of the media impact of allegations of corruption. Furthermore, there is a human risk for the employees, the management and the representatives prosecuted in their own countries or abroad. International corruption also causes a loss of income, as those companies are excluded from public procurement contracts financed by States, local and regional authorities, and investment banks. In this contest, for example, an Italian enterprise carrying out commercial transactions with a British one – or acting under British jurisdiction – may be prosecuted under the UK law if it is found guilty of whatever act of corruption committed anywhere. The same Italian enterprise can be prosecuted under the UK law also if an individual associated with the company bribes another person, in the UK or elsewhere.

As has already been highlighted, the implications of such measures are important for single companies, but also for the market as a whole, as well as for the relations between individual European countries, and at global level. Public and private entities are expected to adopt preventive measures to limit the effects of said regulations and avoid penalties. A hint in this direction is given by Section 7 of the UKBA, pursuant to which any company accused of bribing (committed by a person associated, regardless of where the act was committed) may avoid being prosecuted (because liable) if it is able to prove that it had adopted a structured preventive strategy against corruption.

6 Preventive anti-corruption measures in Europe. Private and public ethics and compliance programs

A risk-based approach promoting integrity is required. As was pointed out by the 2016 OECD Integrity Forum, it is imperative that public and private sector entities conduct comprehensive corruption risk assessment to define their exposure to integrity risks, which allows them to put in place appropriate anti-corruption controls (2016 OECD Background documents).

As underlined with respect to the French case, the fight against corruption and the efforts to avoid the dangerous effects of zero-tolerance countries on bribery affect all companies worldwide trading abroad. In fact, firms may find it extremely difficult to conduct business without bribing in jurisdictions at high risk of corruption. Such lack of integrity in trade particularly affects smaller firms, which are disadvantaged because they are unable to bear the costs of corruption due to a lack of access to appropriate legal resources and sufficient cash flow (2014 OECD Foreign Bribery Report).

However, the private sector may also contribute to a global fight against corruption and to the efforts made to avoid the dangerous effects of zero-tolerance countries on bribery.

The OECD issued an *Anti-Corruption Ethics and Compliance Handbook for Business* to encourage companies to develop and adopt adequate internal controls, ethics and compliance programmes, or measures for the purpose of preventing and detecting foreign bribery (OECD-UNODC, World Bank, Anti-corruption Ethics and Compliance Handbook for Business, 2013). As has been underlined, enterprises should conduct an anti-corruption risk assessment to better understand their risk exposure. Each enterprise's own risk assessment exercise is unique, depending on that enterprise's industry, size, location and so on.

The relevance of good anti-corruption risk assessment is strictly connected with the adoption of a good compliance programme by the enterprises; it may allow business to develop and maintain a compliance program that is tailored and risk-based. An enterprise should update its risk assessment plan periodically, also envisaging the training of those employees whose activities entail higher corruption risks.

First, it is necessary to promote the idea that integrity is the heart of a company's activity. This implies doing business in a responsible, transparent and ethical way. Those values increase the reputation of a company and are the most valuable assets, which could be further strengthened through the adoption of specific compliance policies, procedures and controls. As is well known, integrity is at the basis of a company's activity and has a positive impact on a company's competitiveness. Doing business in a responsible, transparent and ethical manner may increase the reputation of the company and represents the most crucial issue.

On the private side, there are firms or companies that adopt very structured ethics and compliance programs consisting of the adoption of rules, in their implementation within the company and, lastly, in the adoption of a monitoring and enforcement system through the application of sanctions for the infringement of the relevant rules (Siemens Compliance Guide, 2009). The adoption of a Code of Conduct is very important in order to define how the employees should act when they face some widespread forms of bribery. It shall contain general principles and prohibitions applying not only to ordinary employees, but also to consultants and other third parties working for of the company. The Code of Conduct, which is also called Code of Ethics or Disciplinary Code, should be adopted as an official document by the company and should provide for specific rights, duties and responsibilities, also with regard to other stakeholders (including clients, shareholders, public administrations and so on). Each employee shall undertake to comply with said provisions and with the relevant laws and regulations in force in the geographical area in which the company operates.

Staff communication shall be clear and detailed, effective, repeated and periodically updated. Especially in case of doubt, access to and consultation of the relevant compliance rules should be guaranteed. In parallel with the communication activity, the company should provide a specific training programme, tailored to different target groups. Participation in the training sessions should be compulsory and supervised by a supervisory body. The employees should realize how important the company's policy against corruption is, both in legal and practical terms.

A key point is the provision of an adequate enforcement system in cases of breach of the relevant ethical standards. This implies the adoption of a disciplinary system, which is a cornerstone in the US compliance programs. The measures envisaged by the enforcement system shall be appropriate to the nature and gravity of the infringement, and shall always be based on the principles of proportionality and adversarial process. At the national level, it is important to remember the Confindustria Guidelines, adopted on 7 March 2002 and updated in March 2014 on the construction of organizational, management and control models, on the base of Law Decree no. 231 of 2001. Confindustria is the main association representing manufacturing and service companies in Italy. With the above mentioned document, the association aims to offer to the enterprises a model to follow in the adoption of specific compliance programs. This is in order to avoid the responsibility of legal persons issued by the Law Decree no. 231 when a list of specified crimes occurs, which includes corruption. The guidelines stress the importance of the adoption of such a compliance model, including to avoid the consequences related to the application of a foreign legislation against corruption, such as the UK Bribery Act and the Foreign Corruption Practices Act (FCPA). (Confindustria Guidelines, 2002). Such compliance measures may be envisaged for public authorities as well. This strategy implies the adoption of anti-corruption preventive measures based on the specific organization of the individual institution under consideration.

Some measures appear particularly justified, such as risk mapping related to corruptive practices, the adoption of a Code of Conduct with a preventive role with respect to corruption practices, an effective management of the *pantouflage* phenomenon, controls on causes of incompatibility of public mandates and rotating assignments.

The Code of Conduct should provide for appropriate supervisory and rule-infringement sanctioning mechanisms; it should also envisage a system of incentives and specific training courses promoting a culture of integrity.

The need for the adoption of a Code of Conduct by the public authorities is not a new idea. On 17 May 2012, the Presidency of the French Republic released the *Charte de Déontologie des Membres du Governement*, laying down five principles that should guide the action of government members, namely solidarity and collective responsibility, concertation and transparency, impartiality, availability, integrity and exemplary. The adoption of this Code of Conduct is motivated as follows:

> Le bon fonctionnement d'une démocratie passe par l'existence d'un lien de confiance entre les citoyens et ceux qui gouvernent. Cette confiance ne se confonde pas avec la légitimité donnée, directement ou indirectement, par le suffrage universel . . . C'est afin d'aider à la construction et à la préservation de ce lien de confiance qu'il a paru utile de rassembler, sous la forme d'une "charte de déontologie", quelques principes simples qui doivent guider le comportement des membres du gouvernement.

In France, several authorities at the sub-State level adopted said principles, but more efforts are required to give them a tangible value. The effectiveness in the implementation of public authorities' principles could be guaranteed by a civil servant's performance-assessment method. Lacking a sanctioning mechanism designed for any case of breach of conduct rules, a performance-related pay system may have a serious incentive effect.

From a soft law perspective, it is possible to mention the adoption of guidelines for the implementation of legislation on transparency and corruption prevention by the publicly owned corporation, issued by the Italian Anti-Corruption Authority on 15 April 2014. The purpose of those guidelines is to guide all such companies in the application of the Italian anti-corruption and transparency legislation. They also target the authorities, which are tasked with ensuring and promoting the adoption of preventive measures in connection with the powers of scrutiny accorded. According to the guidelines, the supervising authorities should take action in order to ensure the adoption of organizational and management risk arrangements by the companies. Those organizational and management models are required by Law Decree n° 231/2001, with the aim to prevent crime related to company activity, which includes corruption. In particular, with reference to corruption prevention organizational measures, the guidelines require that each company pinpoints the risk areas based on the internal and external environment in which they conduct their activities, and on the type of activity they carry out.

The question is how to assign a value, in the procurement procedure, to the adoption of such soft-law strategies. As is well known, the adoption of specific models of compliance cannot be imposed at the tendering stage. This could result into a market entry barrier; it would also be against the principle of competition, and against the so-called *favor partecipationis* principle, which is particularly invoked at a European level. Relevant judgements of the ECJ on the elimination of practices that restrict competition in general and participation in contracts by other Member States are Joined Cases C-226/04 and C-228/04, February 9th 2006; C-213/07, December 16th 2008; C-538/07, May 19th 2009. According to those statements, MSs can introduce further exclusionary measures, but always abiding by the principles of equal treatment of tenderers and of transparency, provided that such measures do not go beyond what is necessary to achieve that objective.

However, priority may be given to compliance programs at the stage of tender evaluation. The contracting authorities should clarify in the contract notice the selection priority mechanism. Moreover, the contracting authorities should keep control even after the contract awarding, especially during contract execution, in order to verify if the preventive anti-corruption measures are still implemented by the contracting party. It shall furthermore issue guidelines on the basis of which the relevant company might adjust its corruption preventive strategy.

The European Court of Justice asserted the need to separate the stage of the evaluation of the tenderer's qualifying requirements from the stage of the evaluation of the tenders, *stricto sensu*. The first stage is based on qualitative selection criteria, and may include the ethical and moral standards of an enterprise. Instead, the second stage is based on awarding criteria, and those that do not allow selecting the most economically advantageous tender are excluded. For criteria which may be accepted as 'criteria for qualitative selection' or 'award criteria' ECJ, Case C-532/06, January 28th 2008; June 19th 2003, C-315/01 stated as follows:

> Read in the light of the principle of equal treatment of economic operators and the ensuing obligation of transparency, Article 36(2) of Council Directive 92/50/EEC of 18 June 1992 relating to the coordination of procedures for the award of public service contracts, as amended by European Parliament and Council Directive 97/52/EC of 13 October 1997, precludes the contracting authority in a tendering procedure from stipulating at a later date the weighting factors and sub-criteria to be applied to the award criteria referred to in the contract documents or contract notice.

7 Contract renegotiation and risk of corruption

Renegotiation of contracts is a frequent and widespread practice, especially for complex and long-term contracts. According to the 2013 Report of Centre for Economic Study, contract renegotiation in the highways and parking sector in France accounts for 50 percent and 73 percent respectively of the awarded contracts. It is usually useful in case of unforeseen events, or where additional services become necessary and a change of contracting party is not possible or would be a major drawback.

On the other hand, renegotiation may encourage opportunistic behaviours, may discourage honest tenderers and may weaken the result of the procedure. Moreover, if having firm-driven renegotiations of contracts for infrastructure services is a major concern, efficiency should not be the only consideration in selecting an operator. Indeed, consumers may want to award the contract to a less efficient firm if that would reduce the likelihood of renegotiation. Scholars analyze the possibility of trade-offs between efficiency and equity, as well as possible distributional conflicts in the context of renegotiation of infrastructure contracts in developing countries. (Estache and Quesada, 2001). Their work presents a model in which contracts are awarded by auctioning the right to operate an infrastructural service to a private monopoly, and considers the possibility of renegotiation. To identify the potential sources of trade-offs, the possible outcomes are examined of different renegotiation strategies for the monopoly running the concession and for the two groups of consumers – rich and poor – who alternate in power according to a majority voting rule.

The 2014 European Directives on Public Procurement outline the situations in which contracts may be modified over the course of their execution. In particular, the EU legislature recognized that public procurement contracts are incomplete and leave a great deal of room for potential renegotiation at the contract execution stage (article 72, EU Directive 2014/24/UE and article 43, EU Directive 2014/23/UE). In general, modifications amounting to less than 10 percent of the initial value of the contract for supplies and services and 15 percent for works are permitted, along with modifications that are either not substantial or had been incorporated in the contract in the form of price revision clauses or clear options, regardless of their value, defined as modifications for design flaws. In this case, the designer's responsibility remains unchanged. Some scholars argue that the percentage is relatively high and suggest an amount of less than 5 percent. At the same time, there is no consensus in the interpretation of the 2014 EU Directives. In particular, it is not clear whether the estimated percentages of 10 percent and 15 percent of the initial value of the contract relate to each modification or, on the contrary, should be calculated on the total amount of the contract. However, any increase in price shall not exceed 50 percent of the value of the original contract where additional works, supplies or services have become necessary (De Carolis and Trybus, 2016).

Concessions can also be significantly modified under the same conditions and to the same extent as procurement contracts. It is important to recognize the hypothesis of substantial modification of the contract and to provide some terminological clarifications. The 2014 EU Directives mention the term "modification", while the phenomenon is defined differently in the EU Member States. In Italy, for example, changes to the contract after it is awarded are called "renegotiation". Instead, common law countries such as the UK use the terms "adjustment" or "amendment". It is advisable to think of whether, besides terminology, the meaning is also different. According to art. 72 of EU Directive no. 2014/24/EU, these alter the character of the original contract/framework; would have allowed other potential suppliers to participate or be selected, or another tender to be accepted; changes the economic balance in favour of the contractor; extends the scope of the contract/framework "considerably"; a new contractor replaces the original contractor, other than where the change arises from a review or option clause in the original contract or from corporate changes such as merger, take over or insolvency. Clearly, art. 72 of 2014 EU Directive leaves great discretionary power with regard to any substantial modification of the contract. The difficulty to select in advance such hypotheses could be overcome by the interpretation provided by case law.

Furthermore, the ECJ clarified the cases in which the contract could be modified after being awarded with no need for re-advertising in OJEU. In particular, according to Pressetext, C– 454/06, changes in a contract post award could in certain cases lead to a legal requirement for re-advertisement in OJEU. The purpose is to provide a "safe-harbour" for certain types of amendments. This provision should help contracting authorities to ensure that post-award changes to contracts are properly controlled. In particular, a contract may change without re-advertisement where the change, irrespective of its value, is not substantial or the change is provided for in the initial procurement documents in a clear, precise and unequivocal review or option clause, which specifies the conditions of use and the scope and nature of the change; and where the overall nature of the contract/framework is not altered. Moreover, the EU Directives now provide for the cases of major or minor changes, without re-advertisement, in art. 72(1) (b), 72(1) (c), 72(3) and 72(5), 72(6).

However, there is a relevant nexus between renegotiation and risk of corruption. It usually arises at the company selection stage that generally involves a tendering process. At such stage, an illicit agreement might be reached between the public officer and the tenderer, according to which an overly aggressive offer will be submitted which is designed solely to ensure selection, with the aim of renegotiating the contract at a later stage.

Some scholars argue that renegotiation weakens invitation to tender by encouraging opportunistic behaviours (aggressive bids in which the companies willingly submit a low bid in anticipation of the fact that they will renegotiate the contract during the execution stage). A list of recommendations has been drawn up, aiming at increasing the efficiency of the French public procurement system (Saussier and Tirole, 2015). The same could also apply to other countries, such as Italy, for example.

It is worth mentioning the need to recognize that the aim of public procurement is primarily to meet an identified need by achieving the best possible performance in terms of cost and service or expected functionalities. It is also suggested to make it compulsory for the public party to provide and publish online two summary reports on the analysis of the bids both prior to and following the negotiation stage; to centralize information regarding the past performances of contractors for the purposes of facilitating and encouraging the use of such information at the awarding stage, so as to penalize less reliable companies; to introduce electronic advertising and application platforms only at the regional level and upload all the information to a national platform. Making it compulsory for a bid analysis report to be published online, along with the relevant legal information, is necessary to improve transparency, as well as making it compulsory to publish an "amendment notice" when the value of the contract varies by more than 10 percent and to introduce a quick amendment summary procedure that is open to all stakeholders. Transparency requirements should also be applied to directly managed activities, along with appropriate incentives and penalties. It is also very useful to strengthen the professionalization and expertise of public buyers and project managers, and to centralize the purchasing of standard goods and services wherever possible; to give public buyers the option of decentralizing their purchases so as to ensure maximum flexibility where it is required. Last but not least, a good recommendation is that of entrusting the upstream and downstream evaluation of all public procurement tools to an agency for amounts exceeding a given threshold, such as 50 million.

Changing a contract after it is signed reduces the competitive effect of the tender and, therefore, the transparency of the process and compromises its value for money. If, in some cases, an adjustment may be necessary, it is often driven by opportunism and it increases distrust in the country, thus generating market "crowding out" (moving away best skills and capital). Moreover, the asymmetry of information and the lack or difficulty in activating the necessary skills erodes the bargaining power of the PA, thus making the process of review and renegotiation even more critical.

According to this approach, improving the transparency of renegotiation procedures would help to limit the distortion of the initial tendering process and to ensure that the rules governing renegotiation are abided by.

As it has been pointed out above, the will of the contracting parties to renew a contract could be driven by corruption and/or collusion. Such phenomena have been taken into consideration by the international literature conducting an empirical analysis of public-private agreements. It has been observed that if, on the one hand, corruption was facilitating cooperative renegotiations and, therefore, contract renewals, it should be highlighted that, on the other hand, the more frequent the renegotiations, the more corrupt the public authority and the more willing both parties would be to renew a contract (Beuve, De Brux and Saussier, 2014).

How could such opportunistic behaviours be checked?

One possibility is that of improving the transparency of the renegotiation procedure by drafting a specific procedure for amendments to public procurement contracts, starting from the publication of an amendment summary in order to inform the parties concerned (Cuhna Marques and Berg, 2015). This could also involve a special dispute procedure concerning the content of the changes made to the contract.

The French *Conseil d'analyse économique* seems to move in this direction. It has designed an amendments procedure that applies to the French contracting authorities. Such procedure would be quick and improve the transparency and accountability of public authorities. Furthermore, the amendment proposals would be simultaneously published and sent electronically to all bidding companies. The proposals have to specify, at least, the value of the contract, the value of the increase, and the object of the amendment. The right to be notified of any amendment and its characteristics is also envisaged.

Another possibility is that of choosing selection criteria other than the lowest price. In fact, the international literature argues that when the contract is awarded based on the lowest price criterion, there are more chances for opportunistic behaviour. A company could exploit the lack of information or errors made by the Contracting Authority within the project. Therefore, it would offer the lowest price, being aware of the fact that the contract will be renegotiated during its execution. In order to avoid such consequences, focus should be placed on the company's reputation parameter. For example, if special value is attached to the previous performance of the company, the latter will be motivated to improve its reputation. Along the same lines, policy-makers should consider the possibility of awarding the contract based on a negotiation. The 2014 EU Directives on PP offer three options for a negotiation stage between the Contracting Authority and a company: the competitive procedure with negotiation, competitive dialogue and the innovation partnership.

8 Final remarks

A lot can still be done on both the regulatory and the soft-law sides, at a national, European and global level.

On the regulatory side, the existing 2014 public procurement directives put a lot of emphasis on the need to prevent and fight corruption, but with no clear means of action. They should be implemented in single Member States in order to guarantee more transparency in the procurement procedures. Discretionary powers have been strongly increased by the 2014 European directives on procurement.

An example is the rules on negotiated procedures, based on a discretionary choice of the Contracting Authority, concerning the technical characteristics of the works, services or goods. Thus, negotiated procedures are not an exceptional hypothesis anymore. Those procedures imply the adoption of specific rules on transparency, publicity and equal treatment.

The flexibility of these procedures is appreciate, but the EU Commission warns on possible risks of favouritism, because of the greatest discretional power given to public authorities. Among potential remedies is setting up an appropriate project supervision system in order to avoid alterations and changes while work is in progress, and any related cost increase. Furthermore, only specialized experts should be competent to evaluate the project submitted and to set up a mechanism of accountability of public officials with political power, tasked with ascertaining that the project meets public interest.

The new procurement directives move in the direction of attributing the contracting authorities' greater flexibility in the use of the most suitable contract models to meet their specific needs. This approach is not reflected at the national level, where some Member States (including Italy) have always believed that it was necessary to limit discretion through clear rules in order to curb the evolution of corruptive phenomena in the field of public contracts. The Italian legislature has implemented the EU Directives on PP through Legislative Decree n° 50 of

April 18th, 2016. In particular, art. 95 sets forth the awards criteria. It refers to the most advantageous offer as general criterion and specifies the cases in which it is possible to derogate from it.

More discretion means more flexibility of procedures – a growing need much felt in the sector – but also potentially more risk of abuse, which can only be mitigated by introducing (new) rules. The need to mitigate the risk of abuse results in the trade-off between *rules and flexibility – rules and discretion.*

It is not easy to bridge the gap

We do not suggest reducing flexibility, but it is necessary to limit the risk of abuse and asset up a more efficient joint supervisory system of enforcement, at least at the European level. A European model is needed to support integrity but, unfortunately, a comprehensive answer to the issue is strongly affected by political uncertainty in Europe.

On the European soft-law side, an administrative public procurement procedure standardization process (see Renewal model, book IV) could also be implemented, including for example the obligation to adopt private and public ethics and compliance programs. There could be a way to link the above-mentioned soft-law strategies with the existing regulations and procedures, by attaching value to compliance programs at the tender evaluation stage. Only companies that have special anti-corruption programs could be selected.

Along the same lines, it is important to stress the value of a company's reputation and its motivating effects, as well as the beneficial effects of negotiated procedures if conducted in a transparent and non-discriminatory context.

Without challenging the belief of the European legislature regarding the need to ensure discretion to the public administration in order to support the flexibility of procedures, it is possible to "adjust discretionary power" through soft law by adopting corruptive phenomena conflict prevention measures, such as renegotiation procedures. Once again, as is the case for public and private preventive anticorruption measures, soft law may be a means to supplement the existing regulations without reducing flexibility.

References

Acemoglu, D., and Verdier, T. (2000). The choice between market failures and corruption. *American Economic Review*, 194–211.

Aidt, T., and Dutta, V. J. (2007). Governance regimes, corruption and growth: Theory and evidence. *Journal of Comparative Economics*, 36(2), 195–220.

Arrowsmith, S. (2010). Public procurement: Basic concepts and the coverage of procurement rules. In S. Arrowsmith (ed.), *Public Procurement Regulation: An Introduction* (p. 4). Nottingham: University of Nottingham.

Beuve, J., De Brux, J., and Saussier, S. (2014). *Renegotiations, discretion and contract renewals*. Available at http://economix.fr/pdf/seminaires/lien/S_Saussier_2014.pdf

Bribery Act 2010 (2010). Chapter 23, 8 April 2010.

Centre for Economic Study (2013). *The 2013 report of Centre for Economic Study*. Available at www.cesifo-group.de/ifoHome/publications/docbase/details.html?docId=19126461

Cohen-Tanugi, L. (2015). L'application extraterritoriale du droit américain, fer de lance de la régulation économique internationale? *En Temps Réel – Les cahiers*.

Commission of the EU (2011). *Communication from the commission to the European Parliament, the Council and the European Economic and Social Committee, Fighting Corruption in the EU*. Available at http://eur-lex.europa.eu/legal-content/EN/TXT/?uri=celex:52011DC0308

Cunha Marques, R., and Berg, S. V. (2015). *Revisiting the strengths and limitations of regulatory contracts in infrastructure industries*. Munich Personal RePEc Archive. Available at https://mpra.ub.uni-muenchen.de/32890/1/MPRA_paper_32890.pdf

Estache, A., and Quesada, L. (2001). *Concession contract renegotiations: Some efficiency vs. equity dilemmas*. World Bank Policy Research Working Paper No. 2705. Available at http://documents.worldbank.org/curated/en/132061468739536458/Concession-contract-renegotiations-some-efficiency-versus-equity-dilemmas

European Commission SEC (2011). 853 final, Brussels 27.6.2011. Available at ec.europa.eu/internal_market/publicprocurement/docs/modernising_rules/er853_1_en.pdf

The General Confederation of Italian Industry (2002). *Confindustria guidelines, March, 7 2002 on the construction of organizational, management and control models, on the base of the law decree n. 231 of 2001*. Available at www.confindustria.it/wps/portal/IT/AreeTematiche/Diritto-d-impresa/Documenti/Dettaglio-doc-diritto-impresa/4eaa0336-f353-4bc8-aa05-35dfda228a50/4eaa0336-f353-4bc8-aa05-35dfda228a50/!ut/p/a0/04_Sj9CPykssy0xPLMnMz0vMAfGjzOJ9PT1MDD0NjLz83UxNDBxNgpwCfYzdLCzDTPQLsh0VAVhK9gI!/www.elysee.fr/communiques-de-presse/article/charte-de-deontologie-des-membres-du-gouvernement/

Hanousek, J., and Kočenda, E. (2011). Public investment and fiscal performance in the new EU member states. *Fiscal Studies*, 32(1), 43–71.

Houillon, G. (2012). *Le lobbying en droit public*. Bruxelles: Bruylant.

Houillon, G. (2014). Corruption and conflicts of interest: Future prospects on lobbying. In J. B. Auby, E. Brenn, and T. Perroud (eds.), *Corruption and Conflicts of Interest, a Comparative Law Approach* (pp. 53–67). Cheltenham: Edward Elgar Publishing.

Huntington, S. P. (1968). Modernization and corruption. *Political Order in Changing Societies*, 59–71.

The Italian Anti-Corruption Authority (2015). *Consultation paper n. 36 of 2015*. Available at www.anticorruzione.it/portal/public/classic/home/_RisultatoRicerca?id=e09918230a7780425303082827cee41c&search=PREC+151%2F14%2FS

Koelher, M. (2012). Revisiting a foreign corrupt practices act: Compliance defense. *Wisconsin Law Review*, 609.

Lui, F. T. (1985). An equilibrium queuing model of bribery. *Journal of Political Economy*, 93(4), 760–781.

Mendez, F., and Sepulveda, F. (2006). Corruption, growth and political regimes: Cross country evidence. *European Journal of Political Economy*, 22(1), 82 ss.

Méon, P. G., and Weill, L. (2010). Does financial intermediation matter for macroeconomic performance?. *Economic Modelling*, 27(1), 296–303.

Murphy, K. M., Shleifer, A., and Vishny, R. W. (1991). The allocation of talent: Implications for growth. *The Quarterly Journal of Economics*, 106(2), 503-530.

OECD (1999). *An international survey of prevention measures*. Corruption, Public Sector. Available at www.oecd-ilibrary.org/governance/public-sector-corruption_9789264173965-en

OECD (2003). *Recommendation of the council on guidelines for managing conflict of interests in the public service*. Available at www.oecd.org/gov/ethics/managingconflictofinterestinthepublicservice.htm

OECD (2016). *OECD Integrity Forum, Fighting the Hidden Tariff: Global Trade Without Corruption, Background Document*. Paris: OECD. Available at www.oecd.org/cleangovbiz/2016-Integrity-Forum-Background-Report.pdf

OECD – UNODC (2013). *Anti-Corruption Ethics and Compliance Handbook for Business*. Available at www.oecd.org/corruption/anti-corruption-ethics-and-compliance-handbook-for-business.htm

PwC and Ecorys (2013). *Identifying and reducing corruption in public procurement in the EU*. Available at http://ec.europa.eu/anti-fraud/sites/antifraud/files/docs/body/identifying_reducing_corruption_in_public_procurement_en.pdf

Racca, M., and Perin, C. (2014). Corruption as a violation of fundamental rights: Reputation risk as a deterrent against the lack of loyalty. *Ius Publicum Network Review*, 3–4.

Rose-Ackerman, S. (1997). The political economy of corruption. *Corruption and the Global Economy*, 31, 60.

Saussier, S., and Tirole, J. (2015) *Strengthening the efficiency of public procurement*. French Council of Economic Analysis. Available at www.cae-eco.fr.

Scott, J. (2014). Extraterritoriality and territorial extension in EU Law. *The American Journal of Comparative Law*, 62(1), 87–126.

Shleifer, A., and Vishny, R. W. (1993). Corruption. *The Quarterly Journal of Economics*, 108(3), 599–617.

Siemens (2009). *Siemens Compliance Guide – Anti-Corruption*. Available at http://w3.siemens.no/home/no/no/omsiemens/Documents/sc_upload_file_anticorruption_handbook.pdf

Transparency International France (2013). *Transparence et Intégrité du Lobbying, un enjeu de démocratie, report on lobbying*. Available at www.transparency-france.org/e_upload/pdf/transparency_france_lobbying_en_france_octobre2014.pdf

UK Government (2014). *UK anti-corruption plan*. Available at www.gov.uk/government/uploads/system/uploads/attachment_data/file/388894/UKantiCorruptionPlan.pdf

UK Ministry of Justice (2011). *The Bribery Act 2010: Guidance 15*. Available at www.justice.gov.uk/downloads/legislation/bribery-act-2010-guidance.pdf.

White, S. (2014). Footprints in the sand: Regulating conflict of interests at EU level. In J. B. Auby, E. Breen, and T. Perroud (eds.), *Corruption and Conflict of Interest: Comparative Law Approach* (pp. 272–288). Cheltenham: Edward Elgar Publishing.

Wouters, J., Ryngaert, C., and Cloots, A. S. (2012). The fight against corruption in international law. *European Journal of Crime*, 94, 13.

Index

Note: Page numbers in italics indicate figures. Page numbers in bold indicate tables.